Stephen Turner and the Philosophy of the Social

Poznań Studies in the Philosophy of the Sciences and the Humanities

Founding Editor
Leszek Nowak (1943–2009)

Editor-in-Chief
Katarzyna Paprzycka-Hausman (*University of Warsaw*)

Editors
Tomasz Bigaj (*University of Warsaw*) – Krzysztof Brzechczyn (*Adam Mickiewicz University*) – Jerzy Brzeziński (*Adam Mickiewicz University*) – Krzysztof Łastowski (*Adam Mickiewicz University*) – Joanna Odrowąż-Sypniewska (*University of Warsaw*) – Piotr Przybysz (*Adam Mickiewicz University*) – Mieszko Tałasiewicz (*University of Warsaw*) – Krzysztof Wójtowicz (*University of Warsaw*)

Advisory Committee
Joseph Agassi (*Tel-Aviv*) – Wolfgang Balzer (*Munchen*) – Mario Bunge (*Montreal*) – Robert S. Cohen†(*Boston*) – Francesco Coniglione (*Catania*) – Dagfinn Follesdal (*Oslo, Stanford*) – Jacek J. Jadacki (*Warszawa*) – Andrzej Klawiter (*Poznań*) – Theo A.F. Kuipers (*Groningen*) – Witold Marciszewski (*Warszawa*) – Thomas Müller (*Konstanz*) – Ilkka Niiniluoto (*Helsinki*) – Jacek Paśniczek (*Lublin*) – David Pearce (*Madrid*) – Jan Such (*Poznań*) – Max Urchs (*Wiesbaden*) – Jan Woleński (*Krakow*) – Ryszard Wójcicki (*Warszawa*)

VOLUME 116

The titles published in this series are listed at *brill.com/ps*

Stephen Turner and the Philosophy of the Social

Edited by

Christopher Adair-Toteff

BRILL
RODOPI

LEIDEN | BOSTON

Cover illustration: Images from the personal archive of Stephen Turner, used with permission.

The Library of Congress Cataloging-in-Publication Data is available online at http://catalog.loc.gov
LC record available at http://lccn.loc.gov/2021931109

Typeface for the Latin, Greek, and Cyrillic scripts: "Brill". See and download: brill.com/brill-typeface.

ISSN 0303-8157
ISBN 978-90-04-44959-6 (hardback)
ISBN 978-90-04-44960-2 (e-book)

Copyright 2021 by Christopher Adair-Toteff. Published by Koninklijke Brill NV, Leiden, The Netherlands.
Koninklijke Brill NV incorporates the imprints Brill, Brill Hes & De Graaf, Brill Nijhoff, Brill Rodopi, Brill Sense, Hotei Publishing, mentis Verlag, Verlag Ferdinand Schöningh and Wilhelm Fink Verlag.
Koninklijke Brill NV reserves the right to protect this publication against unauthorized use. Requests for re-use and/or translations must be addressed to Koninklijke Brill NV via brill.com or copyright.com.

This book is printed on acid-free paper and produced in a sustainable manner.

Contents

Notes on Contributors   VII

Stephen Turner and the Philosophy of the Social
An Introduction   1
    Christopher Adair-Toteff

PART 1
Overviews

On What There is, Maybe
Turner versus Turner on "the Social"   11
    Paul A. Roth

Rationality and Interpretive Methodology
Transformations in the Apparent Irrationality Debate   30
    Mark Risjord

Practical Normativity
Stephen Turner's Contribution to the Philosophy of the Social   49
    Rafał Paweł Wierzchosławski

PART 2
Practices and Beliefs

What Is in an Account of Practices?   71
    Theodore R. Schatzki

Yes Virginia, Folk Psychological Understanding Really is Explanatory
Towards a Realist Conception of the "Verstehen Bubble"   90
    Karsten R. Stueber

Individualistic and Holistic Models of Collective Beliefs and the Role of Rhetoric and Argumentation
The Example of Religious and Political Beliefs   110
    Alban Bouvier

PART 3
Intentions and Norms

What Does Normativity "Explain"?   133
   Peter Olen

Norms
You Can't Always Get What You Want ... but You Can Get What You Need   150
   David Henderson and Terence Horgan

PART 4
Social Science

Cognitive Theories and Economic Science   177
   Sam Whimster

Interpretivism and Qualitative Research   202
   Julie Zahle

Sociology, Expertise and Civility   221
   John Holmwood

Response

Normativity, Practices, and the Substrate   243
   Stephen Turner

Index   267

Notes on Contributors

Christopher Adair-Toteff

has retired as a professor of philosophy and social theory. He has published widely on classical German social thinkers, especially Max Weber, Ernst Troeltsch, and Ferdinand Tönnies. His current interests are on political philosophy as indicated by *Ernst Troeltsch and the Spirit of Modern Culture* (Walter de Gruyter 2021) and the intersection of social theory and economics as shown in his forthcoming book on Weber for Routledge.

Alban Bouvier

is Emeritus Professor at Aix-Marseille University and Senior Researcher at the Ecole Normale Supérieure de Paris (Institut Jean Nicod). He previously taught at the Sorbonne. He specialized in both the philosophy of the social sciences and theoretical sociology. He is especially interested in the connections between analytic sociology on the one hand and argumentation theory and rhetoric on the other hand in the continuity of Vilfredo Pareto.

David Henderson

is the Robert R. Chambers Distinguished Professor of Philosophy at the University of Nebraska, Lincoln. He works on a wide range of topics in the Philosophy of Social Science and Epistemology. In the latter, he has commonly collaborated with Terence Hogan. In the former, he has long admired and learned from the work of Stephen Turner. Indeed, his own early work, including *Interpretation and Explanation in the Human Sciences* (SUNY 1993) owed much to this engagement. His contribution with Terrence Hogan in this collection reflects a related overlap with Turner's work: the significance of recent cognitive science for the social sciences.

Terence Horgan

is Professor of Philosophy (Emeritus) at the University of Arizona. His philosophical work, often collaborative, spans a number of fields including philosophy of mind, metaphysics, epistemology, metaethics, and philosophical paradoxes. He collaborates extensively with David Henderson on topics in epistemology.

John Holmwood

is emeritus professor of Sociology at the University of Nottingham and senior researcher at the Centre for Science Technology and Society Studies in the

Institute for Philosophy at the Czech Academy of Science. His current research is on multiculturalism and religion and on colonialism and modern social theory. He has recently published a work of public sociology (with Therese O'Toole) on the Birmingham Trojan Horse affair which involved false claims of a plot to Islamicise schools and (with Gurminder K Bhambra) on the role of colonialism in the construction of classical sociology and contemporary accounts of modernity.

Peter Olen
is an assistant professor of philosophy at Lake-Sumter State College in Clermont, Florida. His research focuses broadly on the history of philosophy (especially 19th and 20th century American philosophy). Specifically, Peter's recent publications address issues surrounding Wilfrid Sellars, pragmatism, logical positivism, and historical perspectives on the tension between normative and naturalistic accounts of human agency.

Mark Risjord
is professor of Philosophy at Emory University (USA) and Affiliated Research Professor in the Department of Philosophy and Social Science, University of Hradec Králové, Czech Republic. His research is in the philosophy of science, with special interests in issues arising from anthropology and nursing. His current projects investigate inferentialist approaches to scientific representation and minimalist approaches to joint action.

Paul A. Roth
is Distinguished Professor in the Department of Philosophy at the University of California-Santa Cruz (USA). His research focuses on several areas, including Quine and naturalized epistemology, philosophy of history (particularly historical explanation as debated within the analytical philosophical tradition), and philosophy of social science. He has numerous articles in each of these areas as well as a recent book on historical explanation.

Theodore R. Schatzki
is professor of geography and philosophy at the University of Kentucky and professor of sociology at Lancaster University. He is a social theorist, widely associated with the theoretical stream in the social disciplines known as practice theory. His books have developed an original version of this approach. Schatzki's present research ranged over multiple topics such as materiality and social life, cryptocurrencies/blockchains, and spaces of educating under the Covid-19 regime.

Karsten R. Stueber

is Professor of Philosophy at the College of the Holy Cross. He works at the intersection of the philosophy of mind, philosophy of the social sciences, and metaethics. Among others, he is the author of *Rediscovering Empathy: Agency, Folk Psychology and the Human Sciences* (MIT Press 2006) and more recently the co-editor of *Ethical Sentimentalism: New Perspectives* (Cambridge University Press 2017). In his new book project, he is exploring the relationship between empathy and morality.

Stephen Turner

is Distinguished Research Professor at the Department of Philosophy, University of South Florida. He has published extensively on the history and philosophy of social science. His current research interests are in the relations between cognitive science and the conceptions of the social, and in aspects of democratic theory, especially relating to issues of knowledge and expertise.

Sam Whimster

is a sociologist and is Professor in the Global Policy Institute, London. He is editor of the journal *Max Weber Studies*. He is the co-editor (with Hans Henrik Brunn) of *Max Weber: Collected Methodological Writings* (Routledge 2012).

Rafał Paweł Wierzchosławski

lectures on philosophy and history of science and axiological problems of modern civilization in the Liberal Arts Program at the Adam Mickiewicz University, Poznań. He has published on the philosophy of the social sciences, social ontology, political philosophy and social studies of science. His present focus is on the experts' role in defining republican freedom and forms of government within the context of knowledge societies.

Julie Zahle

is associate professor on the Department of Philosophy at the University of Bergen. Previously, she taught at Durham University and the University of Copenhagen. She received her Ph.D. from the History and Philosophy of Science Department at the University of Pittsburgh in 2009. Her research areas include the philosophy of qualitative methods, values and objectivity in social science, the individualism-holism debate, and social theories of practices.

Stephen Turner and the Philosophy of the Social

An Introduction

Christopher Adair-Toteff

Abstract

This brief introduction has two parts. The first is devoted to the contributors—what their disciplines are and where the contributors are located. This indicates Turner's interdisciplinary influence and his international reputation. It also surveys their responses to questions about Turner's general and specific impact on their work and what they consider to be his most important or influential contribution to scholarship. The second part is a brief overview of the contributors' chapters.

Keywords

Stephen Turner – philosophy – social – scholarship – impact

1   Stephen Turner's Philosophy of the Social

Stephen Turner has been recognized as an expert in a wide range of areas. These include sociology, social theory, expertise studies, cognitive science, and the philosophy of law. His interest has led him to become one of the leading scholars on a number of important figures, including Max Weber, Emile Durkheim, Hans Kelsen, Hans Morgenthau, Michael Oakeshott, Leo Strauss, and Edward Shils. He has also been regarded as one of the major experts in the philosophy of the social and that has been a focus of his interest throughout much of his academic life. This was shown early by his degrees in philosophy and sociology and later by many of his recent publications. It is also revealed by his interest in both empirical sociology and social theory. Turner grew up in the sociologically and culturally distinctive community of Chicago's South Side. Although the community was sociologically studied, Turner recognized that many of the published studies were inadequate or flawed. He came to understand that "the social" was not an ontological object, but the topics which we regard as "social" are constructions. Social categories, social settings, and social groups help determine how we regard the social; thus, there are not social objects but social explanations. It is the idea of practices which help explain by providing persistent patterns of behavior. These prompt reflection on our own practices and reveal that our own practices to be distinctive. Again, the philosophy of the social is not about a thing, but an attempt to explain what we think, what we believe, and how we interact in social and cultural settings.

It is with this in mind that the title of this volume in honor of Stephen Turner's seventieth birthday is the philosophy of the social. This brief Introduction has two parts. The first one is a discussion of the contributors to this volume and to Turner's impact on their scholarly thinking. The second is an overview of the eleven chapters and Turner's response.

2   The Contributors and Turner's Impact

The contributors are primarily philosophers (11) but there are a number of sociologists (5) and then there are those who are regarded as both (3). While most of the contributors are residents of the United States (9) there are a number from other countries: United Kingdom (3), Denmark (1), France (1), and Poland (1). There are some from two countries: the U.S. and Germany (2) and the U.S. and the U.K. (1). All of the contributors have known Turner for a long time; some met him around 2000, but many more have known him since the 1990s. And, many of the contributors noted that they had been reading Turner's writings for a considerable time before actually meeting him. The point is that all of the contributors have known Turner for a long time and have been familiar with his publications for an even longer period.

Each of the contributors were asked two questions: 1) What did they think was their most important professional/personal connection to Turner? 2) What did they regard as Turner's most important/impressive/influential/innovative/suggestive contribution to the philosophy of the social? The answers to the first emphasized Turner's willingness to support them. This included encouragement but tempered with realism. He is always encouraging us pursuing our research but also wants us to have a realistic understanding of the pitfalls and limitations. The answers also reflected Turner's abilities to help us see old problems in new ways and to challenge us to confront our own tendencies to repeat accepted wisdom. The answers also reflected his skepticism of grand ideas and simplistic solutions. Several contributors noted his skepticism, iconoclasm, and his "cheekiness" but almost every one noted his generosity with time, effort, and the willingness to work with us. As one contributor put it: Turner is "an incredibly nice guy." There is no question that he often is but he has his limits: woe to the budding scholar who does not do his homework or worse, the speaker who makes an unwarranted statement. I have been with Turner

AN INTRODUCTION　　　　　　　　　　　　　　　　　　　　　　　　　　　　　　　3

during many conferences when from the back of the room Turner questions the speaker's source or takes issue with his interpretation. Yes, Turner is often an "incredibly nice guy" but one who does not suffer fools gladly—truth and knowledge are too important to him. He acknowledges the difficulty of much of his writing but it is because of the originality of his ideas and the complexity of the issue. He makes allowances for these in other scholars' writings, but as a few contributors have noted, he has little patience for those who engage in "obscurantist explanatory strategies."

Regarding the second question, many contributors had difficulty identifying one thing and instead wrote of Turner's general contributions to scholarship. They were almost all impressed with his breadth and depth of knowledge in various disciplines: philosophy, philosophy of science, social science, sociology and philosophy of the social sciences. Many remarked on his understanding of the relationship between the social sciences and the natural sciences. Some pointed to his work on social practices as his most important contribution while others regarded his writings on the intersection of sociology and cognition to be his most impressive achievement. Several of the European contributors thought that Turner stood out because of his expertise in philosophy and sociology; they pointed out that it was rare for a scholar to be an expert in two disciplines in Europe and that it was almost unheard of the United States. Many referred to his general approach to problems. Specifically, a few commented on his rather unique ability to contextualize ideas and to use historical examples to explain current controversies. Others pointed to his explanations for social practices while others indicated his participation in the debate about rationalism. But all of them mentioned his continuing deep commitment to understanding and the insistence on furthering knowledge. Supportive but realistic, enthusiastic but cautious; these are the contradictory traits that Turner is able to hold together.

From the preceding it should be readily apparent how much Turner has influenced the contributors, both in terms of their scholarly work and in their academic lives. It remains for me to add a note, indicating how Turner's work has influenced my own writings and his comments and advice helped determine my own academic career. Turner had just moved from the Saint Petersburg campus the University of South Florida to the main Tampa campus in 1987 when I was first introduced to him at a faculty meeting. I had returned to USF in 1985 to wait for the implementation of the new Ph.D. in Philosophy program. While waiting, I continued to teach as a member of the adjunct faculty. Turner was instrumental in getting it approved and was more than helpful in getting it moving. I was the first to enroll in this new doctoral program. Because of a dispute regarding academic accreditation, Turner ended up chairing the oral defense of my dissertation proposal and was rather insistent that I should focus on the Neo-Kantian elements of my proposal rather on the Kantian, thus my dissertation was on the Neo-Kantian dispute over the nature of space. Turner's advice helped determine my move from the study of Kant to work on various Neo-Kantians, especially, Georg Simmel, Ernst Troeltsch, Ferdinand Tönnies, and of course, Max Weber. Anyone who has read my work on Weber is bound to recognize Turner's influence; indeed, it is unlikely that I would have ever written anything on Weber if not for Turner's impact. For over thirty years, he has been generous with advice, gentle with criticism, and always helpful with information. I decided years ago that the one way that I could try to repay him was to organize a "Festschrift" for him. I first broached the idea in 2006 when he and I were sitting on a bench on the "*Philosophenweg*" in Heidelberg. I tried to make my most compelling case but he declined. I brought the subject up again a few years ago when we met in Friedrichshafen in connection with Zeppelin University. I again made what I thought was a compelling argument and this time he agreed, although reluctantly. He was uncertain that there would be a sufficient number of contributors, and I assured him there would be. He was doubtful that there would be sufficient interest by a publisher, and I maintained that there probably would be. This volume in honor of Stephen Turner's seventieth birthday is a testament to his importance in philosophy, his influence on our scholarly work, and his impact on each of our academic lives. I did not doubt that I could find so many people who, like me, owe debts of scholarly gratitude to him, and I do not question there could be many more who would be eager to contribute to another volume or two devoted to Turner's work on Durkheim, causality, Weber, or another topic that Turner has investigated and has chosen to investigate. However, we chose this topic to be the theme of this volume: Stephen Turner and the Philosophy of the Social.

3   Chapter Overviews

The eleven chapters are divided into five parts. Part 1 contains three papers that are overviews. Part 2 contains three papers on practices and beliefs. Part 3 has two papers on intentions and norms. Part 4 has three papers devoted to social science. Part Five is Turner's response.

Paul Roth leads the first part with a sketch of Turner's history of trying to find a science of the social. Roth notes that as a major scholar of the history of the social sciences he is highly appreciative of the number of failures to develop a science of the social. In his first book, *Social Explanation as Translation*, Turner found fault in the folk psychologist's attempt to examine culture as an ontological entity. Roth observed that Turner's youthful enthusiasm matured in his *Explaining the Normative* and suggested that Turner regarded the normative as another name for practices. Roth further notes how Turner began to emphasize the connections between social sciences and cognitive sciences, a connection which Turner makes explicit in his recent book *Cognitive Science and the Social. A Primer*. Roth comments approvingly on Turner's emphasis on the social connections between human action and intentions and cognitive science and he commends him not only for his rich history in attempting to define the problems of a science of the social and for his continuing efforts to delineate the relationship between the cognitive science and a science of the social.

Mark Risjord examines Turner's contributions to the idea of the social by examining it in light of the late-century debate over rationality and relativism. Scholars argued then that culture was bounded but rationality was unbounded but Roth argues that anthropologists have disproved the former and cognitive scientists have disproved the latter. Roth notes that Turner considers both culture and cognitive science and has argued that culture is less bound than many have thought and that rationality is bounded more and that Turner's recent writings show how the philosophy of culture and the empirical science of cognition are not two mutually exclusive disciplines but should be viewed as complimentary.

Rafał Wierzchosławski closes out the first part by first noting the various disciplines in which Turner has made remarkable contributions but he maintains that there has been a single over-riding theme to Turner's scholarly writings. Wierzchosławski insists that Turner employs one methodological approach to various social constructs and that is his attempt to take into consideration the various actors' points of view. In other words, it is his attempt to consider how one acts intentionally and under what specific conditions. Wierzchosławski notes Turner's affinity with Weberian social thought, but suggests that Turner applies this not just in his writings in the social sciences, but also in his more historical work such as *American Sociology: From Pre-Disciplinary to Post-Normal* as well as in his expert studies such as *Liberal Democracy 3.0. Civil Society in an Age of Expert*.

Theodor Schatzki examines Turner's conception of practices and he focuses on *The Social Theory of Practices* and *Cognitive Science and the Social. A Primer*. Schatzki believes the Turner conception of practice is prompted by his focus on human activity and social life. Furthermore, Schatzki notes that Turner objects to the classical account of practices because of its preference for the "collective" and its contention that it is a type of causality. Turner argues that practices are more individualistic and that we can regard them as patterns.

Schatzki then offers an account that he thinks comes close to meeting Turner's conception of practices but he acknowledges that his account does not encompass explaining activity.

Karsten Stueber offers a defense of folk psychology. He understands and appreciates Turner's naturalism and his desire to exclude an "unjustifiably enchanted conception of the social realm." Stueber also respects Turner's skepticism regarding claims pertaining to social practices, rules, and norms as well as claims about common beliefs and shared intentions. Yet, Stueber points to Turner's acceptance of a modified form of Weber's interpretive sociology and notes that we often correctly infer certain intentions from observable behavior. Stueber devoted much of the remainder of his chapter to an attempt to address Turner's complaints about folk psychology.

Alban Bouvier focuses on the fact that numerous sociologists and anthropologists recognize that people are generally uninterested in the specific content of the group's general beliefs and have little inclination to reflect on the contents of their collective belief. Bouvier's concern is that many attempts have tended to be individualistic and he suggests that one has a better chance if one considers how Tocqueville and later Max Weber identified and evaluated collective beliefs. Bouvier acknowledges that societies are less homogeneous than they were in the nineteenth and early twentieth centuries but he recognizes the important contributions by Turner and others in investigating the importance of considering intentions and in recognizing the limitations of rational interpretation of human actions.

Peter Olen concentrates on Turner's conceptions of norms and explanations and his focus is *Explaining the Normative*. Olen notes that he had been in Turner's seminar on normativity and that they co-wrote a bibliography about the subject but that he thinks that Turner's anti-normativist stand might be modifiable. Olen agrees with the distinction between explanation and analysis and he also appears to agree that norms are judgments, thus they embody values. What Turner pointed out that scientists often claim that the argument is "good" or "elegant" but these are not explanations but evaluations. Turner also objects to their attempts to universalize these judgments. Olen suggests that Turner is fundamentally correct to complain that Wilfred Sellars' account is normative but he believes that that account might be slightly modified. Olen concludes that such a modification would be a compromise and that neither Sellars nor Turner would be satisfied with it.

David Henderson and Terence Horgan direct their attention to Turner's *Cognitive Science and the Social. A Primer* and note Turner's concern regarding the difficulties that the scholar who works across a number of disciplines faces. This is true in general and it is especially true in Turner's concern with the connections between the social sciences and cognitive science. Henderson and Horgan focus on the idea of social norms and they suggest that while Turner is correct in believing that there is "conceptual mud," that his pessimism may not be warranted. They grant that the attempt to investigate the "internal" is individualistic and difficult to assess, yet they suggest that Turner agrees that internal beliefs can and are shared—cooperation and coordination is indicative of this. And, they are confident that Turner's notion of the "Verstehen Bubble" can be addressed by his conception of "*Evidenz.*"

Sam Whimster investigates the Austrian School of economics and focuses on its founder Carl Menger and two later followers, Friedrich Hayek and Ludwig Lachmann. At first glance, there would seem to be little connection to Turner and the philosophy of the social. That is because many economists think that the individual acts singularly and rationally, but Whimster contends that if economics is the covering of human needs, then economic individualism not only cannot advance human flourishing, but has a difficult time meeting human needs. Whimster argues that it is mistaken to regard Menger as an economic individualist because he recognized that economic transactions are between individuals and groups and they are each informed by their own cultural and social contexts. Furthermore, the idea that individuals operate like machines in rationally determining means and ends is also an error. As Turner has argued, cognitive science and the social sciences are related and since economics is not just concerned with mathematical formulas but with transactions, then cognitive science and social sciences contribute to addressing the behavior of the other person involved in making the transaction.

Julie Zahle examines the interpretivism of Charles Taylor and while she is rather sympathetic, she notes that it is incomplete. The interpreter conducts qualitative research in both honest and forthcoming participants and those who are not. Thus, the interpreter needs to gauge the responses and to formulate her questions accordingly. Furthermore, the interpreter will conduct interviews in familiar and unfamiliar situations. As a native Dane, she will be familiar with the norms, practices, and social customs of her fellow Danes. However, if she interviews participants in a different country, she will lack familiarity with the local norms, practices, and social customs. Zahle's chapter relies on Stephen Turner's conception of practices and his notion of interpretation to correct and to modify Charles Taylor's idea of interpretivism and qualitative investigation.

John Holmwood has the concluding chapter and like most of the other contributors, he is impressed with the range and depth of Turner's work. Although Holmwood has known Turner for decades and has worked with him as an editor, he notes that they do not share the same sociological or political standpoints. Nonetheless, Holmwood is convinced that few other sociologists or social philosophers regularly "force us to rethink how we understand our practices." Holmwood concentrates on Turner's *Liberal Democracy 3.0* and he notes Turner's definition of democracy as a "government by discussion." Public discussion requires civility and openness, but modern democracy increasingly relies on expertise. Holmwood acknowledges that there have been others who have criticized relying on experts because it undermines democracy. However, Holmwood insists that Turner's case is more sophisticated because he focuses on the "institutional conditions for the public discourse." Holmwood acknowledges that Turner has grounds for pessimism—inequality, power politics, and privatization of everything, including public universities. However, like most of the other contributors to this volume, Holmwood contends that Turner's own writings offer us reason to be optimistic.

In the final chapter, Turner provides a response. He has opted not to go chapter by chapter but has chosen to consolidate his reply to groups of contributors. He has chosen to highlight both the areas where there is agreement as well as those in which he voices skepticism and disagreement. The eleven chapters cover a full range of social-philosophical issues, both historically and theoretically. It is hoped that this volume is a sufficient indication of Turner's considerable influence on the contributors and a fitting tribute to Stephen Turner and his conception of the philosophy of the social.

PART 1

Overviews

On What There Is, Maybe

Turner versus Turner on "the Social"

Paul A. Roth

Abstract

Stephen Turner, scholar that he is of the history of the social sciences, deeply appreciates how the history of social science stands littered with failed theories, ones that aspired to formulate a science of the social. But why? A key insight guiding his work from early to late has been a keen appreciation of a need to clarify what such a science is a science of. That is, Turner almost alone among the leading social theorists of the last several decades understood that resolving prospects for a science of the social required first achieving clarity regarding the constituent elements of any such explanation. His guiding question is: Just what is it for something to be both social and yet sufficiently thing-like so there can be something for some science to explain? In tracking how his concerns refocus and evolve in the several decades that span the time from his first book to his most recent with respect to the question of what makes explananda social, one achieves a synoptic view of how debate regarding the idea of a social science reshapes as it moves into the twenty-first century.

Keywords

Cognitive science – explanation – folk psychology – social ontology – social science – *Verstehen* bubble

> "A curious thing about the ontological problem is its simplicity. It can be put in three Anglo-Saxon monosyllables: 'What is there?' It can be answered, moreover, in a word—'Everything'—and everyone will accept this answer as true. However, this is merely to say that there is what there is. There remains room for disagreement over cases; and so the issue has stayed alive down the centuries."
> W.V. O. Quine, "On What There Is"

∵

A striking feature about problems of social ontology—the existence of the state, culture, classes, joint intentions, etc.—is their simplicity: "Do they exist?" Summarizing answers requires only a word—"Maybe." That is, the answer depends on whom you ask. Everyone acknowledges this. By why such disagreement? Failure to seriously pursue this last question helps account for why the problem continues to persist.

Stephen Turner, scholar that he is of the history of the social sciences, deeply appreciates how that history stands littered with failed theories, ones that aspired to formulate a *science* of the social. This sorry judgment results primarily not from some prior notion of science applied to candidate social scientific theories, but from the fact that no social theory actually yields results commensurate with expectations for a science under almost any definition of that term. And so while social sciences remain established areas of research, social *science* remains to be achieved.

But why? Turner in numerous publications over the course of his extraordinarily productive career repeatedly addresses this very question. In tracking how his concerns refocus and evolve in the several decades that span the time from his first book to his most recent with respect to the question of what makes explananda social, one achieves a synoptic view of how debate regarding the idea of a social science reshapes as it moves into the twenty-first century.

A key insight guiding his work from early to late has been a keen appreciation of a need to clarify what such a science is a science of. That is, Turner almost alone among the leading social theorists of the last several decades understood that resolving prospects for a science of the social required first achieving clarity regarding the constituent elements of any such explanation. His guiding question, that is, is *not* what makes for a social *science*, but rather what makes a science one of the *social*. His work can thus be read as persistent attempts to think through how to formulate what the objects of social inquiry are. Just what is it for something to be both social *and* yet sufficiently thing-like so there can be something for some science to explain?

Rereading Turner's first book, *Sociological Explanation as Translation*, 40 years on from its initial publication from this perspective, the wisdom of hindsight reveals that what troubles him there is the putative ontology of sociology, the status of objects of "folk sociology." For from the opening chapter of that book—"the object of sociological explanation"—Turner frames the problem of sociological explanation as one of contrasting a "prescientific understanding" (SET, 1)[1] of human action and a "properly" scientific one. Of course,

---

[1] Turner 1980 is referenced in the body of the paper as SET; Turner 1994 is STP; Turner 2010 is EN; Turner 2018 is CSS.

what fulfills the description of a "properly scientific" account of human actions has itself occasioned much ongoing disagreement even among the *cognoscenti*. But this debate endures Turner realizes not because of disagreement over the status of results, but due to a lack of results about which to disagree.

From early on, Turner asks why those who aspired to a properly scientific sociology, whatever form that may take, failed to achieve their stated goal. The nub of the problem, as Turner conceives of it *circa* 1980, is ultimately ontological. "This problem about modes of explanation turns on a more fundamental one, the problem of the *object* of sociological explanation" (SET, 2; emphasis mine). He distinguishes in this regard between more and less radical diagnoses of the nature and import of this ontological problem. The less radical diagnosis sees no issue with regard to the objects of sociological explanation. Like doting parents, those in that camp counsel time and patience with still immature sciences. The more radical diagnosis "denies that there is anything that demands any special sort of 'sociological' explanation" (SET, 2). The radical view denies a core tenet on which folk sociology insists—that human action has some special characteristic, something that intrinsically distinguishes action from mere behavior. The radical diagnosis acknowledges no ontology of the social constituted in this way. Thus the social appears irremediably part of a scientifically dispensable manifest image.

Young Turner proposes a *via media* that would assimilate the "folk sociological" manifest image as an object of explanation even while acknowledging that this "object of explanation arises through ordinary discourse and does not purport to 'replace' the prescientific understanding." (SET, 2) That is, the crucial move in SET, one for which Turner would later profess atonement, takes the manifest objects as perfectly good ones for purposes of sociological explanation. "In this work, I identify one class of explanatory objects and a pattern of sociological explanation that can reasonably claim to include the crucial concerns of sociology" (SET, 2). Here Turner follows the radical diagnosis of why sociology has failed to flourish as a science by claiming that "these explanatory objects are misconceived as facts that 'general theories' of sociology can explain" (SET, 2). Rather, by identifying a distinctive *pattern* of sociological explanation he hopes to establish that the "explanatory object" emerges by seeing how it functions within this particular account of explanation, one that more closely resembles translation. Replacing ontological concerns with those of puzzle solving neatly sidesteps questions of whether or not sociology has a special ontology—social stuff. He thus offers, Turner there insists, "a defense of sociology as having a legitimate and intelligible explanatory interest apart from these pretensions [those of models of scientific rationality or conceptual analysis]" (SET, 5). Key to this defense is how the pattern "makes sense" of the social phenomena without having to inscribe it on the inventory of the furniture of the universe.

This explanatory pattern Turner analogizes to puzzle solving. "The explanations that constitute the solutions to these puzzles ... are akin to another, familiar, kind of explanation of a game 'by describing one as a variation of another—by describing them and *emphasizing* their differences and analogies.' The different practices in a social group or social context that raises the puzzle is explained in the way that a different rule of a game is explained" (SET, 97). Turner should not be mistaken here as plumping for a purely hermeneutic account. For he neither places prior constraints on what can serve to solve the sorts of puzzles that prove of interest to sociologists, nor does he insist that successful explanations be couched in intentional terms. Rather, he maintains that the "tactics of both ['interpretive' and 'statistical' sociologies] play identifiable parts in the process of setting and solving these comparative puzzles" (SET, 99). In this respect, Turner nowhere seeks to generally explicate 'explain,' or otherwise pronounce on what the form of explanation must be.

Nor need he. For these very attempts to specify "a one size fits all" account of explanation were part and parcel of his survey of the recurring failed efforts at methodological hegemony with which Turner begins that book. "[I]t must be acknowledged that 'rule governed' is a very weak sense of explanation if you are thinking 'determined by' à la classical mechanics. ... If these do not square with some ideal of explanation, imported from other contexts, and there are no other reasons for denying them the status of 'explanation,' so much the worse for the ideal and its importation" (SET, 83). Early Turner proves undaunted by challenges to either the ontological or the causal factors implicated in his favored pattern of sociological explanations. The ontology of folk sociology can be accommodated because the sorts of metaphysical issues implicit in ontological commitment, e.g., causal efficacy and identity conditions, do not impact the use made there of sociological objects in explanation.

Turner of course has much more to say than just noted regarding what makes for a satisfactory puzzle solution. My concern is exclusively with how Turner frames the problem of sociological explanation, and the constraints such as they may be placed on factors proper to the explananda and explanantia in such cases. Turner positions his efforts there explicitly as a defense of the integrity of at least certain types of sociological explanation. As he characterizes his goal, he offers "a defense of sociology as having a legitimate and intelligible explanatory interest apart from these [philosophical or natural scientific] pretensions" (SET, 5). Important to note is that Turner at this point insists on separating and distinguishing what makes for a "legitimate and intelligible explanatory interest" in sociology from what he dismisses as the hegemonic (with respect to what to call an explanation) pretensions of either conceptual analysis or scientific method. And while Turner carefully attempts to circumscribe criteria for rational evaluation of competing explanatory translations (see especially SET, ch. 4), he champions no claim that there exists some general explication of what to count as an explanation.

In this particular respect, it would be wrong to identify Turner's position as anti-naturalist since he does not explicitly countenance any supra-natural entities. Yet neither does he clearly declare allegiance to any particular sort of naturalism.

> The questions that sociologists ask were pictured as limited puzzles, with origins in the *ordinary* experience of encountering social contexts where the practices of familiar context do not fit. ... The cues for the practicing sociologist came down to the suggestion that he reconstrue *his own activities* in accordance with the puzzle-solving pattern. The case for reconstruing them in this is precisely that by doing so very real difficulties can be avoided—the difficulties with other explanatory forms that became evident in the course of the discussion. *Moreover, they can be avoided without thereby sacrificing any of sociology's distinctive concerns.* (SET, 99; emphases mine).

Turner's position here (and throughout, I would suggest) involves more a quest for explanations where the explanantia in particular are obviously compatible with whatever else passes as a science. Turner at this point can be read as counseling a type of Wittgensteinian quietism; what informed sociological folk accept as explanation is explanation enough.

But this conclusion does not continue to satisfy Turner himself. The problem, as he later comes to think of it, was with those unproblematically accepted terms of the folk sociology, the ones sociologists aimed to construct explanations of. This animates his rueful observation some fourteen years after SET. "Philosophy, as I think of it, is a form of atonement for past enthusiasms. This book [*The Social Theory of Practices*] is the product of a long struggle with myself over the ideas of tradition and practice, and particularly with the inadequacies of my own *Sociological Explanation as Translation*" (STP, ix). The issue with which he struggles and the heresy for which he needs to atone proves illuminating. "Originally, I wished to make a contribution to the tradition of conceptualization of 'tradition'. Instead, I have argued for its dissolution, at least in its standard forms" (STP, ix). But this at least hints at and possibly implies a repudiation of that pattern of explanation that so blithely took as "the object of explanation" those notions that arise "through ordinary discourse" and so "does not purport to 'replace' the prescientific understanding" (SET, 2). Indeed, Turner was not only comfortable speaking of practices in that first book, but even formulated and deployed for his own purposes what he there terms the "same practices hypothesis" (SET, 56). This was basic to characterizing the pattern of explanation that translation represents. The objects of folk sociology imagined as inscribed in practices now troubles the conscience of Turner the social theorist.

For Turner comes to appreciate that the notion of practice does not answer the question of what sociology explains, but rather actually constitutes the core of the problem in characterizing what social theory is even about. "Practices, it would appear, are the vanishing point of twentieth-century philosophy. ... The vanishing point, then, is in a domain traditionally belonging to social theory" (STP, 1). *Indeed, the first chapter of STP is nothing less than an entire recasting of how Turner now understands the problematic of specifying what the social is.* "So the legacy of the nineteenth century is a problem about practices, a problem about their status as objects, their causal properties and their 'collective' character—a problem which is unresolved and casts a shadow over the present uses of the term. The classical social theorist did not solve these problems" (STP, 6). What Turner was in 1980 willing to take for granted as unproblematic objects of sociological explanation has become exactly what he now questions under the general rubric of practices.

Turner does wring his hands a bit regarding what this portends for practices, understood as a general notion for whatever people share when they imbibe what binds them socially.

> It is our *shared practices* that enable us to be persuaded and persuade, to be explainers, or to justify and have the justifications accepted. ... But this reasoning lands us right back to the world of the classical social theorists and their puzzles about causality. ... Each of them [various terms that function as surrogates for a notion of social practice] is the name for an analogical object ... Are all these analogical constructions about the same basic stuff? If so, what is it? Or is it a mistake to ask these questions at all? ... My aim in this book is to give an account of the concepts and its uses. But it is an account that will undermine the notion of practices, and especially in the form of the theory that practices are embedded in some sort of social substrate. ... (STP, 11-12).

Clearly his attention has shifted to the purported objects invoked either in the explanantia or explananda. Turner characteristically does not promote this or that alterative conception of social objects in lieu of a practices account. This is what makes his concerns resonate in a very particular way with the issues canvassed in *Sociological Explanation as Translation*. For while the first book sought to vindicate sociological explanation as a particular type of explanatory endeavor, one rooted in a notion of the social that he was there content to treat as undefined—folk sociology, Turner now doubts that there exists an object of explanation in the sense that he previously took for granted. His doubts arise not from the standpoint of some alternative theories of objects, but from his inability to satisfactorily answer rudimentary questions regarding how social stuff can possibly function as objects, full ontological stop. No objects, no science.

As Turner ponders in STP the manifold shortcomings he finds in various accounts of social practice, these coalesce into what he terms the "transmission problem." "However one conceives practices, one must conceive them in a way which is consistent with at least the possibility of transmission, and the ways in which one conceives the possibility of transmission necessarily limits the kinds of conception of practice one may consistently adopt" (STP, 44). The transmission problem, of course, points back to the ontological question of what can be attributed causal efficacy. Social facts may not be analogizable to Hume's billiard balls, but one owes Turner realizes some story as to how social stuff moves about in the world—a social physics. Practices cannot be the ghost in the machine. In this respect, any solution to the transmission problem has clear ontological implications, for both the stuff being transmitted and the manner of its reception would requires a type of social physics—how social stuff interacts with other bodies. Otherwise, how can one explain that social things become part of a causal order?

In a glum tone, Turner concludes that "the case for practices, or practice, understood as a hidden collective object, is faced with such serious difficulties with respect to the means of transmission and acquisition of these objects that it cannot be accepted, and that appeals to 'practice' used in this sense, either in philosophy or social theory, are therefore appeals to nothing" (STP, 100; see also 115). *Ex nihilo nihil fit*. Turner thus concludes STP on this somber note. "My point is that practices cannot be both causal and shared; when we tried to conceive of them as both causal and shared we failed" (STP, 123). So much the worse, then, for the objects of folk sociology as usable posits for purposes of explanation.[2]

---

2 Turner does in STP flirt with an alternative behavioristic explanation of what accounts for even the appearance of same behavior. But this alternative is no social ersatz, but resolutely individualist as Turner there conceives of it. As such, it offers no alternative basis for a folk sociology. It simply underscores the emptiness of folk sociology.

But as difficult as it may be to imagine, the problems for social theory as Turner understands it only get worse. In Turner's mind, the sins against ontology committed in SET were ones for which he had yet to fully atone (See especially the "Introduction" to EN). In no small part, Turner worried that folk sociological notions, including (or even particularly) appeal to practices, invoked normative elements that he believes fall prey to the issues canvassed in STP connected to the transmission problem.

Normativity for Turner turns out to be just practice talk by another name. "The normative is a special realm of fact that validates, justifies, makes possible and regulates normative talk, as well as rules, meanings, the symbolic and reasoning. These facts are special in that they are empirically inaccessible and not part of the ordinary stream of explanation" (EN, 1). Turner does not believe in magic. Magic, in this case, would be the presence in this world of two distinct causal orders, one consisting of the stuff accessible to natural science, and the other the stuff that exists only in a different space, that defined by social physics. One may be tempted to use both to explain how things move in this world, but each would a causal system unto itself.

In this regard, the problems Turner finds with sociological explanation differ from those who contemplate a space of reasons. There is no accepted analog in the sociological case to deliberation or practical reasoning. It is not that the sociological somehow coincides with the space of reason; rather it defines its own causal space. It requires some of the distinctive vocabulary of the intentional idiom and so the space of reasons, but its mechanics belong to its own special social physics. And once again, Turner puzzles over the thought regarding how non-natural entities exert such influence and so merit explanatory credibility. As he observes, "The long history of secularization ... has largely consisted of desupernaturalizing explanation. Claims about 'normativity' seem to imply that this project can never be completed, that the project of desupranaturalization will always be defeated" (EN, 3). Turner doubts that the project of desupranaturalization will be thwarted, even though he recognizes that resistance to it will not be quieted by mere argument.

As he drily observes regarding Brandom, "Brandom proposes to re-enchant the world by reinstating the belief in normative powers, which is to say, powers in some sense outside and distinct from forces known to science" (EN, 4). Turner is skeptical. "So present normativism, as I will call it, is a more or less self-conscious effort to take back ground lost to social-science explanation" (EN, 5). But, contrary to the stance taken in SET, this does not imply that social science has as its object those countenanced by folk sociology. Rather, this remark must be read in light of what Turner argues in STP. Regularities can be observed; it is their explanation that is at issue. Can certain regularities be explained by adverting to social stuff? STP seemingly raises an insuperable problem to an invocation of social stuff as what explains, viz. the transmission problem. For in light of this how could there be a specification either of items with the needed stuff-like properties to be transmitted or a capacity to receive just "the same" stuff? But what now regarding the social as an object of explanation?

Put another way, what Turner perceives happening is that given the failed efforts to specify in sociological terms what sort of stuff gets transmitted, the philosophical move is to deny that the stuff is sociologically natural. "The mere sociological fact that people believe a given practice to be obligatory does not make it so. It is the extra thing that does make it so that needs to be explained" (EN, 5). This ability to interact in substance-like ways, including causal, makes normative notions ontologically *sui generis*. "Science, the normativist would say is a normative concept, not a sociological one, and distinguishing science from voodoo requires the normative sense of science" (EN, 8). This touches on the basis of Turner's unhappiness. The normative, as he construes it, does what folk sociology was supposed to do, i.e., give an account of what binds and acts on people over and above mundane appeals to socialization and the like. In this context, "these new normative facts constitute a rupture in the world of ordinary fact" (EN, 9) But what now is the "world of ordinary fact"? Turner, as previously noted, does *not* seek to champion any particular flavor of naturalism, materialism, etc. Neither does he endorses any particular account of explanation. His strategy, rather, is to ask what would license appeal to a special realm of fact, and so justify an account of explanation that brooked the boundaries recognized by empirical science (See EN, 12 for a concise statement of this issue). In sum, "The case for normativity rests very heavily on the idea that only the normative can account for the normative" (EN, 25). But his cagey maneuver turns on insistently asking what would license adversion to a realm of "normative" explanations. If the normative requires its own special physics, then one should proceed with theoretical caution before embracing any such account.

This underscores just how sharply later Turner breaks with the Turner of SET. For the Turner of SET, the terms of folk sociology could be taken at face value for ontological and explanatory purposes. The puzzle solving pattern early Turner attributes to sociological explanations did not need to break free from the terms in which the folk had set the issues, keeping in mind that the folks in question could all be professional social scientists.

But by the publication of *Explaining the Normative*, later Turner will have no truck with the promiscuous ontologizing of his youth. This impatience surfaces quite explicitly, *inter alia*, when Turner surveys the literature on cognitive diversity.

> What are the implications of all this diversity? ... But there is a way of distilling it, from an explanatory point of view . ... All the diverse folk notions mentioned here (and this is merely the tip of the iceberg) have two relevant features: ... They work in those social settings to enable the participants to interact with each other, understand each other, and coordinate their conduct. None of them is 'true' in the sense of being scientifically true. ...
>
> We can, for convenience, call these diverse notions 'theories', though we should keep in mind that this is only a convenience, and that the whole language of theory ... we use to describe these diverse things does not necessary match up with anything like 'a theory in someone's head,' that is to say, a genuinely explanatory account of what is going on when people use these folk notions. With that qualification, we may describe these various folk conceptions as 'Good Bad Theories', meaning that they are good theories for a particular, unspecified set of purposes in a particular setting, *but bad theories if we are thinking of them as adequate explanations of anything, or as proto-explanations that can be turned into genuine explanations with a little empirical vetting and some minor revision* (EN, 42-3; emphasis mine).

The italicized remark represents a wholesale rejection of the explanatory project endorsed in SET. The key resides in understanding what Turner implies by "None of them [folk theories] is 'true' in the sense of being scientifically true." Again, this judgment does not reflect Turner's imposition of some favored definition of science. Rather, he only asks how to make ontological sense of whatever has been ascribed reality and causal efficacy. Sociological theories do not provide a social physics in any tolerably precise way, and he can locate no science in the vicinity that provides aid and succor to beliefs in objects so imagined. R.I.P. SET.

Turner's use of the phrase "scientifically true" that is must be treated *descriptively* and not as endorsing some prior theoretical position. Turner here (and throughout his post-SET beratings of his earlier self) notes *just as a matter of fact* that no established natural science endorses the ontology of folk theories or anything like it. This discrepancy between theoretically tolerated items establishes the basic tension between the explanatory projects of the social versus the natural science. This shows that the question animating SET remains, alas, alive and well, viz., what is the relation between the social world and the natural? SET tried to set to rest that question. Turner sees that initial attempt on his part as failing because he did not take seriously enough the question of the putative objects invoked for purposes of explanation.

Once the objects are problematized as he argues in STP, the explanatory pattern assuming those objects can no longer be granted a *prima facie* legitimacy—the strategy of SET. EN relentlessly asks if a "special" explanatory pattern for folk normativity can be justified, and finds no such extenuating rationale (See, e.g., his discussion of "causal-normative dualism" at EN, 44–5). A possible caveat here concerns, of course, cognitive science. To this topic we shall return. But note for now that Turner's strategy post-SET is never to say yea or nay regarding folk talk. He remains resolutely agnostic, i.e., unconvinced that the natural sciences can explain the social, but skeptical that this legitimates re-enchanting the social world. Restoring his early faith in the social now requires some plausible solution to the transmission problem.

One can distinguish in this regard between "Turnerized" v. "non-Turnerized" explanations in the following way. Turnerized accounts consist of just those explanation of things social about which no special philosophical assumptions regarding norms or normativity need be made. Put another way, Turner's repeated complaint is that normative explanations consistently presuppose the legitimacy of what they claim to prove, viz., the need for normative facts. "The normative-natural distinction used in this way is a normative distinction, depending on the definition of norms, or the normative theory, that supplies the normative elements that are supposed to be separated out and used to reconstruct the phenomenon free from naturalistic or causal considerations. It is not an explanatory distinction found in nature or social reality. It is visible only to those constructing a normative lens" (EN, 148). In short, Turner's position is not that normative accounts are demonstrably false, but that he remains unconvinced that normative "facts" can be part of a scientific explanation. The explananda in view, e.g., why people take certain actions to be legitimate, simply do not require anything more than mundane facts about social life and socialization (See, e.g., EN, 168, 184).

In the closing pages of EN, however, Turner appears to waver on this key point. His uncertainty about the prospects of re-enchantment emanates from his considerations of empathy and its role in constituting the social. "Empathy is important as an addition to this discussion because it goes beyond the traditional Humean inputs and means of learning. To the extent that we have, and actually employ in ordinary interaction, a primitive capacity for following the thought of another ... we have a surrogate for the kinds of *a priori* content that Kant thought Hume was lacking, a surrogate without the mysteries of transcendental philosophy" (EN, 204). As always, Turner delights in taking away with one hand what the other hand seems to proffer. On offer seems to be what normativists and friends of folk sociology hungered for—non-natural explainers. But, Turner cautions, empathy provides this *"without the mysteries of transcendental philosophy."* One can almost hear the sighs of disappointment.

Why no mysteries, at least just yet? Here is how Turner assesses the matter in the closing paragraph of EN.

> Empathy does the work of explanation that hidden presuppositions did for Brentano's rivals. The reason empathy works to produce genuine *Evidenz* is that there is a natural process underlying it: both the capacity, actually employed, of emulating or following the thought of another and the feedback generated by social interaction. These are facts of social theory (and of neuroscience). This kind of social theory does not involve collective facts ... But it detranscendentalizes 'reason' just as effectively. (EN, 205).

Turner's conviction at this point that even empathy, unavoidable though it may be, requires positing no special realm of fact rests on experiments involving mirror neurons.

> They [mirror neurons] enable the brain to operate on a dual-use basis, so that the neurons used for acting are also used for what Weber would call the direct observational experience of a meaningful action. ... The brain, in short, performs the trick Weber attributes to direct observational understanding—of transforming behavioral cues into action-identifications, which is to say into meaningful actions. And having a location in the brain changes the status of empathy—it ceases to be an intellectual process bound up with the error-prone folk language of intentionality, and becomes a fact of science with a discoverable set of features located in specific neuronal processes. Moreover, it is these processes that deal with *subjective meaning*, in an [sic] recognizable sense of that term. (EN, 176).

Thus does Turner continue to play whack-a-mole with theories that give any sign that there exists something irreducibly normative or social, things that must be explained and yet can only be explained using normative or non-natural terms. For any such candidate explanandum normative theorists suggest, Turner locates a naturalistic surrogate. He does this not out a commitment to naturalism so much as a part of his ongoing *mea culpa,* his continuing atonement for the misplaced faith of his youth in uncritically accepting the ontologies of folk sociologies.

But his youthful sins and enthusiasms are not easily expiated. His restless theoretician's soul turns yet again to the question of whether or not mirror neurons and their ilk prove up to theoretical task he contingently assigns them in EN. Thus, less than a decade after having tried to bring closure yet again to the issue of explaining the normative, one finds Turner openly worrying whether or not things social require explanation in terms that slip a naturalist's net.

Cognitive Science and the Social: A Primer renews Turner's argument with himself on just this ontological and explanatory point. As he observes at the very outset of that work, "topics of concern to social science, such as human action and intentionality, are also of central concern to cognitive science. Nor can social science ignore cognitive science: 'social' phenomena route their causality through human minds, and therefore also through brains" (CSS, 1). The problem is as before a variation on the transmission problem. "The way we can describe the brain does not mesh well with the way we describe our minds and actions" (CSS, 2). Without that mesh, transmission remains an unsolved problem. Solutions counsel either countenancing non-natural facts or showing that there is less to "transmit" than normativists assume.

Turner for his part remains torn. "The focus of this book, accordingly, is on the conflicts in cognitive science and the conflicts between various considerations central to particular approaches to cognitive neuroscience and the larger domain of 'the social,' and with question of how they can be, if not resolved, at least understood. *In doing this, it should be evident the concept of "the social" is also in play*" (CSS, 3; emphasis mine). The italicized remark signals it appears that the confidence originally excited by mirror neurons has waned. For although Turner concludes EN with a declaration that even empathy has been naturalized, he begins CSS with questions on just this point. "Does their efficacy [mirror neurons] confirm the folk theory of mind, or any theory of mind, the 'theory implied by our attempts to articulate our knowledge of other minds?' ... The paradoxical downside to the recognition and neuroscientific ground of these capacities is this: our understanding of ourselves and our own cognitive processes is especially limited" (CSS, 5–6). This limitation raises for Turner yet again the specter that forever haunts social science—how to account for reality of social facts. "[T]he experience and social experience made possible by the *Verstehen* window is 'real'. It is a fact that needs to be accounted for, and whose causal role needs to be understood in order to account for 'mind' or for the social phenomena that are associated with these experiences" (CSS, 6; cp. SET, 5). Having intended to lay the ghost of SET in EN, Turner now finds himself forced to revisit the ontological and explanatory issues that he has continually tried to put to rest. Forty years on, his philosophical conscience clearly remains troubled by the ontological promiscuity of his youth.

Turner introduces early in CSS the neologism "*Verstehen* bubble" (CSS, 11). This should be contextualized in terms of the issues surveyed thus far. Turner always writes with a view to the history of social science as framing the questions that concern him. He invokes basically the same historical lineage and set of issues to begin CSS as he does to begin SET, one dating from Hobbes and concerning questions about constituting "the social" (Cp., e.g., SET, ix and CSS, 3–4). This offers a perspective from which to take to heart Turner's remark that the import of his neologism reflects "the fact that this book [CSS] is a social science and philosophy of social science approach to the issues" (CSS, 12). For seen that way questions regarding what the bubble encloses just encapsulate Turner's continuing worries about what there is, social speaking.

This signature concern surfaces quickly enough.

> Folk psychology is, in some sense, the language we use to express our understanding of others. Indeed, without this ability to understand others we would be hard pressed to do neuroscience at all. ... This dependence on folk psychology, or something like it, is pervasive—Daniel Dennett uses the term 'intentional stance', while in this book I will be using *Verstehen*. ... The social sciences do not merely employ these terms incidentally, but incorporate them ... into their own theories. ... This makes them different from normal concepts in science. (CSS, 19; see also 21).

How different? Turner's answer to that question from early to late remains the same. These terms are implicated in constituting the objects, and the causal relations among those objects, in sciences of the *social*. Without intentional characterizations, there would be no actions, and so nothing collective or social to explain. Without adverting to beliefs, desires, norms and their ilk, there would be nothing social about such explanations, much less a transmission problem to solve regarding the items that move social actors to act. "It is an open question as to what role the body, interactions with the environment, physical and interpersonal, and physical objects play in the processes that correspond to 'mental' terms. Worse, this plethora of concepts of the mental prevents us from getting a coherent way of talking about the subject. The concepts are not merely diverse, they often appear to conflict with one another" (CSS, 22). *Plus ça change, plus c'est la même chose.*

Indeed, as Turner worries the relation between the cognitive sciences and the social, he ponders yet again the problem set by the realization that the "domain of things that 'need' be explained is not given as something well defined. Indeed, as will see in later chapter, it is very difficult to distinguish "the social" as a domain, and perhaps futile" (CSS, 37). Moreover, a variation on the transmission problem that figured so prominently in STP reappears in Turner's discussion in CSS, albeit not by that name. For in his accounts of representation in cognitive science, Turner astutely and in retrospect unsurprisingly finds that the same problems that dogged accounts of transmission of social stuff resurface (See, e.g., CSS, 62–5).

Turner devotes chapter 4 of CSS to the topic "Explaining and Understanding Action." Interestingly, in the context of a discussion of Weber, Turner hints at a way out of the ontological and causal questions that bedevil him (Turner). Turner remarks that for Weber, "folk psychology is indispensable, but only because it is the language of the culture in which we formulate our questions and answers. ... For him, folk psychology need not be a true theory of mind, or even an approximation. It is simply a way of talking about the world disclosed by understanding or *Verstehen*" (CSS, 102). This is an observation with which not only could the author of SET agree, but it is the very sort of remark that author makes (See SET, 21 and 80). The author of CSS concludes that what Weber's strategy yields is

> an odd, and non-reductive, division of labor between social science and biology ... The narrow limits [of social science] are defined by the capacity to empathize, particularly to identify actions ... We can think of his sociology as social science within the limits of understanding, but with a full recognition that many relevant processes lie beyond these limits. ... He gets the full conceptual advantage of being able to use the rich language of his own local speech community, including the language of folk psychology, without any need to commit himself to its 'reality,' or correspondence with the brain, or ultimate causality, for example, in the form of the theory of free will. (CSS, 103).

That is, the Turnerian strategy for licensing talk about the social no longer requires taking folk sociology to have any special ontological status or causal role. Of course, it remains to be clarified what "social science within the limits of understanding" amounts to.

Turner the inveterate agnostic surveys the alternatives that the literature offers. Another vestige of his youth reappears—pattern recognition (See, e.g., CSS, 177ff). Turner suggests that the virtue of this approach is that "it does not depend on positing spooky and problematic mental entities such as intentions" (CSS, 120). And yet he reluctantly acknowledges this view leaves one "still very far from traditional social science issues" (CSS, 120). The survey has drawn cognitive science and social science closer, but fundamental gaps remain. The primary obstacle Turner repeatedly finds is one he himself pioneered in identifying, viz., the dreaded transmission problem. For whatever surrogate he examines for accounting for the self and the social, explanation stumbles just here. "The difficulty, which cognitive science shares with social theory generally, is not with these facts [about culture] but with explanation. ... This puts the focus on a variant of the same problem that we encountered with Chomsky: the question of how, if there are shared cognitive structures, they got where they need to be for the explanation to work" (CSS, 169) What the shared is, and how people share it, remain in Turner's account questions without good answers. And so as before, no objects, no science.

Although Turner continually seeks to expiate the theoretical excesses of his youth, like St. Augustine he keeps his old ways close even while he contemplates the move to a higher (in Turner's case, more explanatorily integrated) plane of being. Consider Turner the Older contemplating "The Self as a Problem" (CSS, 172). This Turner continues to eschew all appeals to normativity as unacceptable mystery-mongering.

> Each of these accounts works by taking something—culture, the body, computational architecture, the organization of memory, narrative—as given and unproblematic, and attempts to build an account of the coherence of the self around it. One might think that it would be possible to integrate the account into a general theory of the self. But the elements are not only too diverse, they also appear to be incompatible. The alternative would be reduction to one controlling consideration, or prioritizing one kind of coherence as representing the core or true self. This does not seem plausible either. (CSS, 172).

But does this imply for Turner that he has decided to do the full Quine and simply forgo the intentional as an object of explanation? No. For in the very next paragraph, the voice of Turner the Younger breaks through the explanatory gloom retailed above.

> The problem of the self *is* its irreducibility to either the material or spiritual side of the subject . ... But we can replace the older language, or at least use the cognitive science data to improve it and specify the issues; there is the self of the *Verstehen* bubble ... The self of the *Verstehen* bubble is the self that is defined by our capacity to understand and distinguish ourselves from others and to identify them as empathic subjects ...

> Then there is the body self. The intractability of the problem of the self is a result of [these] two facts [i.e., integrating intentional characterizations of self and physical accounts of bodies]. ... We can break these issues down by considering the relation between the self of the *Verstehen* bubble and the self or person in the causal sense. (CSS, 172).

Turner the Older cannot live explanatorily with the Verstehen bubble and yet Turner the Younger cannot live without it, in at least two sense of 'without'. One sense is just the root Brentano sense of the intentional—he continues to insist that there is no paraphrasing it away in non-intentional terms. The other sense is that as people we cannot live outside this way of speaking, if only because others then disappear.

But as unavoidable as encounter with mind and world as conceptualized within the *Verstehen* bubble may be, no theory that Turner scouts can clear his core explanatory hurdle, viz., "explaining how the tacit theory or 'program' get inserted: they can't come from normal interaction, except through some hitherto unknown means of transmission" (CSS, 175).

Thus after further review, Turner now sees no way to fully reclaim the optimism of his youth.

> And this leaves us with the unanswered question of the book. Can the standard approach account for practices, social institutions, ideologies, and the like? Are the alternative approaches adequate to the task? Or is the problem of the social the place where the challenges became overwhelming? ... Largely taken for granted social concepts [ones within the Verstehen bubble] ... are cognitively involved. To the extent that they depend on cognitively implausible ideas about the relevant cognitive processes, they are strictly speaking unscientific. *There may be good reason for remaining outside the circle of consilience that is science. But to do so would be to abandon the project of social science as science itself.* ... The social is the great unexplained domain. Is it the place where plausibility goes to die? (CSS, 216; emphasis mine).

This returns Turner to not quite where he began his intellectual odyssey so many years ago. For then as now, he remains committed to the view that "foundational concerns with the philosophical problems of understanding human action remain our problems today" (SET, ix). But unlike the optimism that informs that first book, what remains of "the social" one now finds encapsulated (quarantined?) in a "*Verstehen* bubble." This serves to underline its problematic status as a legitimate object of explanation. Put another way, Turner's early willingness to accept as a working hypothesis "the existence and intellectual substance of sociology" lingers on, albeit in a more attenuated form. Ditto for his view that "the substantive problems of concern to sociology are genuine problems" (SET, ix). That said, whether problems so understood permit of scientific solution remains unsettled.

Early and late, Turner insists that he has no "new theory" to offer. And that is true. This in large part reflects Turner's rhetorical and intellectual positioning himself as primarily an informed observer on the social theory scene. But of course he does much more than that. *Sociological Explanation as Translation* had as its implied thesis a kind of Wittgensteinian quietism about sociology. All is in order as it is. Sociological objects—the stuff of folk sociology—could be assumed to have both their own reality and their own explanatory form.

What Turner concludes over time is that the objects did not have the integrity he initially granted them, and so he embarks on a decades long odyssey to return to the confident position held in his youth. To do so, he must navigate his way over uncharted ontological and causal terrains. The challenges this metaphysical *terra incognita* pose crystalize I have argued in his 1994 discussion of the transmission problem. He must discover a way to navigate past the transmission problem before he can reach his journey's end.

Although still unsolved, Turner remains vaguely hopeful that the transmission problem will yet prove tractable. Put another way, progress with respect to understanding what the social is has been made in philosophy of social science *not* by regimenting all explanations into a particular form, but by discovering how to make its distinctive objects scientifically manageable. Despite the dour note on which Turner concludes his 2018 work, it would be remiss to ignore the optimism he almost unwittingly expresses at its beginning. For in his "Foreword," he states that the book is *not* a critique of efforts bring work in social theory together with that of cognitive science. Indeed, overcome it seems by newfound enthusiasm, he there remarks "It is not too much to say that this is the beginning of a revolution" (CSS, xi).

Put another way, philosophy of social science as Turner well knows begins with debates about how explanations in social science appear to diverge in important and debilitating ways from those in the natural sciences. The original debates also included ones about ontology, e.g., individuals and classes. But debate about the form of explanation initially took precedence. Yet what Turner has relentlessly and compellingly drawn to everyone's theoretical attention is that the root problem resides not with the form of explanation but with the objects to be explained. Turner's own arc of development is driven by this fundamental insight, one that he more than any other thinker has analyzed and explored as philosophy of social science evolved and migrated into the current century. He led the way in charting how any explanation of social objects—whatever falls within the *Verstehen* bubble—might be conjoined with objects of other sorts so as to finally provide explanations of how they all interact. In doing this, Turner has also determined the route that must be followed to make progress in an understanding of the social.

References

Turner, Stephen P. 1980. *Sociological Explanation as Translation.* Cambridge: Cambridge University Press.

Turner, Stephen P. 1994. *The Social Theory of Practices.* Chicago: The University of Chicago Press.

Turner, Stephen P. 2010. *Explaining the Normative.* Cambridge, MA: Polity Press.

Turner, Stephen P. 2018. *Cognitive Science and the Social: A Primer.* New York: Routledge.

Rationality and Interpretive Methodology
Transformations in the Apparent Irrationality Debate

Mark Risjord

Abstract

The problem of apparent irrationality was a question about how to understand speech or behavior that was, from the interpreter's point of view, irrational. The ensuing debate concerned the role of rationality in interpretation. Localists contended that norms of rationality were embedded in cultural practices, and the range of discoverable variation was as broad as the possible variation of cultures. Neo-rationalists contended that norms of logic were presupposed by the activity of interpretation, and hence that there were a priori limits on the forms of rationality. Expanding on the mutual constraints of the cognitive and social sciences for which Turner argues in *Cognitive Science and the Social: A Primer*, this essay contends that the debate over apparent irrationality depended on two assumptions: that culture is bounded while rationality is unbounded. Both of these assumptions have been shown false by developments in anthropology and psychology. In its canonical form, then, the question that generated the problem of apparent irrationality cannot be answered, and the canonical positions in the debate are undermined.

Keywords

Culture – rationality – explanation – apparent irrationality – anthropology – cognitive science

1 Introduction: Two Senses of Naturalism

In the late twentieth century, the problem of apparent irrationality was an outstanding issue in the philosophy of social science. Ethnographers described many examples of puzzling belief that seemed to be beyond the bounds of rationality. In the first part of the twentieth century, such examples prompted a theoretical debate in anthropology about "primitive mentality." In philosophy, the question became whether ethnographic interpretation presupposed rationality in the traditional, philosophical sense, or whether it was possible to discover culturally specific norms of rational thought and action. The debate touched deep themes in philosophy, and Stephen Turner's first book, *Sociological Explanation as Translation* (1980), contributed to this conversation.

Turner's most recent book, *Cognitive Science and the Social: A Primer* (2018) argues that cognitive neuroscience and the social sciences present deep and potentially transformative challenges to each other. He proposes that cognitive neuroscience and the social sciences are linked by a web of "issues and constraints" (Turner 2018, 10–11). This essay will expand that list of mutual constraints to encompass issues of rationality. It will argue that the apparent irrationality debate of the late twentieth century depended on two assumptions: that culture is bounded and that rationality is unbounded. Both of these are now dubious. The first was called into question by anthropology, the second by cognitive science. Arguably, then, the questions that animated the rationality debate in the philosophy of social science can no longer arise, though related issues remain.

In his synoptic reflection on the rationality debates in the philosophy of social science, Paul Roth concluded that "The ghost of a nineteenth century philosophical dispute about rationality should at last finally be exorcised, and the dead hand of tradition made to release its grip on the philosophy of social science" (Roth 2011, 117). This essay concurs in that opinion, though argument here differs from Roth's in important ways. Roth was concerned with the relationship between *scientific* rationality and the practical rationality of the subjects of a social science. One way to see the question of naturalism—whether the sciences have a unified method—is as a question about whether understanding the practical rationality of agents requires different methodologies than other kinds of inquiry. Roth traces this philosophical dispute back to the nineteenth century, arguing that the question presupposes a metaphysics of determinate objects of inquiry and fixed methods for finding out about them. With the fall of this larger edifice, the idea that an interpretation could capture a stable and independent world of meaning must fall too. The philosophical arguments that brought down logical positivism and its attendant philosophy of science thus undermine the metaphysical assumptions of the rationality debate.

As distinct from Roth's focus on scientific rationality, this essay will be concerned with the broader conception of human rationality and the character of presuppositions specific to the apparent irrationality debate. These presuppositions, it will be argued below, have been undermined by developments in the sciences, not by broader changes in the philosophy of science (or, perhaps, not *only* by such changes, since there is no sharp distinction between philosophy of science and the sciences). Anthropologists rejected the idea of determinate and bounded cultures at least in part because it distorted their understanding of human behavior. The idea of bounded rationality has flourished because it provides superior explanations of human thought and action. This essay will thus raise the issue of "naturalism" in its other philosophical sense—the relationship between philosophy and the sciences—which was an important theme of Turner's work throughout his career.

2   The Problem of Apparent Irrationality and Its Presuppositions, 1958–2000

In the form to be discussed here, the problem of apparent irrationality can be traced to Peter Winch's *Idea of a Social Science* (1958) and the companion piece "Understanding a Primitive Society" (1964). Winch provided arguments for some startling conclusions:

> … criteria of logic are not a direct gift of God, but arise out of, and are only intelligible in the context of, ways of living or modes of social life (1958, 100).
>
> Reality is not what gives language sense. What is real and what is unreal shows itself *in* the sense that language has (1964, 309).

Winch's position was that concepts like "reason," "reality," or "truth" got their sense from their use in particular speech communities. He argued that ethnographic or historical interpretations must therefore be sensitive to the differences in forms of reasoning between the interpreter and those interpreted. It would be a mistake to assume that, to use a standard example, Azande witchcraft was a proto-scientific theoretical system that might be falsified by empirical evidence. Winch's arguments were challenged by those, such as Martin Hollis (1967b, a), Alasdair MacIntyre (1967, 1970), and Stephen Lukes (1967), who wanted to argue that substantive commitments about the rationality of one's interlocutors were presupposed by the activity of interpretation. The ensuing debate between what this essay will call "localists" and "neo-rationalists" created a rather well-defined literature, and it can be clearly divided into two phases.

The key essays from the first phase of the debate were collected in Bryan Wilson's *Rationality* (1970). The questions focused on methodology, and centered on a few vivid examples drawn from cultural anthropology. The main question was whether an interpreter could treat the apparently irrational behavior as rational "by the lights" of the local norms and standards, or whether interpretation required the application of universal norms of rationality. In the second phase, arguments for the presumption of rationality were given a boost by Donald Davidson's essays, particularly "The Very Idea of a Conceptual Scheme" (1984c). The principle of charity became a key to the neo-rationalist position. On localist side, the arguments were kept alive by the new currents in the sociology of science, especially the so-called Edinburgh School. Hollis and Lukes's *Rationality and Relativism* (1982) crystallized the second phase of the debate and set the agenda for the 1980s and 1990s, where questions of translation (Turner 1980, Roth 1987, Feleppa 1988) and explanation (Henderson 1993, Risjord 1993) were the focus.

The claims that culture is bounded and rationality is unbounded were presuppositions of the debate in the sense that they were commitments shared by parties to the rationality debate and they shaped the scope of possible responses. The first presupposition concerns the concept of culture as well as its philosophical cognates, such as linguistic community and language-game. The commitment is that humans can be divided into relatively homogenous groups that share a language and a body of beliefs, values, habits, institutions, life-ways, and so on. Cultures (language communities, etc.) are taken to be bounded in the sense that individual persons can be identified as members of the culture. Moreover, beliefs (values, etc.) can be sorted into those that are typical of, or shared by most, members of the culture and those that are atypical or imported. Of course, both philosophers and social scientists recognized the existence of borderline cases. Questions of culture change and individual acculturation were also acknowledged, but all of these questions were understood in the context of a commitment to clear cases of community membership. Given the boundedness of cultures, it made sense to name them and to use this name as the subject of ascriptions of word meaning, belief, and value (hence the intelligibility of a sentence like "the Azande believe in witchcraft").

The second presupposition concerns rationality. Herbert Simon coined the phrase "bounded rationality" to contrast with the idea that human rationality could be modeled with formal logic and decision theory (Simon 1957). Bounded rationality now encompasses a range of disciplines, theoretical stances, and research programs (Evans 1989, Gigerenzer and Selten 2001, Jones 2001, Kahneman 2002, Elster 2007, Gigerenzer 2008, Thaler and Sunstein 2009, Kahneman 2011). They share a commitment to the realistic description of the cognitive processes that constitute human reasoning, and agree that the description will involve a cluster of processes that explain both valid and invalid reasoning. The second presupposition of the rationality debate might be called *unbounded* rationality because it is precisely the picture of rationality

Simon was resisting. The idea is not that humans have unlimited powers of deduction. Parties to the rationality debate were quite clear that humans make mistakes, get tired, and sometimes are simply dim-witted. Rather, the rationality debate presupposed that human rationality consisted, at least in part, in the capacity to follow the rules of logic, including deduction, induction, and practical rationality. In other words, humans are rational insofar as they conform to logical norms.

In the first phase of the rationality debate, both commitments were manifest in the centrality of *rules* to the conceptualization of human thought, language, and action, and to the conceptualization of social scientific understanding itself. Drawing on Wittgensteinean themes, Winch articulated a view that made meaning a matter of correct rule-following. The meaning of a word is its use in the language, and rules determine correct use. Winch conceived of rules as constituted by the behavioral regularities and activities of a group of people (their form of life). The very idea of a rule, then, depended on the existence of well-defined groups (bounded cultures), since a rule could have determinate content only insofar as the group was determinate. Since reasoning was understood as a matter of correctly following the rules of logic, rationality was unbounded.

Winch argued that because the rules constituting meaning and rationality were dependent on community behavior, and since communities could vary, meaning and rationality could vary as well. The range of possible forms of rationality is as wide as the range of possible forms of life. This is what he meant when he wrote "... criteria of logic are not a direct gift of God, but arise out of, and are only intelligible in the context of, ways of living or modes of social life" (Winch 1958, 100). The consequence for social scientific understanding was that social scientific methods needed to focus on the practices that constituted the rules and the way in which these practices are different from our own.

Those who responded to Winch's arguments maintained the focus on rules in social scientific understanding. But they disagreed with Winch over the possibility of discovering certain kinds of variation. Because of his capacity for elegant synthesis, Lukes nicely illustrates the neo-rationalist position (Lukes 1967). Lukes distinguished between what he called "rational (1)" and "rational (2)" criteria of rationality. Rational (1) criteria are universal, and they will be the "general" criteria of rationality for any given society. They include the distinction between truth and falsity, basic principles of logic, and the practical rationality of everyday behavior. Rational (2) criteria are local and context dependent. They differ among cultures, and within any particular culture, they are applied only to a special class of belief, typically those associated with religion and mysticism. On this view, it was possible for a social scientist to identify in a culture a special "ritual logic" or form of reasoning that deviated from universal logical norms. But doing so did not entail the pervasive differences in rationality envisioned by Winch. In the neo-rationalist response to Winch's localism, unbounded rationality is clearly visible. Even in rational (2) criteria, the local form of rationality is a matter of following (local) rules.

In the second phase of the debate, Lukes' distinction between rational (1) criteria and rational (2) criteria were given a boost by Donald Davidson's work in the philosophy of language. In a series of influential essays, (Davidson 1984a), Davidson argued that the meaning of a sentence could be identified with its truth conditions. Drawing on Tarski's semantics for first order logic, Davidson argued that translation required identifying the logical structure of the language. Nothing could be identified as a language unless it conformed to classical logic, at least in large part. The presupposition of unbounded rationality is clear, since someone can be interpreted as a speaker of a language, and a rational agent, only insofar as they conform to the rules of classical logic and decision theory.

The evidence for an interpretation, on Davidson's view, was a matter of empirically verifying that the truth conditions of a sentence in the target language were the same as a sentence in the home language. The T-sentences of a Tarskian semantics are tailor-made for such a role:

> ... positive instance of 'Speakers (of German) hold "Es schneit" true when, and only when, it is snowing' should be taken to confirm not only the generalization, but also the T-sentence, ' "Es schneit" is true (in German) for a speaker x at time t if and only if it is snowing at it (and near x)'. ... The general policy, ... is to choose truth conditions that do as well as possible in making speakers hold sentence true when (according to the theory and the theory builder's view of the facts) those sentences are true.
>
> DAVIDSON 1984b, 152

In these early formulations,[1] meaning in a language depended on a best fit between the logical semantics and the behavior of a group of speakers. Davidson's view thus presupposed both unbounded rationality and bounded cultures, since insofar as the group is indeterminate, assigning meanings will be impossible.

---

1   In the 1980s, Davidson's view evolved away from the commitment to bounded linguistic communities. "A Nice Derangement of Epitaphs" (1986) represents an important development in his thinking, but its lessons were not absorbed into the rationality debate.

The empirical tractability of interpretation, in Davidson's view, requires the "the principle of charity." An empirically well-grounded interpretation will confirm many T-sentences, and this means the interpreted speakers will have mostly true beliefs. It was quickly pointed out—and Davidson himself recognized—that making speakers plausibly right or wrong depends on considerations of the speaker's culture and context. The principle of charity was thus often reformulated as the "principle of humanity:" do not attribute inexplicably false beliefs to the speakers (Grandy 1973, Macdonald and Pettit 1981). The principle of humanity entails that there is a difference between the attribution of beliefs that are true (by the interpreter's lights) and those that are false. The attribution of true beliefs needs no explanation, while the attribution of false beliefs does. This became known as the "asymmetry thesis," and it was central to the second stage of the rationality debate.

In the second stage of the rationality debate, the localist side of the argument was buttressed by work in the sociology of science. One of the main thrusts came from the Edinburgh School, which had clear lines of influence from the same Wittgensteinean ideas that influenced Winch (Barnes 1974, Barnes and Bloor 1982, Bloor 1983). They targeted the asymmetry thesis, arguing that even in the sciences, true belief stands in need of the same kinds of explanations we give false belief. Barnes and Bloor moved away from the unbounded rationality assumption by rejecting any role for considerations of whether a belief is justified or arguments are valid. The question shifted to the "credibility" of belief and the causes by which scientists take conclusions to be acceptable. Beliefs are credible when they are sanctioned by the community of scientists through their practices. While their appeal to practices was more causal than rule oriented, this phase of the sociology of science maintained the Winchean assumption that communities of scientists were identifiable and bounded.

Turner's first book, *Sociological Explanation as Translation* (1980), developed the idea that explanation and translation are tightly linked. Turner proposed that "comparative sociology" (a broad term which includes much of cultural anthropology, as well as some strands of history and political science) had a distinctive pattern of explanation. A comparative sociologist looks to compare the practices of two groups. In the comparison, tentative hypotheses about similarities are made: practice A in group X is similar to a practice B in group Y. This "same practice hypothesis" will break down when members of group Y don't respond or act in ways that would be expected, were they were doing something analogous to A. When a hypothesis fails, explanation is called for. New explanations require new evidence, and Turner emphasizes the broad range of factors that can be explanatorily relevant. Sometimes the call for explanation is rejected by rejecting the point of analogy; *B* is not analogous to *A*, but to anther practice, *A'*. In other cases, the analogy is maintained, but new explanatory burdens must be shouldered. On Turner's view, explanation and translation are two parts of the same activity, since to translate is to make an analogy between their practices and ours. Like Barnes and Bloor, Turner did not give a prominent role to reasoning in his account of cross-cultural interpretation. That a group reasons in this or that way is another possible point of analogy between us and them. Turner was therefore not committed to the unboundedness of rationality.

Mark Risjord (2000) generalized Turner's conclusion about the deep link between translation and explanation. He deployed an account of explanation that applied to a wider variety of explanatory forms than Turner's comparison of practices. Risjord, however, did not follow Turner's approach to rationality. He returned to the notion that following rules of reasoning is constitutive of rationality. Risjord treated these rules as explanatory postulates made by the interpreter, but regarded rationality as a matter of following the local rules. Risjord was thus committed to unbounded rationality in a way that Turner was not.

While they differ on the role of rules, and hence differ in their commitment to unbounded rationality, the turn to explanation found in Turner and Risjord retains an underlying commitment to the boundedness of culture. It persists in a somewhat weaker form than found in Winch or (early) Davidson. For Winch and Davidson, content of rules or linguistic meaning could be fixed only insofar as community boundaries could be fixed. Turner's and Risjord's appeals to explanation were broadly based, and thus did not link content to community boundaries. Their deployment of explanation, however, assumes an intelligible general distinction between "us" and "them." For Turner, the distinction is presupposed by the idea of a comparison, while for Risjord it is presupposed by the asymmetry between the explainer and the practices being explained. Both views assume the intelligibility of a clean comparison between "our" practices and "theirs."

As the rationality debated evolved between 1958 and 2000, then, the twin presuppositions that culture is bounded, while rationality is not, shaped the problematic. While not all views depended on rules deriving their content from a well-defined community, these assumptions influenced the kinds of moves that were made in critique of Winch, as well as those that developed of his idea of a social science.

3 Culture and Rationality

As the rationality debate was unfolding, its central assumptions were being steadily undermined. Anthropologists were having serious doubts about the utility of the culture concept by the 1980s. Herbert Simon proposed his notion of bounded rationality about the same time that Winch wrote *The Idea of a Social Science*. But it was not until experimental work by scholars like Wason (1968), Johnson-Laird (1969), or Kahneman and Tversky (1982) that the proposal had real substance. A full history of these developments in the history of science is well beyond the purview of this essay. The object of this part is to sketch some of the main reasons why culture is no longer thought of as bounded, and rationality is no longer considered unbounded. Part 4 assesses the consequences of the breakdown of these assumptions.

3.1 *Culture Unbound*

The anthropological notion of culture began its life as a description of the phenomenon to be explained in anthropology. Before it was 50 years old, the notion of culture transformed from the explanandum into the explanans. Nineteenth century anthropologists like Tyler or Morgan tried to understand the reasons for the scope of human variation along linguistic, religious, technological, aesthetic, economic, and related dimensions. In this early work, "culture" and "civilization" were often used synonymously, and they assumed that culture or civilization progressed in a regular, perhaps even law-governed, way from lower to higher forms. By the early twentieth century, the evolutionary perspective of the nineteenth century was superseded by a kind of relativism. Each human group was to be understood in its own terms, not as a waystation on the historical march toward "civilization." Differences in culture explained differences among human groups. The anthropological theories of functionalism and structuralism gave content and explanatory power to the concept of culture. It had all the marks of a theoretical entity in the sciences: it could not be directly observed, it played an important role in theory, it unified a wide variety of phenomena, and it was explanatory.

As an explanatory posit, culture has fallen out of favor for several reasons. First, even within small, relatively isolated groups, there is substantial variation among individuals, families, or villages on whatever point of cultural difference is under consideration: clothing, social norms, cooking, storytelling, economic practices, religious belief, ritual practice, and so on. Elements of culture, traits, are communicated from parents to children, but not in consistent or homogenous ways. Within a group, the ethnographer is typically confronted with a family resemblance of similar traits and practices. As a result, proposing that there is some abstract, shared core has little explanatory value (Sperber 1996). A second, closely related point is that within a group of people who live in proximity and maintain close social relationships, there are conflicting norms and conflicting interpretations of commonly acknowledged norms. The points of friction and conflict follow lines of power and control in the group. As a result, resistance to a norm, or strategic reinterpretations of what a norm demands, are part and parcel of how agents negotiate their position in social structures (Bourdieu 1977). Whatever "culture" might be, it is not a hidden theoretical entity that explains behavior.

Another line of critique argued that the very idea of such a thing as a unified, homogenous culture is a problematic illusion of ethnographic writing (Clifford 1983; Clifford and Marcus 1986; Rosaldo 1989). Ethnographers traditionally synthesize their experiences into a unified narrative. They abstract away from the mess of individual, family, or village differences and paint a coherent picture of the group's activities. Anthropologists have become convinced that doing so is not simply a benign abstraction. Its function as both explanans and explanandum creates a problematic circularity. The ethnographic narrative is the data for anthropological theory, and culture is the theoretical entity that explains the data. But the ethnographic narrative creates the unity under the guise of describing "the culture." Writing an artificial unity into the very data to be explained introduces an epistemic circularity into ethnography: the ethnographer is creating the very reality they seek to use as an explanation for behavior.

The critique of culture has two important consequences for the discussion here. First, while the notion of "culture" remains a useful way to highlight a certain kind of human variability, cultures do not have clear boundaries. Boundaries are imposed on human differences by ethnographers for the sake of a narrative, and by members of the group for reasons of politics, identity, or power. Cultural boundaries do not reflect deep natural divides. Second, cultures do not have pure forms or essential traits. While people do conform to the practices or norms of those around them, there is much variation within a given group.

3.2 *Rationality*

Since the 1960s, there has been a mass of experimental research on the processes of human reasoning and decision-making. It has consistently shown that humans fall well short of the standards set by the norms of first order logic, inferential statistics, and decision theory. Moreover, we deviate from these norms in systematic, predictable ways, and we do so when working under optimal conditions. While theorists differ on the best way to understand or explain the results, they are agreed on one point: our cognitive processes do not strictly conform to the demands of classical logic or decision theory.

The most famous, and among the earliest, results in the program of experimental manipulation of human reasoning is Wason's "selection task" (Wason 1968). In Wason's experiments, subjects were presented with four cards and told that each had a letter on one side and a number on the other. The visible side of the cards showed "D," "3," "B," and "7." They were then asked to evaluate the truth of the sentence "If there is a D on one side of the card, there is a 3 on the other." The experimenter indicated each card and asked whether "knowing what was on the other side would enable [the subject] to find out whether the sentence was true or false" (Wason 1968, 275). According to the truth table for 'P → Q,' the subject needs to turn over both the card with the visible "D" and the card with the visible "7." In Wason's experiment and the literature that followed, few subjects get the correct answer. The effect can be modified by expressing the problem in concrete terms about which the subjects have some background knowledge, but the phenomenon persists nonetheless.

Experimental paradigms since the 1960s have explored a variety of logical forms, as well as various deontic and practical modalities. Among the results are a set of biases and heuristics. Biases are persistent ways in which subjects fail to conform to logical norms. These include the "negative conclusion bias," where subjects resist conclusions phrased in negative terms, even when logically equivalent to an accepted positive conclusion; the "matching bias," where subjects tend to make inferences with a lexical match to elements in the premises; and the "belief bias," where subjects are more likely to judge arguments as valid when the conclusion was believable than when it was not, regardless of the logical validity of the form (Evans 2002). Heuristics were introduced into the literature by Tversky and Kahneman (1974). Heuristics are ways of simplifying problems to reach answers quickly. While they introduce efficiencies into human reasoning, heuristics can be fooled or misled. Hence, heuristics often have corresponding biases. Two well-known examples of heuristics are the "availability heuristic," where subjects draw conclusions based on the most accessible or memorable examples available, and the "representativeness heuristic," where subjects draw inferences based on similarity or salience.

The current state of the cognitive science of reasoning is too varied to survey in any detail here. In its broad outlines, however, the shape of current scholarship conforms to a pattern that Turner explores in the *Primer* (2018). Cognitive theories differ about the way in which the social dimensions of thought and action are related to their cognitive dimensions. Cognitive theories on one end of the spectrum lean toward methodological solipsism (Fodor 1980). On such views, social phenomena are largely consequences of the way in which the cognitive system processes information and produces action. For all the cognitive system cares, other people need not exist; the system need only contain *representations* of other people. In the literature on the reasoning, the popular "dual process" theories of reasoning illustrate the solipsistic side of the spectrum. The extreme opposite end of the spectrum is marked by approaches that are embodied, embedded, enactive, and extended, the so-called "4E" approaches to cognition. On these views, cognition is part and parcel of social interaction, perhaps even constituted by it. While they do not jump on the 4E bandwagon, Mercier and Sperber's "interactionist" program understands reasoning in terms of the social function of persuasive argumentation (Mercier and Sperber 2017). As Turner points out, while individually-oriented and socially-oriented accounts of cognition have deeply different consequences for social theory, they both underpin potentially major shifts in the way we think about social phenomena. And with respect to the problem of apparent rationality, theories from opposite ends of the spectrum point toward the same lessons.

Dual process theories treat logical judgments—such as those elicited by the Wason selection task—as the product of two distinct cognitive systems (Evans 1989; Kahneman 2011). One set of processes, often called rationality$_1$, are typically identified as those that are unconscious or implicit. They engage automatically with little or no conscious control, and they produce answers quickly. Some have speculated that they are shared with other animals and are evolutionarily more primitive. While rationality processes produce biases, they are reliable enough for survival in the environments that shaped them. Rationality$_2$ processes are slower, and more deliberate. They are typically are regarded as linguistically inflected, and they may invoke rules of logic, statistics, and decision theory.[2]

In *The Enigma of Reason* (2017), Mercier and Sperber take a more socially-oriented approach. They argue for a different kind of difference between the intuitions generated by unconscious (or only partly conscious) cognitive processes and the linguistically inflected processes of reasoning. Their innovation, and difference from the dual process views, is to treat the latter as part of the social processes of communication, not as a higher cognitive system. On their view, our cognitive system contains a wide variety of modules that make inferences. These generate intuitions, which are "judgments ... that we make and take to be justified without knowledge of the reasons that justifies them" (Mercier and Sperber 2017, 64). A distinctive feature of human cognition

---

2 For a comprehensive review and evaluation of dual process theories see Evans (2008).

is metarepresentation, that is, the capacity for representing one's own representations and the representations of others. The metarepresentational capacity to represent inferences yields intuitions about reasons. These intuitions support the social function of communicating reasons that justify beliefs or actions. These justifications are social interactions; justification is a matter of providing reasons for a belief or action so that one's audience will come to see them as justified.

On Mercier and Sperber's view, then, rules of logic are not built into the higher functions of the cognitive system. Rather, they are social norms for shaping the presentation of arguments:

> In argumentative reasoning in particular, the use of logical relationship plays a heuristic role for one's audience. It helps challenge them to examine and enrich or revise their beliefs or else to defend them with arguments in their turn. Thanks in part to its logical garb, argumentation, if not always convincing, is at least quite generally challenging."
> MERCIER and SPERBER 2017, 168

Reasoning, on this view is *interactive.*

The upshot of both the more individualistic dual process theories and the more socially oriented interactionist program is that the process of human reasoning is the result of mechanisms that explain both valid and invalid reasoning and decision. Whether the norms of logic are eternal or culturally variable, we would expect humans to persistently deviate from them. The asymmetry thesis, which played a crucial role in the later stages of the apparent irrationality debates, is false. Reasoning stands in need of explanation whether or not it conforms to valid forms and yields true conclusions.

4 Dispelling the Shadow of a Bad Philosophy of Logic

The problem of apparent irrationality was a vehicle for a larger discussion of the presuppositions of interpretation. The survey of the positions conducted in Part 2 showed that the traditional positions were committed to at least one of the two presuppositions. If those presuppositions are false, then the various positions are untenable, at least in their canonical formulation. Indeed, it is not even clear that the central question of the debate can be posed as originally formulated. Recall that the problem of apparent irrationality had this form: "When an ethnographer decides that an apparently irrational practice is really rational after all, what guides the ethnographer's change in interpretation?" (Risjord 1993, 247). The question presupposes that "an apparently irrational practice" can be identified, and this identification invokes two contrasts: the difference between "our" culture and "theirs," and the difference between "shallow" and "deep" problems of irrationality. Both contrasts depend on the notions that cultures are bounded and rationality unbounded.

Throughout the debate, translation was the frame within which difference was both problematic and understandable. A difference between the target language ("their" language) and the home language ("ours") is what makes the "apparently irrational practice" a problem of interpretation at all. Problems of translation and interpretation lay just beneath the surface of the debates between Winch and his interlocutors. And later, it was explicit in both those who relied on a Davidsonian view of translation, such as Root (1986) or MacDonald and Pettit (1981), as well as those who rejected it, such as Turner (1980) and Risjord (2000). Once we lose the boundedness of culture, the problem of "translation" is just as pressing between members of the "same culture" as it is between those who are purportedly different. Navigating the puzzling behavior of human beings is a perfectly general problem of understanding, and there is nothing about it that might shed special light on how we might Understand a Primitive Society.

Turning from culture to rationality, in setting up the problem of apparent irrationality, parties to the debate routinely discounted cases of error, fatigue, or stupidity. Lukes again provides admirably clear example. In his 2007 review of the literature on the problem of apparent irrationality, Lukes devoted several pages to sorting examples into "shallow" and "deep." He placed the results of the heuristics and biases research in the shallow end, while witchcraft and magic were deep (Lukes 2007, 591–596). This distinction is crucial to setting up the question, but it is unsustainable. It supposes that a core of human activity is definable by rational norms, and therefore that the violation of those norms is a special problem for interpretation. The experimental research into reasoning and decision making has done more than exhibit systematic mistakes. If we fully accept the idea of bounded rationality, the difference between shallow and deep irrationality is effaced. The propensity to make—and fail to make— particular kinds of inferences is part of who we are, no matter what the explicit rational norms are. We should expect to find people routinely violating logical norms, whether those norms are local or universal, and not just because they were drunk or duped. And while an interpreter may be surprised by behavior that violates his or her expectations, conformity to norms should potentially be as surprising as violations of them. Contrary to its traditional framing, then, the problem of apparent irrationality is not a uniquely troubling phenomenon for interpretation. Unexpected behavior is nothing more than one of the many things that an adequate social science must account for.

While the question that generated the apparent irrationality debate may be undermined, it is possible that the answers—or some of them—stand as true and justified. To what extent, if any, can any of the protagonists of the debate claim victory? One point of contention between the parties to the debate was whether the identification of rational norms could be an empirical matter. In this area, a vestige of neo-rationalism seems to survive. Even if rationality is bounded, if a being is to be the subject of interpretation, the interpreter must treat it as having the capacity for representation. This will require cognitive processes of making inferences. This prerequisite is recognizable as a form of the principle of charity, in its guise as a precondition of interpretation (Ramberg 1989; Risjord 2000). The neo-rationalists might take heart, but their hopes are soon dashed. As has been argued elsewhere (Henderson 1993, Risjord 2000), this presupposition is too weak to support the claims of the neo-rationalists and is consistent with a localist view. Moreover, research into the psychology of reason, in both its individualist and socially-oriented guises, presumes that patterns of reasoning are something to be determined empirically. The time is long past when logic might set the standard and all human deviation from those norms could be understood as a form of irrationality (Evans 2002). In this respect and to this extent, then, the localist position in the rationality debate is vindicated.

Another point of dispute between the localists and the rationalists was the character and scope of variation for norms of reasoning. Rationalists argued that variation was possible only against a background of agreement. Within the "bridgehead," an interpreter had to find that the local norms of reasoning were similar to the interpreter's. Deviation from the universal norms could be found in the fringes, such as discourse about the supernatural. Localists wanted to defend the possibility that difference could be found anywhere, and that the interpretations of the bridgehead were revisable. On this point, there is partial vindication of the rationalist view. The bounded rationality programs assume that dispositions to reason in certain ways are the product of evolution and are found in all humans. There is, then, something like Lukes' distinction between "rational (1)" (universal) and "rational (2)" (locally variable) criteria, but the distinction does not have the content he envisioned (Lukes 1967, 1982, 2007). For Lukes, rational (1) criteria were built into the presuppositions of interpretation, while rational (2) were locally variable and discovered empirically. The bounded rationality programs propose the existence of universal human cognitive processes of inference, but their character is determined empirically, not as *a priori* characteristics of interpretation. There is, then, only a limited vindication of the rationalist position about interpretation.

If we reject the twin assumptions of bounded culture and unbounded rationality, rationality has a much weaker relationship to interpretation than the debate over apparent irrationality supposed. Both localists and rationalists thought that norms of rationality had a central role in structuring interpretation. If we take rational (1) criteria to be the heuristics and inferential processes of the bounded rationality programs, and rational (2) criteria to be explicit norms used in social evaluation and criticism, then an interpretation does not need to find that *any* behavior is rational in the light of classical logical norms. Understanding inference and decision in ethnographic or historical contexts is an empirical matter, not something guided or constrained by philosophical accounts of either rationality or interpretation.

5   Conclusion: Naturalism, Normativity, and Questions of Method

There is a metaphilosophical lesson to draw from this story. One important source for Winch's reflections on apparent irrationality was Evans-Pritchard's writing about the Azande and Nuer. In the essays to which Winch refers, Evans-Pritchard was engaged in a debate with Levy-Bruhl about primitive mentality. (Recall also that Levy-Bruhl's postulation of pre-logical mentalities also informed Quine's writing on translation.) Evans-Pritchard and Levy-Bruhl took the question of whether some humans exhibited primitive or pre-logical forms of mentality to be an empirical question, answerable by anthropological research. In the 1960s, this question became a philosophical question, answerable by argument and conceptual analysis. If the arguments of this essay are correct, then the question has returned to the realm of the empirical, albeit somewhat transformed by its trip through the abstract realms of philosophy. The questions have changed both because of the philosophical debate and because of the way in which empirical presuppositions of the philosophical question and its answers have evolved.

This brief episode in the history of ideas illustrates the intimate relationship between philosophy and the sciences. While philosophy can (and should) critique the sciences and examine the conditions that make them possible at all—such as an inquiry into the structure and justification of interpretation—it does so against a background of empirical commitments justified by the very sciences under the philosophical microscope. Critics of this sort of pragmatism have often worried that such intimacy between empirical science and philosophical critique is circular. The rise and fall of the problem of apparent irrationality shows that tugging at one's bootstraps can result in progress after all.

Acknowledgement

Work on this chapter was supported by the research grant "Steps towards the naturalization of inferentialism" supporting international research teams at the Philosophical Faculty of the University of Hradec Králové.

References

Barnes, Barry. 1974. *Scientific Knowledge and Sociological Theory*. London: Routledge.
Barnes, Barry, and David Bloor. 1982. Rationality, Relativism, and the Sociology of Knowledge. In *Rationality and Relativism*. Edited by Martin Hollis and Steven Lukes. Cambridge, MA: MIT Press, 21–47.
Bloor, David. 1983. *Wittgenstein: A Social Theory of Knowledge*: Macmillan International Higher Education.
Bourdieu, Pierre. 1977. *Outline of a Theory of Practice*. Cambridge: Cambridge University Press.
Clifford, James. 1983. "On Ethnographic Authority." *Representations* 1 (2):118–146.
Clifford, James, and George Marcus, eds. 1986. *Writing Culture: The Poetics and Politics of Ethnography*. Berkeley: University of California Press.
Davidson, Donald. 1984a. *Inquiries into Truth and Interpretation*. Oxford: Clarendon Press.
Davidson, Donald. 1984b. "Radical Interpretation." In *Inquiries into Truth and Interpretation*. Oxford: Clarendon Press.
Davidson, Donald. 1984c. "The Very Idea of A Conceptual Scheme." In *Inquiries into Truth and Interpretation*. Oxford: Clarendon Press.
Davidson, Donald. 1986. "A Nice Derangement of Epitaphs." In *Philosophical Grounds of Rationality: Intentions, Categories, Ends*. Edited by Richard Warner and Richard E. Grandy. Oxford: Clarendon Press, 157–174.
Elster, Jon. 2007. *Explaining Social Behavior: More Nuts and Bolts for the Social Sciences*. Cambridge: Cambridge University Press.
Evans, Jonathan. 1989. *Bias in Human Reasoning: Causes and Consequences*. Mahwah, NJ: Lawrence Erlbaum Associates.
Evans, Jonathan. 2002. "Logic and Human Reasoning: An Assessment of the Deduction Paradigm." *Psychological Bulletin* 128 (6):978.
Evans, Jonathan. 2008. "Dual-Processing Accounts of Reasoning, Judgment, and Social Cognition." *Annual Review of Psychology* 59:255–278.

Feleppa, Robert. 1988. *Convention, Translation, and Understanding*. Albany, NY: State University of New York Press.
Fodor, Jerry A. 1980. "Methodological Solipsism Considered as a Research Strategy in Cognitive Psychology." *Behavioral and Brain Sciences* 3 (1): 63–73.
Gigerenzer, Gerd. 2008. *Rationality for Mortals: How People Cope With Uncertainty*. Oxford: Oxford University Press.
Gigerenzer, Gerd, and Reinhard Selten, eds. 2001. *Bounded Rationality: The Adaptive Toolbox*. Cambridge, MA: MIT Press.
Grandy, Richard E. 1973. "Reference, Meaning, and Belief." *Journal of Philosophy* 70: 439–452.
Henderson, David K. 1993. *Interpretation and Explanation in the Human Sciences*. Albany, NY: State University of New York Press.
Hollis, Martin. 1967a. "The Limits of Irrationality." *Archives Europeenes de Sociologie* 7: 265–271.
Hollis, Martin. 1967b. "Reason and Ritual." *Philosophy* 43: 231–247.
Hollis, Martin, and Steven Lukes, eds. 1982. *Rationality and Relativism*. Cambridge MA: MIT Press.
Johnson-Laird, Philip N, and Joanna Tagart. 1969. "How Implication is Understood." *The American Journal of Psychology* 82 (3): 367–373.
Jones, Bryan D. 2001. *Politics and Tte Architecture of Choice: Bounded Rationality and Governance*. Chicago: University of Chicago Press.
Kahneman, Daniel. *Maps of Bounded Rationalty*. Nobel Media 2002. Available from http://www.nobelprize.org/nobel_prizes/economic-sciences/laureates/2002/kahneman-lecture.html.
Kahneman, Daniel. 2011. *Thinking,Fast and Slow*. New York: Macmillan.
Kahneman, Daniel, Paul Slovic, and Amos Tversky, Eds. 1982. *Judgment Under Uncertainty: Heurstics and Biases*. Cambridge: Cambridge University Press.
Lukes, Steven. 1967. "Some Problems about Rationality." *Archives Europeenes de Sociologie* 7: 247–264.
Lukes, Steven. 1982. "Relativism in its Place." In *Rationality and Relativism*, edited by Martin Hollis and Steven Lukes. Cambridge, MA: MIT Press.
Lukes, Steven. 2007. The Problem of Apparently Irrational Beliefs. In *Philosophy of Anthropology and Sociology*, edited by Stephen P. Turner and Mark W. Risjord. Amsterdam: Elsevier.
Macdonald, Graham, and Philip Pettit. 1981. *Semantics and Social Science*. London: Routledge and Kegan Paul.
MacIntyre, Alasdair. 1967. "The Idea of a Social Science." *Proceedings of the Aristotelian Society, Supplementary Volume* 61: 95–114.
MacIntyre, Alasdair. 1970. Is Understanding Religion Compatible with Believing? In *Rationality*. Edited by Bryon Wilson. Evanston: Harper and Row, 62–77.

Mercier, Hugo, and Dan Sperber. 2017. *TheEenigma of Reason.* Cambridge MA: Harvard University Press.

Ramberg, Bjørn. 1989. *Donald Davidson's Philosophy of Language.* Oxford: Basil Blackwell.

Risjord, Mark. 1993. "Wittgenstein's Woodcutters: The Problem of Apparent Irrationality." *American Philosophical Quarterly* 30: 247–258.

Risjord, Mark. 2000. *Woodcutters and Witchcraft: Rationality and Interpretive Change in the Social Sciences.* Albany, NY: SUNY Press.

Root, Michael. 1986. Davidson and Social Science. In *Truth and Interpretation.* Edited by Ernest LePore. Oxford: Basil Blackwell.

Rosaldo, Renato. 1989. *Culture and Truth: The Remaking of Social Analysis.* Boston: Beacon Press.

Roth, Paul. 1987. *Meaning and Method in the Social Sciences.* Ithaca: Cornell University Press.

Roth, Paul Andrew. 2011. The Philosophy of Social Science in the Twentieth Century: Analytic Traditions: Reflections on the Rationalitatstreit. In *The Sage Handbook of the Philosophy of Social Sciences.* Edited by Ian Charles Jarvie and Jesus Zamora-Bonilla. London: SAGE Publications, 103–118.

Simon, Herbert. 1957. *Models of Man.* New York: Wiley.

Sperber, Daniel. 1996. *Explaining Culture.* Oxford: Blackwell.

Thaler, Richard H, and Cass R Sunstein. 2009. *Nudge: Improving Decisions About Health, Wealth, and Happiness.* London: Penguin.

Turner, Stephen. 1980. *Sociological Explanation As Translation.* Cambridge: Cambridge Univeristy Press.

Turner, Stephen P. 2018. *Cognitive Science and the Social: A Primer.* London: Routledge.

Tversky, Amos, and Daniel Kahneman. 1974. "Judgment Under Uncertainty: Heuristics and Biases." *Science* 185 (4157): 1124–1131.

Wason, Peter C. 1968. "Reasoning About a Rule." *Quarterly Journal of Experimental Psychology* 20 (3): 273–281.

Wilson, Bryan R., Ed. 1970. *Rationality.* Oxford: Basil Blackwell.

Winch, Peter. 1958. *The Idea of a Social Science.* London: Routledge and Kegan Paul.

Winch, Peter. 1964. "Understanding a Primitive Society." *American Philosophical Quarterly* 1: 307–324.

Practical Normativity
Stephen Turner's Contribution to the Philosophy of the Social

Rafał Paweł Wierzchosławski

Abstract

In the first part of my text, I draw attention to some general philosophical assumptions accepted by Stephen Turner. I start with his early work Sociological Explanation as Translation (1980) and the relationship between ordinary and scientific knowledge as important for the understanding of the two categories analyzed: social practices (The Social Theory of Practices [1994]) and normativity (Explaining the Normative [2010]), both are discussed briefly in the following parts. In the next step I discuss the meaning of Good Bad Theories, as a key concept in the understanding of Turner's view of normativity. Then I consider the GBT problem in the context of the relationship between the scientific and local perspectives. The problem is presented as an example of understanding religious beliefs (as evading empirical verification) both from the point of view of a specialist (theologian) and local worshipper, especially in case of believers from another culture (problem of missionary translation and explanation of alien beliefs). In my analysis I refer to the considerations of Mike Singleton: anthropologist and theologian. I consider whether GBT applies in this case, and if yes, in which way? In consequence, I claim that GBT might be a useful analytic tool in dealing with religious (worldview) contexts. In final remarks, I point out the potential application of the GBT concept in contemporary sociology of culture in context of Hubert Knoblauch's analysis of popular religion.

Keywords

Social practices – normativity – Good-Bad Theories – *hau* – rationality – understanding (interpretation) – Turner – Singleton – Knoblauch

Avant-propos

∴

On every side the weeds of error grow;

"Vengeful logician, at them with the hoe!"
"Weeding? For that just now you must not ask!"
"Why not?" - "Tool-sharpening is my present task."
(TADEUSZ KOTARBIŃSKI (1957: 12)[1]

• • •

Reaching into the clear depths – he could not find the right place.
One herring, talented with a fastidious nature
Wherever he wandered, it was always in vain:
Here it's clear, but shallow – deep over there, but dark.
(TADEUSZ KOTARBIŃSKI (1957: 13)[2]

• • •

Entia non sunt multiplicanda praeter necessitatem
WILLIAM OCKHAM

• •
•

Stephen Turner is an author of many books and articles, and editor of collected works and Handbooks. He is in many fields: as philosopher of society and cognitive sciences, philosopher and methodologist of social sciences, historian of social thought and development of sociological institutions, philosopher of politics and sociologist of institutions and organizations which results in his being a pioneer in the field of experts studies. In his analysis he takes into

---

[1] Tadeusz Kotarbiński (1886–1981): Polish logician, moral philosopher and epistemologist; Professor of Warsaw University and eminent member of the Polish Lemberg-Warsaw School. He proposed minimalist ontology of reism (there are only material objects), which evolved to semantic theory of names: names refer to objects only; other terms (like abstract names) are quasi-names (referring to properties, relations, features etc.).
  Gdziekolwiek myślą sięgnąć, tkwi błędu łodyga. Logiko, karcicielko, po badylach śmigaj! - Na chwasty moja praca później się rozpostrze. - A teraz czym się trudnisz? - Sama siebie ostrzę (*Wesołe smutki*, s. 12) translation by Anna Maria Mickiewicz.

[2] Do jasnych dążąc głębin - nie mógł trafić w sedno Śledź pewien, obdarzony naturą wybredną. Dokądkolwiek wędrował, zawsze nadaremno: Tu jasno, ale płytko - tam głębia, lecz ciemno (Wesołe smutki, 13); translation by Anna Maria Mickiewicz.

account the social and institutional context: Theories do not arise out of thin air; rather, theories are created by people who are situated in a certain place and time, who act within a certain framework and respond to a certain social demand. Thus, there are social practices which are guided by social norms. But the question is: how do they happen?

Is it possible to pin down the work of an author who is active in so many areas: philosophy of social sciences, philosophy of society, sociological theory, history of social thought, conceptual analysis, etc.? Can we find one (even complex) term?! Obviously, this type of expression will always be a certain idealization (the ideal type) referring to and integrating into one (combining) concept (a) various and sometimes different threads (problems) undertaken by the author, or (b) the method he used in relation to the issues he was undertaking, or (c) the areas on which he was focusing his attention, or (d) in the perspective from which he was looking at those issues he was dealing with (discussing).

It seems that the key concept to capture all mentioned above might be the term of: practical normativity. Obviously, it refers to his two important books *The Social Theory of Practices* (1994) and *Explaining the Normative* (2010). I would claim that it reflects some fundamental ontological and epistemological principles that he endorses (like ontological and methodological individualism under certain reading, soft naturalism, or minimal realism as far as social reality is concerned). What I mean by this conceptual junction, is regardless of what issue he is considering (or has considered), his method (or approach) to the problem is to play two pianos at the same time; that is, to take into account the actors' point of view. In other words, Turner wants to consider how one acts in intentionally in one's life-world practices and under what conditions (the tacit, knowledge, practices, normative frameworks). We may consider whether it is a [permanent] confrontation adopted by him of a Weberian perspective with what science adds or revises as far as our common understanding of ourselves and of our interactions with our neighbors within the social framework.

Since it is not possible to focus on all the issues that could be put into this key concept in such a short text, I will focus primarily on the problem of the relationship between common (local) knowledge and scientific (expert) knowledge in the context of modern knowledge-based societies. I would like to reflect on whether it is possible to apply the issues of social practices and normativity (practical normativity) analyzed by Turner in the context of the relations between the two levels, which are currently under discussion among some sociologists of scientific knowledge. The key issue here will be the concept of GBT [Good-Bad-Theories], which might be promising as far as the descriptions of relation between the two are concerned. One strategy is an elective modernism (Collins and Evans 2002, 2017), another one is post-truth condition (Fuller et al. 2014; Fuller 2018). My question deals with the problem to what extent one can make use of more theoretical considerations dealing with the status of practices (do practices make our actions, or the other way round, do our actions foster our practices), and normativity (how it happens that, we can use some set of beliefs, which we do not believe in)?

At the same time, I would like to indicate my own point of view (interpretation) which is conditioned both by my biographical (situation/history) and certain conceptual framework (positionality) which grounds my reading of Turner's works. When I made contact with Turner 30 years ago, I was a recent graduate in philosophy at the Catholic University of Lublin, the only relatively independent university in Poland at that time. As a young man, I was looking for readings to formulate the subject for a planned doctoral dissertation on the philosophy (methodology) of social sciences.

Turner sent me copies of his two works, which, for various reasons, could not be bought in Poland in the late 1980s. It was a photocopy of *Search for a Methodology of Social Science: Durkheim, Weber, and the Nineteenth-Century Problem of Cause Probability, and Action* (1986) and a copy of his book with Regis Factor, *Max Weber and the Dispute over Reason and Value: A Study of Philosophy, Ethics, and Politics* (1984) and a connection to Weber. Max Weber was undoubtedly an important author who should have been read, if one had ambitions to study the philosophical foundations of social sciences. Inside the book, I found a nice dedication: *To Rafał – in scholarly fraternity Stephen Turner*. One can imagine what did it meant for a greenhorn in academia to receive such a generous gift and invitation to the international academic community from a well-established star of philosophy of social sciences and sociology. Especially when you take into account, that a Ph.D. scholarship was about 10 USD according to the 'black market' exchange rate at the end of Communist Poland in the late 1980s.

I mention this not only to express my gratitude for the help and support, but also as a sociohistorical illustration of the functioning of a peculiar book Cargo-cult in Polish science at the time. which, apart from its Wallerstein peripheral position, was additionally attributed to a different theoretical system: for years the official domination of political Marxism, especially in the social sciences, and the management of science by party apparatchiks. Our begging letters asking to send these or other publications were an expression of Merton's faith in the CUDOS (communism, universalism, disinterestedness, and organized skepticism) of science and of the academic solidarity across borders.

At the same time, this reminiscence is important in pointing out my position in defining the inter-contextual reception of what was obtained due to Cargo-cult packages, but also in understanding what has been noticed recently by Turner about how collaboration and cooperation in science has changed in recent years (Turner and Chubin 2020; Turner 2020).

This invitation is still important for me and Steve has become one of my *maîtres à penser*; and in particular as pioneering explorer of unknown territories he is an inexhaustible source of inspiration in ways of thinking about the social world. As recently Willam Outhwaite commented in one of the emails we have exchanged: "As always, Stephen was there before us" (22. 01. 2020, 05:51).

At the same time, thanks to various opportunities, I have spent part of those years in Germany (summer 1986 and spring 1989) and France (spring 1988). My stay in Germany resulted in a study of social phenomenology initiated by Alfred Schutz, as I had contact with Richard Grathoff in Bielefeld, Ilia Srubar from the *Sozialwissenschaftliche Archiv* in Konstanz, and my stay in Paris in the long term in the study of political philosophy, in particular Republicanism, as I attended several Quentin Skinner seminars which he conducted around the English idea of freedom at *l'Institut Raymond Aron* at rue Jean Calvin. As it later turned out, these experiences were important both in my reading of Turner's works, and in my attempts to use his view of the social world, which has always been of interest to me. The study of social phenomenology in the context of Turner's early work *Social Explanation as Translation* (Turner 1980) which I photocopied from the Library of Maison des Sciences de l'Homme, at that time still at 54 boulevard Raspail, made me aware of the very important issue of different forms of social knowledge and their mutual relations. These include phenomenological constructs of the first and second order, which today may manifest itself as local and universal knowledge. The study of the Republican tradition (not only its history), but above all of the neo-Republican project focused on the implementation of political freedom as a lack of domination, shows the importance of normativity problem in relation to collective and institutionalized individual and community actions. At the same time, it is connected with the first, by taking into account axiological issues, especially axiological pluralism—both in the individual dimension (experiencing of the life-world) and in the collective dimension (community)—institutional structures and functional *modi operandi*.

The study of Tuner's work was an experience of how important the analysis of the classics is for the application and adaptation of their solutions to the problems they were struggling with in the contemporary context. The author states the importance of the history of social thought for the analysis of contemporary times (it follows the intuitions of the Cambridge School in historical research).

The evocation of certain biographical threads aims not only (not so much) at the commemorative dimension of the relationship with the addressee of this *Festschrift*, but also (and perhaps most importantly) at drawing attention to a very important substantive aspect that can be metaphorically expressed by following the title of the famous book by Jon Elster, *Making Sense of Marx* (1985). In Turner's case we can talk not only about *Making Sense of Max Weber*, but also about *Making Use of Max Weber*.

For we are dealing with the author of the studies on various aspects of analysis of what the author actually meant, but also the meaning of those in understanding the problems we are currently struggling with. Thus, the rational reconstruction of meaning may in a further aspect translate into its use in the understanding of contemporary problems concerning the functioning of various dimensions of social knowledge, social, political, or economic institutions.

That is what I mean metaphorically by the phrase *Making Use of Weber*: Turner can be treated metaphorically as a *porte-parole* of Weber, not only as a means of understanding the social world (and thus a certain ontological option), but also in the epistemological-methodological sense. Turner inherits from Weber the choice (selection) of certain aspects (cognitive perspectives) from which he accepts certain tools of cognition (*Wertbeziehung*). They are important, but only as an example or instance of certain more general problems in relation to which Turner utilizes his *Sonderweg* to cope with them[3].

In this context, it is worth noting some points that make up the basic ontological-epistemological assumptions that characterize Turner's methodological attitude defined as "using Max Weber." It seems that it can be described as (a) subject-oriented ontology, in the sense that the description and explanation of the functioning of individuals in social structures, institutions, or groups does not have to involve the adoption of a collective (holistic) element (in a strong sense, and not derivative or metaphorical) to recall his excellent analysis of the "we" category, which he carried out in opposition to Searle's category of collective intentionalities, even if these were to have their habitat only in human minds (or rather in individual brains to emphasize the naturalistic strand). In this sense, one can metaphorically say that Turner follows the Ockham maxim: *entia non sunt mulitplicanda praeter necessitatem*. This

---

[3] I write more about the categories of knowledge uses in the context of historical studies in a text on Paul Roth's irrealism. I mean, first of all, the pragmatic aspect, which influences the different understanding of various semantic aspects of the described event, the historical process, depending on which one is chosen by the user. Particularly interesting are the cases of antinomic use (contentious, and sometimes contradictory, and sometimes exclusive descriptions or interpretations). In this text I make use of interesting analyses by Turner of the category of antinomy in Michael Oakeshott (Wierzchosławski 2018).

attitude can be called minimalist realism in terms of existence and irreducible properties of social entities.

At the same time his approach escapes the classification scheme of *bottom-up* versus *top-down* positions (Hollis 1994, 18–21). For there is no collective social *top* from which to derive the patterns that are the cause of individual behavior, and the observed individual actions do not lead at all to the creation of some collective practices that would emergently be founded in/on them, while at the same time would not be reduceable to the sum of individual interactions.

In this context, it may be worth noting that the term "methodology" can be understood as the philosophy of sciences (including social sciences), i.e., the analysis of their ontological assumptions and applied methods, i.e., meta-objective reflection on various current projects that are present on the market more or less. It can also be treated as a specific methodological theory which is proposed either by a single author or as a representative of a certain school or theoretical orientation (structuralism, functionalism, ethnomethodology, etc.). In the first sense, the (historically understood) methodology serves rather as a comparative analysis of different positions, focusing on the issue of the "costs" that one has to pay for the promised cognitive gains. In the second sense, it is an expression of a specific argumentation in favor of one's own theoretical position. I mention this distinction because it has some significance in the context of my deliberations on the use of a certain methodological attitude in the Weberian spirit, which Turner takes in context (relation to) other competitive approaches. At the same time, I think he is using it skillfully to consider the issue of social practices and normativism in the context of defining relationships between different types of social knowledge. In that context, as I suggest, Turner's approach may be important in the ongoing discussions on the status of scientific knowledge in contemporary knowledge-based societies.

In Turner's *Sociological Explanation as Translation* (1980) we may find an interesting point. He refers to the observation made by Leo Strauss, a scholar of antiquity and a political philosopher in exile, who distinguished two approaches to the social and political reality which are characteristic of the ancient and modern authors respectively (Strauss 1953, 8).

The great political philosopher Leo Strauss distinguished the modern project in political philosophy from the classical political philosophy of Plato and Aristotle by pointing out that the ancients sought the perfection of the pre-scientific or ordinary understanding of human things in their philosophy or science, whereas the modern "sciences" of human things, such as sociology, seek to replace this ordinary understanding and are founded on its rejection (Turner 1980, 1).

For Strauss the principal example of modern approach was Max Weber. Since:

> [...] ordinary person understands and accounts for the occurrences of political life evaluatively. Weber denied the possibility of rationally evaluating action. In the last analysis, he argued, there are conflicts among various positions that are irreconcilable by human reason. So, for Weber, scientific knowledge of human action must be non-evaluative (*Wertfreiheit*) and thus radically unlike the prescientific knowledge it replaces.
>
> TURNER 1980, 1

In other words, Max Weber is an example of the modern paradigm, a paradigm which suggests that any ordinary and prescientific cognition cannot lead to real knowledge because of the latter's normative and evaluative attitude. It seems that in the case of the Moderns, knowledge should be value free and respect the *Wertfreiheit* postulate—despite Weber's commitment to the value relevance thesis (*Wertbeziehung*). This postulate has been proposed due to our being condemned to the unavoidable dilemmas of axiological polytheism, in the bedrock of which we undertake our choices. Weber's point is that there are many values which are not only inconsistent but that they contradict one another in certain situations. Moreover, there is no rational way to choose among them. The situation can be overcome only by acceptance of "value polytheism" in the value-free scientific considerations. This can be reached at the expense of deposing the queen-ethics from her throne, which she has occupied until now, and placing her among various life-styles.

In order to avoid sinking into details I would like to follow Turner's remark about the Moderns. He claims that the classics of sociology have gone even further than Weber in their rejection of the prescientific understanding. One of them, Émile Durkheim, denies that ordinary explanations of actions might be any guide to the true causes of action since our comportment depends on the laws of the *conscience collective*. They are nothing more the Baconian *Idola*, and, as cognitive obstacles, should be overcome. Another of the "foundering fathers" of modern social sciences, Vilfredo Pareto, dismissed prescientific understanding entirely. Any action that has moral or religious purport is labeled by him as "non-logical," and any attempt at such an explanation is counted by him as pseudo-explanation, as "derivation." We can be saved by referring to a deeper level on where we can find real causes, "which are radically unlike the reasons that figure the ordinary explanations."

As we know from the ongoing history of the social thought none of those projects has been fulfilled and they have failed to live up their expectations of their proponents. Since:

> There are neither Durkheimian "laws of the collective consciousness" nor Paretian laws of social equilibrium, and Weber's elaborate constructions of categories for historical causal analysis have not served to give the account of the unique character of Western society that he sought (1980, 1).

What is the lesson we can draw from that story? First of all, that there is a serious problem to be solved, i.e., what relationship obtains between our common world and our cognitive equipment we apply to it in order to get reasonable and sound explanations? One positive formulation of the diagnosis amounts to a claim that the social sciences have been an attempt to apply causal explanatory methods to attain an understanding of that which is already properly understood or can be properly understood by noncausal methods, such as classical teleology and "idealism."

The quoted excerpt from Turner's early work can be read, finding in it a current significance which manifests itself in the context of the postulated category of practical normativity. I will develop this point later.

As the reviewers concluded, *The Social Theory of Practices* (1994) is "an interesting, important, provocative and amusing book" (Pickering 1997, 325), "Weighing in at a mere 145 pages [...] has the highest value-per-page ratio of any social theory text I have read in a long time" (Fuller 1997, 23). "Steve Turner takes aim [...] which pervades the more epistemologically self-conscious lines of social theory, cultural studies, and science studies" (Lynch 1997, 335). "Without embracing either postmodernism or naturalism, Turner accepts a kind of epistemological behaviorism for the social sciences" (Bohman 1997, 95), "Ironic empiricism (apparently) versus the demon of analogy" (Acourt 1995, 107). They are some quotations from reviews which have been devoted to the first book which pretends to one of the key-concept (or umbrella concepts) which might cover some essential patterns of thinking about the social world.

The most important consequence of the dense erudition and multiplicity of aspects of Turner's book is the conviction that we have to accept a certain cognitive specificity, which involves the need to accept, on the one hand, the understanding of the basic categories in explaining the social world, which are beliefs and desires of intentional subjects. Regardless of the sophisticated methods (e.g., statistical) used in social sciences, one cannot avoid referring to the individual dimension, on the other hand, accepting that this understanding of actions will always be imperfect (possibility of misreading rules, practices, etc.). Simultaneously, the orientation to the level of an individual actor is connected with the necessity to abandon dreams of finding something magical beyond this dimension. What is essential for his theory of practices is that there is no social stuff (in collective or holistic ontological or explanatory sense) beyond ongoing interactions between individuals.

As it seems, this problem is reflected in the passage from Turner's article "Where Explanation Ends" (2013a) on the issues of statistical explanation (and any explanation of social reality from the macro level that refers to causal relations) in social sciences:

> If we are to take the idea of direct understanding seriously, the distinction between the social sciences and the natural sciences with respect to where explanation ends comes down to this: explanation in the natural sciences can end with an understood model. In the social sciences, to the extent that models are concerned with conduct that is subject to direct understanding, there will always be an additional question: does the model fit with our direct understanding of the conduct which is being modeled?
>
> TURNER 2013a, 537-8

This does not mean, as Turner rightly points out, that we do not use different idealizations, models, etc., which aim to bring out the factors that are important in explaining social activities or the functioning of individuals in institutions at different levels, but also in a naturalistic approach to social sciences, the final and original level will be the level of direct understanding:

The need for background knowledge involving intentions and beliefs, the need to explain why a model applies or fails to apply to a particular case of conduct, and the role of intentional elements in "mechanisms," as well as the question of whether a particular description of an action "fits," all require that models attach at some point to direct understanding. (Turner 2013a, 538)

A second book devoted to explaining the normativity phenomenon (Turner 2010) has been discussed from different positions, like analytical "hard-liner" Jaroslav Peregirn (2011) and a group of Spanish holistic "inquisitors," Antonio Gaitán-Torres, Jesus Zamora-Bonilla, and José A. Noguera (2013), who tend to criticize Turner (2013b, 2013c) for lack of faith in collective normative beings and their abstract *modi* of existence. I myself had an occasion to discuss the book when making my presentation at the ENPOSS and POSS-RT joint conference in Venice 2014. My aim at the time was to put Turner's attempts to grasp the normativity problem within a wider ontological framework, claiming that we may better understand his point when grasped in terms of a soft naturalism position, which tries to avoid threats of both radical naturalism and antinaturalism. One of the problems deals with the question of how scientific are, or might be, normative issues when they appear in the context of the social.

In getting Turner's point in solving the normativity problem it is important to focus on the concept of Good Bad Theories. As Turner observes we can use a collective (umbrella) term which covers diverse notions by means of "theories," i.e., normative terms which he discusses in different contexts and discussed by authors he refers to (Turner 2010, 29–42). They function as "theories" due to the very fact that they serve as conventions, due to convenience in spite of not necessarily matching up with anything like "the theory in one's head": a genuinely explanatory account of what is going on when people use these folk notions. Using "theory" means in that context "extending our folk language to talk about our folk language (2010, 43).

> We may describe these various folk conceptions as "Good Bad Theories" meaning, that they are good theories for a particular unspecified set of purposes in a particular setting, but bad theories if we are thinking of them as adequate explanations of anything, or as proto-explanations that can be turned into genuine explanations with a little empirical vetting and some minor revision. They are in short kludges.
> WIMSATT 2007, 137-8; TURNER 2010, 43

A good example of the phenomena in question may by an example discussed by Turner in the context of problems which meet anthropological interpretations of alien cultures which are the object of translation into the language of social sciences. Turner refers to Marcel Mauss and his description and explanation of Maori belief in *hau* – normative force, which enforces the obligation it embodies by causing pain or death (Turner 2010, 60). The problem deals with sociological change of the subject that the sociologist considers in their interpretative understanding; since they do not accept the descriptions and explanations which are provided from inside the narrations (sets of beliefs), they try to grasp and express them in terms of social sciences. The clash is evident not only in cases of understanding of primitive societies, which are alien to the cultural bedrocks we have grown up with, but also, in the case of religious beliefs, (still) persistent in modern societies. Sociological descriptions might be criticized by both believers and theologians (who are trained specialists, i.e., experts in the domain), since in their descriptions of the rituals they omit reference to the actual presence of God, which is an essential feature of what is happening. The sociologist is not talking about genuine communion, as the believer or theologian understands the ritual (Turner 2010, 60–61). The problem of social explanation in such cases deals with not only whether the social scientist endorses or rejects the claim that there are supernatural forces she refers in her descriptions, but whether she provides adequate explanation congruent (in this or another way) with their users (believers).

> "Explaining the effects of such ideas and the reasons they might appear to be real forces of this kind doesn't require us to believe them. [...] We can explain this belief arises in and is sustained in the epistemic situation of the ordinary Maori, [...] this explanation would not depart form the ordinary stream of explanatory fact, and of course would at no point appeal to the normative fact of *hau* itself.
> TURNER 2010, 61

The sociological explanations are rival explanations to those, which are given by representatives of primitive and alien cultures or other religious believers accepting existence unobservable entities and causal powers they can exercise on them. They can claim that sociological explanations are insufficient, since they do not grasp some facts, which are indispensable or inevitable for proper understanding their practices or believes in question.

> One of the insufficiencies would be the failure to account for the normative facts described in terms of *hau*, "facts" which do involve a rupture in the ordinary stream of explanation. But he would say that this rupture is warranted: if the events that befall the person who fails to satisfy *hau* are described as mysterious, they demand a suitable explanation, in terms of mysterious force, which *hau* supplies. He would complain that the normative language of the practice, which is a pervasive part of the life of the community, would be bogus if the sociological explanation were true. He might go on to complain that the sociologist has re-described the practice in such a way that the normative element, the genuinely binding character of the fact of *hau*, had been left out. And he would of course reject the idea that *hau* was a fiction. In this respect, the Maori lawyer would be a classic normativist.
> TURNER 2010, 61-2

The point I would like to develop is the context of practical normativity as Turner's key concept. And, his understanding of various aspects of social reality in consideration of whether the Strauss observation about the Ancients and the Moderns might be of importance in his mature considerations in the pursuit of the social. The two concepts bring many questions and problems, which Turner and his critics have discussed in many ways. My suggestion is to examine whether referring to Good Bad Theories (GBT), treated as an explanatory device in context of normativity, might be useful in better understanding various forms of knowledge which have been discussed by Turner in other writings (Turner 2003a, 2003b, 2014). I would like to consider whether Turner's idea of GBT provides any resources for placing experts' (universal) and non-experts' (local and contextual) knowledge within the framework of knowledgeable societies. The rival approaches are elective, but we have here an example of a discussion between the values of science in relation to common (local) knowledge, which from various ups and downs is assessed by science as being not only engaged in the valuations (Leo Strauss problem), but also with references to various concepts such as *hau*.

However, unlike the more fundamental issues that Turner discussed in his book ten years ago, the context in which I want to focus on the question of GBT is somewhat different. For we are not dealing here with the beliefs of primitive cultures or religious beliefs, whose contents inherently go beyond empirical observation and the testimonies available to us.

But, on the contrary, the beliefs and collective worldviews at stake are born out of the use of science, its reception among people who have undergone the process of education, often going beyond the average, and at the same time they are the representations of the contestation (to varying degrees) with regard to established science.

If, in explaining certain practices and the underlying normative elements that escape reduction to what is observable (though rational at some understanding), we cite the GBT scheme as a form that allows us to understand the actual interactions taking place (the Maori exchange of gifts), then we can ask ourselves a question, whether this scheme will also be suitable not only for cultures that are radically different from the contemporary rationality of knowledge-based societies, but also for situations in which we can try to put our own beliefs (of a normative nature) into these categories. As a form of thought experiment, we can consider the situation of a contemporary theologian (regardless of denomination, it may be Judaism, Islam, Christianity, etc.). Theologian of some (any) religion in which he is an expert on faith and morality for believers who accept his knowledge and spiritual leadership. The theologian has grown out of a certain set of life practices that are saturated with theistic beliefs and the moral norms that flow from them, in the belief that he has grown up since his youth (unless he converted at a later age). Choosing theology as the subject of his study, he grew up in religious practices (local knowledge), but the theological study assumes not only a study of the *Sacra Doctrina*, but also of many humanities, knowledge of which is required in the specialist understanding of writings considered canonical (revealed) in a given religion. Thus, an adept of theology learns a standard lecture of dogma and moral theology, which in one form or another is codified as an authorized interpretation of the religious content which he passes on to the faithful members of the congregation in which he serves. This can be authorized by a special institution if such an interpretation is accepted in a given religion, or there can be a situation in which an unambiguous interpretation is not sought, leaving a certain margin of interpretation (they assume, however, that the really important issues are not subject to any greater divergence—because they are governed by the principle of coherence and coherence of interpretation).

This issue is important for the interpretation of the content and normative precepts that relate to the relationship of Transcendence (the Other) to creation. However, in the context of both the practical normativity and the relationship between expertise and local knowledge, two aspects are of interest.

First of all, I mentioned that the theologian we are discussing (at least as ancillary sciences) studies fields other than just the *Sacra Doctrina*, so there is sometimes not only a difference in languages (conceptual grids) that refer to the same reality that the theologian speaks about, but which do so in a different way. The theological interpretation (in a standardized version) gives a proper (orthodox) understanding of the content of the holy books in a specific way and assumes a certain kind of legitimacy which, however, can be challenged in the humanities and social sciences used by the theologian (e.g., comparative history of religion, history of mentality and everyday life in given historical periods, etc.). I do not mean to suggest that the theologian does not read critically and hermeneutically the contents of certain texts considered by a particular community to be founding for a particular system of religious beliefs. But I do mean that the descriptions of victorious wars, the super powerful status of Israel from the time of King Solomon, or certain social practices from the time of Jesus or Muhammad may be undermined (both in the sense of the narrative and the allegorical approach to it) by the results of these teachings.

Thus, the methodologically self-conscious actor occasionally finds himself in caught up in a schizophrenic way in attempting to describe the situation. On the one hand, as a man of faith within a particular religion, he accepts a standard interpretation as true; on the other hand, as a critical expert in the biblical sciences or as a comparative historian of societies, he must consider a different image from that which emerges from the Jewish, Christian, or Muslim "History of Salvation." Clearly, they can refer to the practice relativism mentioned by

Turner and state that the truthfulness of the accounts of the various events described in the Bible has a different "truthful" meaning for the theologian and a different meaning for the historian.

The first one is not about establishing facts in the spirit of *Wie es eingenlich gewesen*, but about pointing out, for example, Yahweh's pedagogical dialogue with the chosen people, who once are rewarded by them, and another time are punished for not being faithful to God's law and fall into slavery. Regardless of the peculiarly understood Imaginative Variations—if we may use this phenomenological term in that context—which tend to change the status of the subject, depending on the accepted perspective of the observer (interpreter), the scholarly theologian would have to speak about and the possibilities of reconciling them, the fact is that he has to make a peculiar leap between paradigms, perspectives, interpretative practices, etc., which can be described as intellectual *bricolage*.

In such a situation, they have two choices: to consider that there is no special conflict and that there is a certain continuity in interpretation, or *vice versa*, that certain general concepts that define continuity are a certain idealization that can be recognized from the perspective of "faith," that is, a member of a congregation, but from the point of view of a sociologist or anthropologist, this continuity is highly questionable because historical implementations (realizations) in different epochs are quite different.

I am referring here to a recent and unpublished text by Michael Singleton, the theologian, philosopher and, above all, social anthropologist from Louvain-la-Neuve, who, on the basis of the post-conciliar changes in the Catholic Church is carrying out a certain deconstruction of the conviction of a certain substance continuity of social and institutional (not only religious) institutions.

> When they were not in a position to enforce conversion, missionaries resignedly told the pagans to "either take it or leave it". The "it" being what in good faith they supposed to be the whole truth and nothing but the truth deposited by God (*depositum fidei*) once and for all in a biblical repository. Hence Rome's dogmatic belief that instructions for the use of the divine had been definitively drawn up on the death of John, the last Apostle and confided exclusively till the End of Time to the infallible successors of Peter, the first Pope.
> SINGLETON 2020, 4

At the same time, from a sociological and historical perspective and in the spirit of post-Khunian relativism, it suggests that we are actually dealing with a whole series of revolutions in history that lead to different paradigms (epochs) within a whole that looks different from the outside than it is presented from the inside—as an essential *continuum* despite the changes:

Hence "Christianity" is a mere convenient blanket term. Its value is purely heuristic and taxonomic—allowing us to distinguish a global phenomenon from similar analytical generalizations such as Islam or Judaism within the even less meaningful generic category of "monotheistic religion." In no way should this kind of residual, lowest common denominator description be taken as essentially and identically present in the disparate, successive configurations delimited by historians such as the Apostolic Age, the Patristic Period, Middle Age Christianity, or Post Vatican II Catholicism. Even less should Christianity be conceived as the transcendent, archetypical cause of accidental avatars, some less perfectly Christian than others. Just as the God of Abraham, of Thomas of Aquinas, and of Teilhard de Chardin has only a name in common, so too the Church of Constantine, of Charlemagne, or of Napoleon represent three (re)locations not of substantially the Same but of successively the quite Other (Singleton 2020, 10). Whether or not we are inclined to agree with Singleton's suggested picture of the intermittent and revolutionary development of various social institutions such as religious communities, and universities, he undoubtedly poses an important question from the point of view of the practice normativity about the *hau* factor.

The second problem deals with the aspect of knowledge transfer (and normative structure of beliefs) into a different culture, described by Singleton. The process in question seems to be different from the figure of an expert on the Maori rules of the exchange of gifts reconstructed by Turner. In his example, a lawyer explaining the rules applicable to all participants in the process of the exchange of gifts and stressing the importance of *hau* as a normative factor in the threat of a possible breach of the rules applicable to the community. In the Singleton example we have a reverse situation: how to learn about different religious reality, which goes beyond local and empirical modes of perception. One may ask whether and, if yes, to what extent do we have to cope with the GBT pattern when "the rational religion is transmitted into realm of former superstitions"? It should be noted, that Singleton has worked for many years as a Catholic missionary in Tanzania, doing his anthropological research as well. Thus, as an expert on theological issues, in a pastoral dimension, he had to reflect on an appropriate form of pragmatic communication of complex theological semantics for audiences whose mental structures functioned in categories completely different from the neo-scholastic version of Christian dogmatics, or any other version promoted in the framework of the *Vaticanum Secundum* at least. He has been inspired by the conciliar guidelines on the need to enculturate the truths of the faith, and above all the liturgical forms, i.e., the necessity of their functional translation into the categories of local communities which, in the case of the WaKonongo people, had only recently come into contact with Christianity.

> Though they might not have realized the extent to which they relativized the phenomenon when the Scholastics proclaimed that whatever was received could be so only in keeping with the receptive capacities of the receiver (*Quidquid recipitur ad modum recipientis recipitur*) they implied that no matter how much the recipient of a "revelation" might feel it came from Above or Outside, it could only be comprehended in keeping with his culturally conditioned capabilities - foremost among which his language. Consequently, one cannot hand down the Gospel either intra- or inter-culturally as one does an heirloom.
> SINGLETON 2020, 4

It seems that also in this second dimension, i.e., in the context of activities of a pastoral nature (i.e., persuasive towards the recipients of religious messages), we can consider whether and to what extent the GBT scheme is applied here. Perhaps it is reversed because the rational individual, on the one hand, wants to avoid Europeanisation, whether in the Roman or Lutheran, Calvinist, Methodist, etc., and on the other hand, by participating in everyday life, he faces the dilemma of what and how he can implement from the religion he wants to transmit in his missionary activities in order to allow for the preservation (or at least respect for the traditional culture to date). At the same time, as he recalls his missionary activity:

> Having written a thesis on Teilhard de Chardin in Rome before another on Nilotic religion in Oxford, I had come to believe that sooner or later intercultural contact gave rise not to the transfer of a weaker to a stronger culture but to the emergence of a completely new provisional halt. In participating actively in witchcraft trials and spirit possession séances rather than observing them with scholarly passivity my aim was not to suggest sorcery was a superstitious illusion or that group psychotherapy worked better [...] from *ad gentes* to *cum gentibus* via *inter gentes*: from working *for* the salvation of others through living *amongst* them towards the *nec plus ultra* of inventing *with* them more salutary outcomes for all concerned.
> SINGLETON 2020, 18

The fundamental question remains whether the Good Bad Theories device proposed by Turner is a one-way street: it determines what, from the point of view of scientific knowledge, we can consider as an element explaining the functioning of certain normative practices, even though they refer to concepts that escape rational (empirical) perception. Yet, if the problem I have referred to in the example of certain relations within religious knowledge and the issue of social distribution of knowledge is plausible, then perhaps the question of a certain "two-way street" GBT is justified.

The theological-missionary excursion was to show that GBT can function in both directions. Thus, the concept of normativity proposed by Turner may have interesting applications not only for practices and related beliefs that may seem unreasonable (or even false) from a scientific point of view, but also for the study of very diverse contemporary forms of popular culture, which Hubert Knoblauch described as a popular religion (2009). What he has in mind is not an old term *la religion populaire* (*Volkstümliche, folk religion*), but "When I speak of popular religion, I do so in the sense that religion adapts to the new form of popular culture" (Knoblauch 2009, 198).

As Knoblauch notices, it is no coincidence that the boundaries of specialized institutions are sharper than between social milieus, for example, since popular culture itself is supported by institutions that follow different rules than the "religious system," the "science system" or the "education system." He points out that among these institutions of popular religion are the many "institutes" of the New Age, alternative therapy facilities or free church seminars, which are located on the edge of the religious system (Knoblauch 2009, 199). Those systems—I suggest—might be treated in a similar way as the Maori GBT normative explanations referring to various *hau* in spite of their modern and, in significant amount, secular formulations.

And while showing to what extent GBT can be applied to the analysis of different forms of expression and communication of contemporary spirituality in secularized times, as Kipling would say, this is another story, that is, it would require the writing of a second consecutive text for which this would be an initial point of reference. Nevertheless, I suggest that the project proposed by Turner to understand what is normative has (potentially) quite broad application. It seems that the problem of *hau* does not only concern primary cultures, but perhaps much more relevant in the analysis of the spiritual transcendence of our contemporary everyday life-worlds.

References

Acourt, Paul. (1995). Ironic Empiricism (Apparently) versus the Demon of Analogy." *History of the Human Sciences*, 8(3): 107–127.

Bohman, James. (1997). "Do Practices Explain Anything? Turner's Critique of the Theory of Social Practices." *History and Theory*, 36(1): 93–107.
Collins, Harry, and Robert Evans. (2002). "The Third Wave of Science Studies: Studies of Expertise and Experience." *Social Studies of Science* 32(2): 235–96.
Collins, Harry, and Robert Evans. (2007). *Rethinking Expertise*. Chicago: University of Chicago Press.
Collins, Harry, and Robert Evans. (2017). *Why Democracies Need Science*. Cambridge: Polity Press.
Gaitán-Torres, Antonio. (2013). "Normativity, Explanation, and Social Sciences: A Symposium on Stephen Turner's *Explaining the Normative*." *Revista Internacional de Sociología* (ris) 71(1): 191–225.
Gaitán-Torres, Antonio. (2013). "Normativity for Social Sciences. The Expressivist's Recipe: A Symposium on Stephen Turner's *Explaining the Normative*." *Revista Internacional de Sociología* (ris) 71(1): 213–225.
Ginev, Dimitri. (2018). *Toward a Hermeneutic Theory of Social Practices: Between Existential Analytic and Social Theory*. London, New York: Routledge.
Hollis, Martin. (1994). *The Philosophy of Social Science: An Introduction*. Cambridge: Cambridge University Press.
Elster, Jon. (1985). *Making Sense of Marx*, Cambridge: Cambridge University Press.
Fuller, Steve, Mikael Stenmark, and Ulf Zackariasson, eds. (2014). *The Customization of Science: The Impact of Religious and Political Worldviews on Contemporary Science*. London: Palgrave Macmillan.
Fuller, Steve. (1997). Why Practice Does *Not* Make Perfect: Some Additional Support for Turner's *Social Theory of Practices, Human Studies*, vol. 20(3), pp. 315–323.
Fuller, Steve. (2018). *Post-Truth: Knowledge as a Power Game*. London: Anthem Press.
Knoblauch, Hubert. (2009). *Populäre Religion. Auf dem Weg in eine spirituelle Gesellschaft*, Frankfurt/Main: Campus Verlag.
Kotarbiński, Tadeusz. (1957), *Wesołe smutki [Merry Sorrows]*, Warszawa: Państwowe Wydawnictwo Naukowe.
Noguera, José A. (2013). "Social Science and 'Normative Facts' What's the big deal?: A Symposium on Stephen Turner's *Explaining the Normative*." *Revista Internacional de Sociología* (ris) 71(1): 200–220.
Lynch, Michael. (1997). "Theorizing Practice." *Human Studies*, 20(3): 335–344.
Pickering, Andy. (1997). "Time and a Theory of the Visible." *Human Studies*, 20(3): 325–333.
Peregrin, Jaroslav. (2011). "Stephen Turner's *Explaining the Normative*." *Organon F*, 18: 405–411.
Singleton, Michael. (2020). *Jesus, Livingstone ... and me! Evangelical Explorers* (manuscript).
Strauss, Leo. (1953). *Natural Right and History*. Chicago: University of Chicago Press.

Turner, Stephen. and Regis A. Factor. (1984). *Max Weber and the Dispute over Reason and Value: A Study of Philosophy, Ethics, and Politics,* London: Routledge.

Turner, Stephen and Daryl Chubin. (2020). "The Changing Temptations of Science." *Issues in Science and Technology* (Spring): 40–46.

Turner, Stephen P. (1980). *Sociological Explanation as Translation,* Cambridge: Cambridge University Press.

Turner, Stephen P. (1986). *Search for a Methodology of Social Science: Durkheim, Weber, and the Nineteenth-Century Problem of Cause, Probability, and Action,* Boston Studies in Philosophy of Science, vol. 92, Dordrecht/Boston: D. Reidel.

Turner, Stephen P. (1994). *The Social Theory of Practices: Tradition, Tacit Knowledge and Presuppositions,* Chicago: Chicago University Press.

Turner, Stephen P. (2003a). *Liberal democracy 3.0: Civil Society in the Age of Experts,* London: Sage.

Turner, Stephen P. (2003b). "The Third Science War," *Social Studies of Science* 33(4): 581–611.

Turner, Stephen P. (2010). *Explaining the Normative,* Cambridge: Polity Press.

Turner, Stephen P. (2013a). "Where Explanation Ends: Understanding as the Place The Spade Turns In The Social Sciences." *Studies in History and Philosophy of Science,* (44): 532–538.

Turner, Stepher.P. (2013b) The Argument of *Explaining the Normative.* A Symposium on Stephen Turner's *Explaining the Normative Revista Internacional de Sociología* (ris) Vol.71(1): 192–194.

Turner, Stephen. P. (2013c). The Tacit and The Explicit: A Reply to José A. Noguera, Jesús Zamora-Bonilla, and Antonio Gaitán-Torres A Symposium on Stephen Turner's *Explaining the Normative Revista Internacional de Sociología* (ris) Vol.71(1): 221–225.

Turner, Stephen P. (2014). *The Politics of Expertise,* New York: Routledge.

Turner, Stephen P. (2020). "Relativism in the Social Sciences," in *The Routledge Handbook of Philosophy of Relativism,* edited by M. Kusch, London: Routledge, 416–424.

Wierzchosławski, Rafał Paweł. (2018). Antinomies, Multiple Realities and the Pasts. In: K. Brzechczyn (eds.). *Towards a Revival of Analytical Philosophy of History. Around Paul A. Roth's Vision of Historical Sciences. Poznań Studies in the Philosophy of the Sciences and the Humanities,* vol. 110. Leiden/Boston: Brill, 166–203.

Wierzchosławski, Rafał Paweł. (2020). The "Post-Truth" Condition and Social Distribution of Knowledge: On Some Dilemmas with Post-Truth Uses. In *History in a Post-Truth World: Theory and Praxis,* edited by Marius Gudonis and Benjamin T. Jones. London: Routledge, 66-83.

Wimsatt William C. (2007). *Re-Engineering Philosophy for Limited Beings: Piecewise Approximations to Reality.* Cambridge, Mass.: Harvard University Press.

Zamora-Bonilla Jesús. (2013). "Normativity without Normativism: A Symposium on Stephen Turner's *Explaining the Normative Revista Internacional de Sociología*" (ris) 71(1): 195–199.

PART 2

Practices and Beliefs

∴

What is in an Account of Practices?

Theodore R. Schatzki

Abstract

This chapter engages Stephen Turner's comments on practices by asking what accounts of practices are up to and encompass. It begins by considering two conceptions of practices: practices as organized actions (theories of practices) and practices as patterns of activity (Turner). These conceptions connect to two notions of what an account of practices is up to: whereas Turner's account starts from patterns and seeks to explain them, theories of practice begin from the question, How best conceptualize social phenomena?, and propose that researchers analyze such phenomena as practices.

The chapter then spells out Turner's well-known criticisms of "classical" collective accounts of practices. These criticisms, it claims, vex Giddens's account but pass by Bourdieu's. Bourdieu's account in fact converges with Turner's. The chapter next outlines Turner's account of practices, according to which patterns of activity are explained by complexes of habits. These complexes are unique due to people's individualized paths of learning but sufficiently aligned to generate patterns in action.

The final section presents my own "postclassical" collective account of practices. This account skirts Turner's criticisms and both affirms the individualized nature of learning and is compatible with each person having unique cognitive machinery. It might, I suggest, be combined with Turner's account to yield a more robust theory of practices. Still, it remains unclear whether the kind of explanation of action Turner advocates jibes with those implied by postclassical accounts.

Keywords

Conceptions of practices – patterns of activity – organized activities – habits – collective mental elements – learning

From time to time Stephen Turner writes something about practices. He calls the principal target of his critical comments on the topic the "classical" or "standard social science" model of practices. He also offers an alternative account of the phenomenon. Turner's engagement with the topic merges his interest in accounting for human activity with his interest in accounting for social life. He has declined, however, to join those who center a social ontology on the concept (e.g., Giddens 1979; Reckwitz 2002; Shove et al. 2012; Schmidt 2012; Kemmis et al. 2014). Seemingly by default, his remarks about practices have remained individualist in character: practices come into his sights only in so far as they have something to do with the activities of individuals.

In this essay, I want to ask what accounts of practices are up to and encompass. Turner is fond of formulating questions that he takes himself and his interlocutors to be addressing as questions of "accounting" for something, for example, human activity, interactions (Turner 2014, 91), or mutual understanding (Turner 2014, 191; 2017, 371). By "accounting for" something, Turner means giving an explanatory account of it that shows how it fits into the causal structure of the world. Turner, moreover, holds that science is the domain of human endeavor that uncovers the causal order of the world. This position implies that an account of practices in his sense must draw on, or at least avoid being incompatible with, what science pronounces about the world—where "science" includes cognitive science but not the social disciplines. However, other theorists have developed "accounts" of practices of sorts different from his. This raises the question: What is in an account of practices?

This chapter proceeds as follows. I begin by asking what a practice is. Answers to this question connect to different ideas about what an account of practices is up to. I then summarize Turner's criticisms of the classical model of practices, show how the criticisms vex Giddens' account, but question their applicability to Bourdieu's. Following this, I present Turner's alternative. I then spell out how my own nonclassical views on practices skirt Turner's critique and are compatible with the ideas about learning and cognitive machinery that are central to his analysis. Nevertheless, I conclude, this compatibility leaves open whether the kind of action explanation that Turner advocates jibes with those marshalled in nonclassical accounts of practices.

1 What is an Account of Practices Up To?

Perhaps the most widespread conception of practices equates practices with human activities. This sense of the term is almost always involved when theorists mention practices more or less in passing. It is also a nontechnical conception. Theorists who mean activities by the term "practices" make no systematic use of it and instead employ the word simply to refer some phenomenon or subject matter to the realm of human activity. As a result, this use of the term is also found outside social thought in both academic work more broadly and the public sphere.

WHAT IS IN AN ACCOUNT OF PRACTICES? 73

Three important technical uses of the term "practices" exist. The first construes practices as situated actions. This conception dominates so-called "practice-based studies," which is popular in organizational studies and education (e.g. Gherardi 2006; Nicolini 2013). This conception holds, in sync with a long tradition in sociology, that human activities are inherently tied to the situations in which they transpire. I will set this conception aside in the following to concentrate on the next two. The second technical conception dominates so-called "practice theory." It holds that practices are composed of organized activities, that is, activities that hang together through arrays of elements different from them. Whereas some practice theorists conceptualize practices as organized regularities in actions (e.g., Giddens, Reckwitz, Shove et al.), others treat them as a kind of open organized manifold that encompasses, not just regularities, but irregularities, unique or occasional actions, and idiosyncrasies, too (e.g., Bourdieu 1990; Rouse 1996; Schatzki 2002).

A third conception of practices treats them as patterns, or uniformities, in action. This, I believe, is Turner's conception. In *The Social Theory of Practices*, for example, Turner opposes the idea that practices are shared causally-effective mental entities (1994, 104) but remarks that it is innocuous to construe practices as "patterns of behavior" (1994, 117). At the end of the book, he further warms to the notion in declaring that the word "practice" denotes the "individual formations of habit" that, he claims, generate utterances, performances, and patterns of activity. In later work, Turner embraces the term more straightforwardly. For example, he acknowledges that it is legitimate to explain "the uniformities of overt conduct that practice theory is an attempt to account for" (2014, 118), elsewhere describing these uniformities as "commonalities of reaction" and of behavior (2017, 361). Turner's subsequent claim that practices arise, inter alia, from shared focuses of attention and processes of pattern recognition (2018, 216) reinforces the idea that practices are patterns. The domain of practices, as a result, includes joint actions (2018, 129), which are "collective form[s] of action constituted by the fitting together of the behavior of separate individuals" (Blumer 1969, 70). Practices are also normative in the sense of carrying explicit normative claims or doctrines.

This third conception of practices dovetails poorly with those found in theories of practice. Above all, it exhibits no sense of organization. A pattern of activity is just a regularity or general configuration of actions. The idea that practices are patterns also sits uneasily with those practice theoretical conceptions that treat practices as open manifolds that embrace actions and sequences of action that are not part of patterns.

According to Turner's "scientific" self-understanding, accounts treat that for which they seek explanations—patterns of activity, for example—as empirical facts or phenomena. It is because practices, that is, patterns of activity, are phenomena in the world that it makes sense to account for them. This is true even if, as Turner holds, noticing such patterns, for instance, how French nurses walk (e.g., 1994, 20–4; 2014, 75) requires contrasts. In discussing practices, therefore, Turner starts from the existence of patterns of activity.

Practice theories do not share this starting point. They do not take the point of discussing practices to be, in the first place, accounting for patterns of activity. Theories of practice are not disinterested in individuals, in the actions of individuals, or in the patterns these actions form. But these matters are not the primary focus of attention: they are instead phenomena one gets to starting from a different issue. This starting issue is how best to conceptualize social life. Theories of practices, furthermore, *propose* that researchers treat social life as composed of practices and that they theorize and conduct research on this basis. Practices are not, in the first place, something in the world to be accounted for. Theories of practice instead suggest that social researchers conceptualize social life as practices and proceed accordingly.

Given their interest in the issue of how best to conceptualize social life, theorists of practice will find the idea of simply taking practices, without discussion, to be patterns revealing. For it dovetails with an individualist social ontology. This idea need not abet individualism—patterns of activity can be "accounted for" with the resources of a nonindividualist ontology. But taking practices as patterns goes well with the thesis that social phenomena are built out of individuals' actions. Indeed, Turner, as mentioned at the start, seems to be an individualist. For instance, he mentions, approvingly, Weber's analysis that what there is to social life and social phenomena is people's actions (2018, 187). What, moreover, he counterposes to *collective* conceptions of society are *social* conceptions, which highlight interactions (2014, 104; chap.11). And the two conceptions of the social that he opposes in chapter eight of *Cognitive Science and the Social* are both versions of individualism.

Theories of practice are primarily interested in conceptualizing and accounting for social life and only derivitively concerned with accounting for patterns of activities. They propose giving center place to the notion of practices in accounts of what social life is. As I see things, moreover, their proposals are good ones if the resulting accounts underwrite insightful social research. For the acid test for the goodness of a theory of social life is whether it funds insightful empirical research (Schatzki 2009, 2019). Whether it leads to good accounts of patterns of activity is only part of what counts.

Hence, in regard to the topic of practices, Turner's account aims to explain patterns in activities, drawing on existing research above all but not only in cognitive psychology. By contrast, practice theoretical accounts aim to conceptualize social life and social phenomena and to develop concepts and ideas that are useful in understanding these. Their views on activity, interaction and patterns of activity become part of this effort. According to these accounts, moreover, explanations of practices cite phenomena other than those studied in cognitive psychology, for instance, evolutionary processes (e.g., Harré 1993), routine reproduction and modes of deroutinization (Giddens 1979), the structure and dynamics of social spaces (Bourdieu), or nexuses of activity chains and material events/processes (Schatzki 2019).

Turner relates (2017, 360–3) that social theory exhibits two opposing sets of concepts. One set includes such notions as culture, society, norms, and values, the other such notions as interaction, imitation, habit, and empathy. He takes these two sets to crystallize alternative ways of accounting for the same subject matter (2017, 362). It might be, however, that these two sets of concepts, equally or more directly, bespeak two general views on social ontology, namely, nonindividualism and individualism. On the one view, social life encompasses such matters as institutions, structures, and practices. On the other view, social life encompasses the activities, interactions, and joint actions of individuals. Some theories, including some theories of practice, might combine elements from the two sets. Characterizing the difference between the two sets of concepts as a matter of ontology points toward issues different from Turner's, for instance, What sorts of ontology fund insightful social research, and on what subject matters? It also opens the possibilities (1) that disparate ontologies lie behind the different accounts of given subject matters that theories from the two camps provide and (2) that overlaps in subject matters that such theories seek to provide accounts of can vary depending on the specific theories involved.

2 Turner's Critique of the Standard Model

Turner is well known for his critique of the "social," or better "collective," theory of practices (2014, chap. 11). The critique is beautifully straightforward. The collective theory of practices holds that patterns of activity exist because shared, that is, "the same," causally-efficacious mental entities exist in different people and determine how they act. The theory is "collective," moreover, because it further holds that these shared entities come to be in different people because people download or internalize them from a common source in the world.

> [There is] a long line of historical figures as well as contemporary thinkers who believe that there is some sort of collective mental element that

is out there, in some sense, is assimilated or acquired by the participants, and functions as a shared structure which is in turn a condition for certain performances that cannot be explained or accounted for in any other way. (2014, 191).

This way of thinking exemplifies what Turner calls the "standard social science model:" "The model is that there is a set of norms or a culture out there in 'society' that gets inserted into people's heads via socialization, and the individuals in society use this culture or enact it" (2017, 360). According to Turner, mental entities that are both common and shared come in two basic varieties: cognitive elements such as presuppositions, representations, and rules and "subcognitive" elements such as skills, habitus, and ways of life (2014, 67; cf. 103).

Turner's primary argument against the standard model is that no account has—stronger, can—be given of how the collective mental elements out there get into different people, in particular, of how this transmission works such that the same causally-efficacious entities become part of different people's mental apparatuses. Other arguments Turner offers are (1) that no sensible account exists of where the collective elements reside and (2) that partisans of the standard model typically describe what is to be accounted for in a way that presupposes what their versions of the model deem responsible for these matters. Turner also holds against the standard model the fact that there exists a multiplicity of conceptions of the collective element involved.

These criticisms impugn especially well the ideas of a practice theorist that I am not aware Turner discusses, Anthony Giddens. Giddens analyzes practices as routines that are governed—constrained and enabled—by structures that for present purposes can be taken as composed of rules: "rules generate—or are the medium of the production and reproduction—of practices" (Giddens 1979, 67). A key difference between practices and their structures is that practices are extended over time and space, whereas structures, that is, sets of rules (and resources), lie outside time and space. At the same time, rules are contained in actors' practical consciousnesses, taking the form of memory traces (Giddens 1979, 64). Giddens' structures are a collective object that is downloaded into the practical consciousnesses of participants in practices, where they become shared action-governing entities. Giddens, moreover, gives more or less no account of how this downloading works. In addition, Turner's worries about location are made acute by the gymnastics Giddens performs to make structure something that exists at once outside time and space and in individual brains.

The cogency of Turner's critique, however, is less clear-cut concerning Bourdieu, a practice theorist he does discuss. Bourdieu famously accounted for practices—that is, activities, more precisely, activities-in-social-spaces—by reference to habitus. Habitus is batteries of dispositions. The dispositions involved are responsible not just for interventions in the world but also for acts of perception and thinking. Bourdieu argued that the habitus a person acquires is tied to, among other things, the positions that that person occupies in the distributions of capitals that define positions in the social spaces (e.g., fields) in which he or she grows up. People who occupy the same positions in these spaces, and who thereby grow up facing much the same opportunities amid much the same practices transpiring in much the same layouts of the material world, acquire much the same sets of dispositions. In this sense, they "share" dispositions.

Contrary to what Turner argues, people do not share dispositions because a collective habitus, a collective set of "core or underlying" (2014, 106) dispositions—or any other kind of collective mental element such as a quasi-telos (2014, 103, 105)—is downloaded into them. What is "collective," or better common, in Bourdieu's account of how people come to share dispositions are such matters as (1) the distributions of capital, together with the positions that these distributions define, in the domains of practice in which people act, (2) the stakes that people pursue in these domains, and (3) the material layouts of the world through which people active in these domains move. It is true that a "singular habitus" is associated with each position in social space. But this singular habitus is not a collective or common habitus that is downloaded into individuals. Indeed, Bourdieu, in a difficult passage, seems explicitly to reject this view:

> Class (or group) *habitus* ... could be regarded as a ... non-individual system of internalized structures, common schemes of perception, conception and action ... [A]nd the objective co-ordination of practices and the sharing of a world-view could be founded on the perfect impersonality and interchangeability of singular practices and views. But this would amount to regarding all the practices and representations produced in accordance with identical schemes as impersonal and interchangeable.
> BOURDIEU 1990, 60

He continues: "In fact, the singular habitus of members of the same class are united in a relationship of homology, that is, of diversity within homogeneity reflecting the diversity within homogeneity characteristic of their social conditions of production." In other words, people who occupy the same position in social space, and are subject as a result to much the same conditions, still have varying life histories through these spaces subject to these conditions—and these varying life histories produce divergent habituses, which are nonetheless versions of one another. What, then, is class or group habitus? It is "individual habitus in so far as it expresses or reflects" (Bourdieu 1990, 60) the class or group. I interpret this characterization to mean that class or group habitus is a person's habitus in so far as it reflects the conditions—the much the same capitals, practices, material lay-outs, and opportunities—that members of the class or group encounter. An analyst then gives content to class or group habitus by *constructing* (statistically) what the habituses of members of the class or group owe to these same or similar conditions, as opposed to what their habituses owe to the particular courses their lives take subject to these conditions. Class or group habitus is not a collective entity in Turner's sense.

At an earlier stage of his career, Bourdieu sought to develop a kind of neo-structuralist practical logic that would at once explain (1) how living through much the same conditions results in people sharing habitus. i.e., possessing batteries of dispositions that are versions of one another, and (2) how sharing habitus in this sense at once reproduces these conditions and makes them understandable to people. He rooted, materially, the structural element of this logic in opposed movements of the human body (Bourdieu 1976, 119). Later, Bourdieu settled for the thesis that correlations exist among these matters. At both stages, his account of habitus recognizes that practices in social spaces drift and evolve and are not just "reproduced" as the same.

Many criticisms can be made of this account. For example, because Bourdieu never said much about what a disposition is, it is unclear what it is for a disposition to be the same or similar. But it is not the case, as Turner charges (1994, 47–8), that Bourdieu evaded the issue of how shared dispositions get into people (and how these shared dispositions explain practices) by simply invoking the notion of reproduction. It is true that Bourdieu did not say much about how the acquisition of dispositions works. He primarily emphasized (e.g., 1990, chaps. 4 and 6) that explicit pedagogy is doubled by a wordless pedagogy that works by people simply living through—participating in and observing—practices in particular material settings. He also held, pace Turner (2014, 115), that individual histories shape what individuals "know," that is, that people, through the particular series of overt or wordless pedagogical moments they undergo, learn different things and thus have different habituses, which are nonetheless versions of the habituses possessed by others who live through much the same practices, materialities, and opportunities. Bourdieu's dispositions also possess the causal powers that Turner attributes to habits. As will become clearer in the following section, Bourdieu's and Turner's accounts converge in important ways.

3   Turner's Alternative

Turner develops a social, as opposed to a collective, account of practices. This account holds that human practices, like human activities more broadly, are generated by habits. By "habits" Turner means "skills and cognitive machinery" (2014, 103) involving, most prominently, neuro nets, mirror neurons, and pattern recognition. The possession of such habits represents a kind of "tacit knowledge," whose tacitness consists in the skills and machinery involved being "occluded" (2014, 162) from consciousness: inaccessible to (2014, 209) and inarticulable by (2014, 8) those who possess them, though not to or by scientists who study this machinery.

In turn, habits arise from learning, which is a process that individuals undergo primarily, though not exclusively, through interactions with others. The importance of interaction in this context has partly to do with feedback, which occurs in interactions and is crucial to the tacit learning process (2014, 10). It also has to do with joint focal points of attention, including objects and events in the world, that mark matters of social significance or concern and around which skills and cognitive machinery accumulate (2014, 214–16). Through interaction, an individual acquires abilities to recognize and perpetuate patterns. Probably the most crucial feature of the learning process for present purposes is its individualized character. The particular series of interactions and situations a person undergoes differ from those that others undergo, and even when people experience the same interactions and situations what they learn through them can vary (2014, 117). As a result, the complex of habits that is deposited in an individual through learning is unique to that individual (e.g., 2014, 106). At the same time, these complexes, by being acquired under similar (or the same) conditions, and developing over time as people interact with one another and jointly focus on the same matters, are calibrated with one another. This alignment both develops while and underlies the fact that individuals get along with, cooperate with, and form relations to one another:

> A practical activity can succeed with skilled practitioners whose skills are not identical but are acquired in such a way that they enable the practitioners to act cooperatively and even to improve their skilled performances in relation to one another, to adjust to one another, and to learn more generally to adjust to others, as in, for example, the joint activities of skilled practitioners and in the improvement and adaptation gained through practical cooperative activity involving other skilled practitioners. (2014, 128).

By virtue of these processes, people also come to act uniformly: to exhibit "commonalties" (2014, 361) and patterns of activity.

Learning involves another process, which Turner alternately calls mirroring, empathy, simulation, or emulation. This process is rooted in the existence of mirror neurons and has two aspects: grasping what is going on with a person whom is observed to act and "imitating" what that person does. The grasping aspect is crucial to understanding other people, thus to the mutual understanding that enables interaction and the shared attention, mutual adjustment, and learning that takes place in and through interaction. The imitation aspect is crucial to people going on to act in particular ways, thus to the acquisition of the cognitive machinery that is responsible for behavior. In sum, the process of learning embraces habituation and mirroring (2014, 75, 162) and both conscious and tacit elements. Joint attention and overt instruction are two examples of the former sort of element.

As explained, the products of learning are individualized complexes of habits that reflect individuals' learning histories. Because these histories are social histories, that is, paths through multitudes of interactions with and relations to other people, people's individualized complexes of habits are "good enough " "matches" (2014, 166) of one another. A person's activities result from (1) focuses, including joint focuses, of attention and (2) individualized cognitive mechanisms, including the recognition of patterns in the world (i.e., the situations the person confronts). Due to the alignment of habits, people who are attentive to the same matters successfully interact with one another and pull off joint activities, and their behavior forms patterns. The result is social life.

The convergence of this account with Bourdieu's is palpable when Turner writes that because a given person's habits are "in rough but imperfect correspondence to others, there is a loose sense in which there is an external 'shared' thing, a concept or representation, that corresponds to the individual's habituated patterns." (2014, 166) Class or group habitus is precisely such an external (i.e., constructed) shared thing, which corresponds to the habituses and practices of individuals who occupy the same positions in social spaces. Turner's claim that institutions combine "physical artefacts, explicit rules … and tacitly learned automatic responses both to training and to the patterned experiences of performing actions in the institution" (2018, 134) is likewise highly reminiscent of Bourdieu's account of practices-in-spaces.

4 Another Take

I want now to outline a practice theoretical position that Turner characterizes as "post-classical." This position bears a different relation to Turner's account of practices than do conceptions of practices—such as those of Giddens and Bourdieu—that Turner characterizes as "classical." I suggested that Giddens' account succumbs to Turner's criticisms but that Bourdieu's account, properly interpreted, converges in important ways with the latter. My own account, by contrast, is compatible with Turner's, and this compatibility suggests the possibility of combining them.

I analyze practices as open spatial-temporal arrays of doings and sayings (activities) that are organized by pools of practical and general understandings, rules, and teleoaffectivities. The part of this analysis that is presently relevant is the pool that organizes doings and sayings: this pool, composed of understandings, teleologies, emotions, and rules, looks like the sort of collective societal element targeted by Turner's objections.

By "practical understandings" I mean understandings of how, in particular circumstances, to carry on particular intentional activities (e.g., greeting a friend) through performances of bodily actions (e.g., waving an arm). By "general understandings" I mean ethoses or general senses of things, for instance, of Calvinist work as sanctification of the earthly sphere of existence or of the venerableness of bourbon. Such understandings are expressed in activities and articulated in sayings. A rule, meanwhile, is a formulated directive, instruction, or remonstration. Rules are uttered by people and written in texts, including children's books, government documents, rule-books, and signs. Finally, the teleologies (ends and end-task combinations) and emotions that organize practices are normativized, that is, are the teleologies and emotions that are acceptable or enjoined/prescribed in particular practices.

Practices are organized by pools of such items. Such organizing pools are self-same structures that indefinitely many people relate to. They are collective elements in social life. I agree with the standard social science view, as Turner specifies it, that these pools are "out there" in the world (as opposed to "in here" in individual people; cf. Taylor 1985). This conviction begs an objection that Turner raises to the standard view, namely, where are such pools located? I am not sure, however, what sort of answer Steve is looking for. My answer is that the pools are *in* the practices, that is, *in* the open arrays of doings and sayings. What it is for such a pool, or structure, to be in an array is multiple: certain elements of the structure are expressed or reacted to in the doings and sayings composing the array, other elements—including unexpressed ones—are connected to these elements, and the doings and sayings involved hang together through these elements. A practice is a certain clumping of doings and sayings that hang together through a pool of items of the above sorts. Whether, furthermore, a given activity belongs to the clump (the practice) is established by reference to this pool. There is no need, as Turner charges standard social science models of doing, of lodging these structures in "group minds" (2014,

196), "collective heads" (2014, 166), or "societies" (cf. 2017, 360). They are out there in the practices mediating the hanging-together of the activities that compose the practices, including the patterns of activity that Turner wants to account for. Of course, doings and sayings that compose a practice also hang together via interactions and chains of action. Indeed, Turner would probably say that the only ways activities "hang together" is through interactions and joint actions. For these are the only ways that activities, which are properties of individuals, can hang together on an individualist ontology.

These organizing structures, moreover, are not "stable determinant object[s]," as Turner (2014, 209) claims collective elements are. The pools of understandings, rules, teleologies, and emotions that organize practices change over time. For example, the bodily movements that people perform in order to greet people evolve, as do the formulated directives to which they are subjected, the ends that are acceptable to pursue in greeting, and even the emotions that are supposed to be exhibited when doing so. Nor are these pools fully determinate. Any pool (at a specific period of time) definitely contains certain elements. But the edges of the pool can be indefinite. It can be indeterminate, for example, whether a particular bodily movement was a greeting, whether the sentence, "Elders should be respected" (or distrusted), articulates a rule, whether it is acceptable for advisors to pursue personal monetary gain in investment brokerage practices, and whether it is wrong not to shed tears at your husband's funeral. Matters such as these are topics of discussion and disputation, which might settle the matter and firm up a component of the organizing pool or end inconclusively and leave the limits of the pool undecided.

The character of discussions and disputes about organizing elements offers one reason for thinking that organizing structures are out there in manifolds of activity. Interests and power differentials can obviously inflect the courses and upshots of discussions and disputes about what organizes practices. People, moreover, might orient what they say on the matter to the particular interlocutors they address. But it is also indisputable that people often, including often when they pursue personal interests when dialoguing or tailor what they say to their audience, try to get the matter right. When people discuss whether such and such is a rule or an acceptable end to pursue—just like when they say that a person or group whom they are studying or interpreting has assumed such and such (e.g., 2014, 20, 200–3)—they often are oriented toward the truth of the matter. There presumably is, therefore, a truth of the matter, at least in most cases. (Turner is right that there are no psychological entities called "assumptions." But statements to the effect that people assumed such and such can still be true or false and also true or false independent of whether the statements explain particular misunderstandings to particular audiences.)

The pools that organize practices are not in their entireties "downloaded" into individuals. Participants in a given practice become familiar over time with *different* subsets of the elements that organize it: they express in their activities and possess or have knowledge of different subsets. Each participant in a practice possesses and acts out of (1) some of the know-how's that organizes the practice and (2) a grasp of the ethoses involved. Each participant also upholds (or actively contravenes) some subset of the rules, pursues some of the ends, expresses some of the emotions, and otherwise possesses or knows of wider ranges of both understandings as well as rules that are at work, and ends, tasks, and emotions that enjoy normative status, in the practice. In this regard, though not in others, the structures that organize practices resemble what Cassirer called the symbolic realm, which embraces objective relations among symbols that individuals differentially draw on in their symbolic acts (see Turner 2014, 196). People, moreover, come to express and to possess and know of these elements by virtue of learning to carry on practices and then doing so. The different subsets of these matters that they possess, know, and express reflect different histories of experience, participation, and learning, and also such matters as the roles or positions they have occupied or presently occupy in the practices involved.

These subsets overlap. Where they overlap, "shared" understanding, knowledge, or expression exists. What it is, however, for understanding and knowledge to be shared varies. People share a know-how when it is the same thing that they know how to do (e.g., greet others), and they do the thing intelligibly to other participants. One person's knowing-how to greet people is shared with others when each knows how to greet people, and their greetings of people are intelligible as greetings to one another. By definition, moreover, participants share a general understanding when the same sense of some general matter is expressed in their activities and articulated in what they say. The existence of shared general understandings is most directly manifested when what participants say on some general topic possesses sufficient unity that a common sense of the matter can be identified (by participants or observers). Note that possession of a shared general understanding is compatible with disagreements on central topics. Calvinists could share an understanding that work sanctifies earthly existence and act and talk accordingly while disagreeing about why this is and even about exactly what it means and implies. If the disagreement had been so large, even encompassing what the basic topics are, there would have been no shared understanding. People, moreover, might assume that, i.e., act as if (2014, 169) they share a general understanding, perhaps because they use the same words or hear the same sentences and do not think much about the matter, and then find out through discussion that this is not the case. Finally, people share knowledge of the rules upheld, and of the ends and emotions that are acceptable or prescribed, in a practice when multiple participants know this of particular formulations, ends, and emotions. Likewise, they observe the same rules when they affirm or enforce the same formulations, and they pursue shared ends or share emotions when the end one person purses or the emotion she exhibits is an end that others pursue or an emotion others express.

When I write that people "possess" understandings and "know" that rules, ends, and emotions organize a practice, that is, have normative status in it, the possession and knowledge I have in mind are accessible and articulable. In Turner's (2014, 160) words, the knowledge involved "relate[s] to conscious thought:" it is conscious or explicit knowledge and usually formulable. It is not tacit knowledge in the sense Turner uses this expression. Conscious knowledge is acquired, that is, learned. It is acquired as people are exposed to, instructed in, watch and talk about, and (come to) participate in practices (cf. Lave and Wenger 1991). It is because people are exposed to, instructed in, and come to participate in different practices, and because the paths they take through and the experiences they have while being exposed to, instructed in, watching and talking about, and participating in these practices likewise vary, that people come to possess or know of different combinations of the elements that organize practices (and to express these in their activities). They take different paths through similar circumstances to become knowledgeable practitioners. To use Stephen Kemmis' (Kemmis et al. 2017) metaphor, they are "stirred into" practices along different, but convergent or parallel routes.

As explained, Turner criticizes the classical model on the grounds that there is no accounting for how the same mental element gets into different people's action-generating apparatuses. Admittedly, the processes of acquisition by which, in participating in practices, one becomes familiar with elements organizing them, are not well understood. But there is nothing more mysterious about these processes than the sort of learning that occurs when people learn how to multiply by doing multiplications, learn vocabulary by memorizing definitions, or learn to be tactful by observing tactful people. What's more, cognitive processes of the sorts Turner discusses, or of sorts that are discovered in the future, might spell out how these accomplishments are effected. So Turner's concerns about acquisition/transmission seem misplaced vis-à-vis shared understandings and shared knowledge of practice structures.

As indicated, the acquisition of knowledge and understanding possesses the individualized character that Turner ascribes to learning. As a result, shared knowledge and shared possession of elements that organize practices are compatible with individualized learning. People can have the knowledge and understanding that others do even though each of them undergoes individualized paths of learning, and even though each possesses individualized cognitive machinery. Different people's possession of the same understandings and knowledge comes out in how they act, in what they say to each other, and in the intelligibility of their actions to one another, not in their possession of identical cognitive machinery. Turner writes that "the only ... 'sharing' [i.e., of cognitive machinery-TRS] we need to account for social interaction is sufficient similarity for understanding to occur." (2018, 133) This is correct since shared understandings and knowledge, like the expression of the same organizing elements in different people's activities, does not require that people possess identical cognitive machineries.

Learning practices involves acquiring know-how's, becoming familiar with ethoses, and acquiring knowledge of rules and of acceptable or enjoined ends, tasks, and emotions. These processes can be nonconscious, or not explicit: people can and sometimes do acquire knowledge without being aware that this is going on or being aware of what they have acquired knowledge of. Accordingly, two sorts of things can be tacitly learned, where "tacit" now means not explicit or not conscious: matters that simply go unnoticed and those that cannot be accessed. People acquire knowledge, understanding, and other ways of being without being aware of it, though they can become aware of what they have learned and of the fact that they learned it. People also acquire the cognitive machinery Turner is interested in without being aware of it, but it remains occluded. Of course, lots of explicit learning is also involved in people acquiring familiarity with the structures that organize practices.

This discussion indicates how my conception of practices skirts another problem Turner poses to the standard model, namely, that of explaining the relation of the collective element, here the structures of practices, to the "causal world" (2014, 209). Understanding and knowledge are not causally-efficacious mental states of the sort Turner criticizes. Although they contribute to "causing" activity in a broader Aristotelian typology of causality, they do not contribute in the way cognitive mechanisms do. This fact removes any oddity from the fact that people who share understanding or knowledge nonetheless possess different "psychological causal structures" (see 2014, 190–1). What's more, my account can fully draw on those causal aspects of interaction identified by Turner that align different people's habits through feedback, adjustment, and joint focuses of attention. For these very same aspects provide instruction, call people's attention to things, and create a context in which people "pick up" understandings and knowledge of practice-organizing elements. Indeed, elements of practice structures can be objects of joint attention, around which cognitive machinery accumulates. As suggested, finally, I am happy to call on the causal discoveries of psychologists, educational theorists, and others to elucidate how people "pick up" understanding and knowledge, though recognizing these discoveries is not the same as affirming whatever these researchers say on the matter. The causal discoveries involved include processes of the sorts that Turner advocates, and thus a mix of explicit and tacit processes and learning.

All in all, Turner's account of practices qua patterns of activity is substantially compatible with my conception of practices as open organized arrays of doings and sayings. It might be compatible with other post-classical conceptions of practices as well (e.g., that of Shove et al. 2012). The practices I describe form constitutive contexts in which the actions, interactions, and patterns of activity that Turner claims are generated by individualized cognitive mechanisms, transpire. The two accounts of practices might thus be combined, each contributing something to a more robust account of human life that theorizes, inter alia, (1) activity, patterns of activity, and chains of activity (see Schatzki 2019); (2) the cognitive mechanisms that underlie activity and patterns thereof, people's understandings and knowledge of elements that organize practices, and the individualizing learning processes through which these mechanisms develop and these understandings and knowledge are acquired; and (3) practices (in my sense), bundles of practices and material arrangements (see Schatzki 2002), constellations of such bundles, and the material events and processes that occur to material arrangements and bodies (see Schatzki 2019).

Knowledge, understanding, ends, rules, and emotions are ordinary concepts that people use in their lives to comprehend one another. They operate on what Turner calls the level of ordinary "functional intersubjectivity" (2014, 117; he now [2018] calls the level of functional intersubjectivity the "*Verstehen* bubble"). The level, or better sphere, of ordinary functional intersubjectivity encompasses everything that can be grasped with common ordinary ways of understanding things. This sphere underlies another sphere that is not distinct from it, namely, the sphere of technical-scientific functional intersubjectivity. This sphere encompasses everything that can be grasped with common technical or scientific ways of understanding things. It might seem that Turner's and my account of practices are incompatible because the former exists in the scientific sphere of functional intersubjectivity and the latter in its underlying ordinary relative. However, my conception of practices, like those of other theorists of practices, is technical-theoretical in character. The ordinary concepts that are appropriated to spell out this conception become technical in being incorporated into it.

Concepts of cognitive mechanisms are likewise technical or theoretical in nature. Consequently, the more robust account of human life just envisioned does not split its existence between two connected spheres of intelligibility but is firmly ensconced in the scientific one. Or better, it is ensconced in a particular sociohistorical sphere of functional intersubjectivity that encompasses elements of ordinary and scientific understanding. In any event, the difference between ordinary and scientific spheres of understanding poses no barriers to combining Turner's account of practices with at least some post classical accounts of the matter.

5   Conclusion

There remains an issue about explanation. Turner claims that the cognitive machinery he discusses explains activities and practices. I have said almost nothing about explaining action. As noted, the point for practice theories of conceptualizing practices is to develop theories and theoretical concepts that illuminate social life; explaining activity is just one part of this broader task. Theories of practices, however, do provide resources or even templates for explaining activity, and it will surprise no one that the phenomena that a theory of practice calls on to explain activities are tied to the phenomena it claims organize practices. On my account, for instance, activity is explained by reference to ends, motives (what people react to), rules, and emotions.

There is no reason in principle why what a conception of practices claims or implies about human activity cannot be compatible with further ideas about activity that are neither part of nor implied by the account. Explaining activity by reference to cognitive mechanisms is an example of such a further idea. Indeed, conceptions of practice, and theories of the social world more broadly, must be compatible with what the nonsocial sciences conclude about their subject matters. This general principle raises particular issues vis-à-vis psychology and cognitive psychology since these disciplines offer explanations of something that many social theories, including theories of practice, likewise support explanations of, namely, human activity. So, the question becomes whether explanations of action that appeal to neuro nets or pattern recognition are compatible with explanations that cite ends, motives, rules, and emotions or the phenomena marshalled in other theories of practice to explain activity (e.g., habitus in Bourdieu; practical consciousness, wants, and articulated intentionality and reasons in Giddens). I am optimistic about the matter. But this is a complicated topic for another occasion

References

Blumer, Harold. 1969. *Symbolic Interactionism*. Berkeley: University of California Press.

Bourdieu, Pierre. 1976 [1972]. *Outline of a Theory of Practice*, trans. Richard Nice. Cambridge: Cambridge University Press.

Bourdieu, Pierre. 1990 [1980]. *The Logic of Practice*, trans. Richard Nice. Stanford: Stanford University Press.

Gherardi, Silvia. 2006. *Organizational Knowledge: The Texture of Workplace Learning*. Oxford: Blackwell.

Giddens, Anthony. 1979. *Central Problems in Social Theory. Action, Structure and Contradiction in Social Analysis*. Berkeley: University of California Press.

Harré, Rom. 1993. *Social Being*, 2nd edn.. Oxford: Blackwell.

Kemmis, Stephen, Jane Wilkinson, Christine Edwards-Groves, Ian Hardy, Peter Grootenboer, and Laurette Bristol. 2014. *Changing Practices, Changing Education*. Singapore: Springer.

Kemmis, Stephen, Christine Edwards-Groves, Annemaree Lloyd, Peter Grootenboer, Ian Hardy, and Jane Wilkinson. 2017. "Learning as Being 'Stirred In' to Practices." In *Practice Theory Perspectives on Pedagogy and Education. Praxis, Diversity and Contestation*. Edited by Peter Grootenboer, Christine Edwards-Groves, and Sarojni Choy. Singapore: Springer, 45–66.

Lave, Jean and Etienne Wenger. 1991. *Situated learning. Legitimate Peripheral Participation*. New York: Cambridge University Press.

Nicolini, Davide. 2013. *Practice Theory, Work, and Organization: An Introduction*. Oxford: Oxford University Press.

Reckwitz, Andreas. 2002. "Toward a Theory of Social Practices. A Development in Culturalist Theorizing." *European Journal of Social Theory* 5 (2): 243–263.

Rouse, Joseph. 1996. *Engaging Science: How to Understand its Practices Philosophically*. Ithaca, NY: Cornell University Press.

Schatzki, Theodore. 2002. *The Site of the Social. A Philosophical Exploration of the Constitution of Social Life and Change*. University Park: The State University of Pennsylvania Press.

Schatzki, Theodore. 2009. "Dimensions of Social Theory." In *Reimagining the Social in South Africa: Critique and Post-Apartheid Knowledge*. Edited by Peter Vale and Heather Jacklin. Pietermaritzburg, South Africa: University of KwaZulu Natal Press, 29–46.

Schatzki, Theodore. 2019. *Social Change in a Material World*. Abingdon: Routledge.

Schmidt, Robert, 2012. *Soziologie der Praktiken*. Frankfurt am Main: Suhrkamp.

Shove, Elizabeth, Mika Pantzar, and Matt Wilson. 2012. *The Dynamics of Social Practice. Everyday Life and How it Changes*. London: Sage.

Taylor, Charles. 1985. "Interpretation and the Sciences of Man." In *Philosophy and the Human Sciences: Philosophical Papers 2*. Cambridge: Cambridge University Press, 15–58.
Turner, Stephen. 1994. *The Social Theory of Practices: Tradition, Tacit Knowledge and Presuppositions*. Cambridge: Polity.
Turner, Stephen. 2014. *Understanding the Tacit*. Abingdon: Routledge.
Turner, Stephen. 2017. "Naturalizing the Tacit." In *Das interpretative Universum. Dimitri Ginev zum 60. Geburtstag gewidmet*. Würzburg: Königshausen & Neumann, 355–76.
Turner, Stephen. 2018. *Cognitive Science and Social Theory: A Primer*. Abingdon: Routledge.

Yes Virginia, Folk Psychological Understanding Really is Explanatory

Towards a Realist Conception of the "Verstehen Bubble"

Karsten R. Stueber

Abstract

In thinking about the nature of the social sciences, Stephen Turner has always been a resolute naturalist arguing for the eradication of any remnants of an unjustifiably enchanted conception of the social realm. Accordingly, he has been skeptical about notions such as practices, norms, or even folk-psychological concepts such as beliefs and intentions. At most, such concepts belong to what he calls the "Verstehen Bubble," within which members of a social community provide each other with an intellectual hug in terms of narratives that allow them to somehow endow their lives with significance.

In discussing Turner's views, I will argue for a realist conception of the "Verstehen Bubble." I will defend the causal explanatory potential of our folk-psychological framework and argue that it constitutes an autonomous domain vis a vis the explanatory practice of the cognitive neurosciences. I will do this also by discussing why I regard my conception of our folk psychological practices to be fully in accord with Weber's complex manner of thinking about our grasp of the significance of human agency. Finally, I will discuss why I regard talk of mere patterns and of responses to affordances outside the realm circumscribed by our empathic capacities and folk psychological repertoire to be explanatorily blind.

Keywords

Naturalism – Empathy – Weber – Verstehen – Mirror Neurons – Causal Explanation

1   Introduction

Throughout his distinguished career, Stephen Turner has argued from a perspective of resolute naturalism for the eradication of the remnants of an unjustifiably enchanted conception of the social realm. Accordingly, he has been skeptical about claims that the notions of practices (Turner 1994), rules and norms (Turner 2010), or even folk-psychological concepts such as beliefs and intentions describe real structures of social reality (Turner 2018). At most they seem to belong to what he calls in the later book the "Verstehen Bubble," within which members of a social community provide each other with an intellectual hug in terms of narratives that allow them to somehow endow their lives with significance. Despite acknowledging what one might call its phenomenal reality he seems to be tempted by a non-realist conception of the contents of the "Verstehen Bubble" by pointing out that most of its categories fail to be validated from the perspective of the cognitive brain-sciences, that is, most of its categories are not "brain-ready" (Turner 2018, 127). Accordingly, the folk-psychological categories of the intentional stance, particularly the concepts of beliefs and desires, cannot be regarded as allowing us to construct adequate causal explanatory accounts of human behavior within the social realm that are acceptable within the impartial and culturally unbiased perspective of the scientific stance. Rather, good old-fashioned action theory (GOFAT), which constitutes the conceptual core of the "Verstehen Bubble" and which explains human behavior in terms of mental states such as beliefs and desires, is only part of our manifest image, to use Sellarian terminology; a "cultural artefact" (Turner 2018, 211) whose explanations come with a big warning label: they are culturally relative and reflect our limited capacities to understand and articulate our own mental process" (Turner 2018, 186).

Nevertheless, while Turner is generally suspicious of the central categories of the intentional stance, he is also keen to account for the emergence of the manifest image from the perspective of the scientific stance (see in this context also Turner 2019). Within this context he acknowledges that Max Weber in his conception of an interpretive sociology (Weber 1968 or 2014) is quite correct in thinking that we have direct observational and epistemically foundational access to the significance of human behavior. In this manner we perceive immediately that swinging an ax constitutes the act of cutting wood or that yelling at another person expresses anger. Such direct observational understanding can indeed be conceived of as providing us with an epistemically reliable access to the structure of social reality because the category of direct observational understanding is "brain-ready," since it can be directly linked to the activity of so-called mirror neurons. Similarly, Turner acknowledges categories of more complex and inferential forms of understanding as scientifically legitimate if they are liberated from the conceptual cage of folk psychological theorizing. Such forms of understanding would no longer conceive of the central features of human behavior as having to do merely with internal features of the human mind but would understand human behavior as being essentially embedded in and responding to the affordances provided by a larger natural and social environment. Most importantly, such complex forms of understanding can be regarded as legitimate, since they correspond closely to the activities of our brain when recognizing patterns in our environment that are important for us to track in order to flourish (see Turner 2018, particularly chp. 5; Turner 2019).[1]

I have always admired Stephen Turner's sophistication in his relentless effort to save the social sciences from an overreliance on the conceptual framework of what he regards as the mere manifest image of humanity, a humanity imprisoned in its "Verstehen Bubble." Yet as a hardcore (but non-dogmatic) interpretivist who feels that there is not much of social reality left worth thinking about outside of the "Verstehen Bubble," I must admit that my gut reaction has always been that on a fundamental level Turner must be plainly wrong. Most importantly, Virginia, even if there is no Santa Claus, there certainly has to be some way to account for the reality of norms and for our reality as rational agents who rationally respond to their environment in virtue of their evaluative commitments and of how they conceive of their surroundings. To think otherwise seems to be "affected by the skepticism of a skeptical age," as Francis Pharcellus Church expressed it in his famous editorial in the *New York Sun* in 1897, a skeptical attitude that one nowadays might also link to an unhealthy obsession with the STEM disciplines.

Yet merely asserting the objective adequacy and causal explanatory potential of our folk psychological categories without further arguments is certainly philosophically inadequate. It, rightfully, would be seen as an illegitimate attempt to hold on to an enchanted conception of the world and as a form of wishful thinking that avoids facing reality in all of its dreadful and scientific weariness associated with a world of plain facts and mere patterns. In the following, I will attempt a philosophically more rigorous defense of the causal explanatory potential of our folk psychological framework. Rather than addressing Turner's objections in a piecemeal fashion, I will proceed by first articulating programmatically a conception of our folk psychological practices that regards them to be autonomous vis a vis the explanatory practices of the cognitive neurosciences. I indeed do agree with Turner that our folk psychological notions are not "brain ready." Yet I disagree with his implicit assumption that their primary purpose consists in referring to internal neurological states and that their explanatory and causal potential can only be validated from the bottom-up by showing them to be "brain-ready." Folk psychological concepts are not intended to refer to events in the brain but to causal powers

---

[1] Turner seems to be favorably inclined towards Dan Hutto's enactivism and narrativism (Hutto and Myin 2012). I do not have space to fully do justice to this aspect of Turner's position. For a constructive discussion of narrativism see however Stueber 2018.

that persons have within a larger social context. Moreover, I regard folk psychological practices to be epistemically unique in that they are closely tight to our empathic capacities. In this context, I do not merely emphasize what I call basic empathy, which, like Turner, I view as being tied to the activities of mirror neurons. More importantly, I focus on our cognitively more advanced ability to imaginatively put ourselves in the perspective of another person and see and deliberate about the world from that perspective, a capacity that I refer to as reenactive empathy. Such imaginative and empathic capacities are not solely focused on internal features of other persons, but they are oriented towards the situation that other persons face. Given these unique epistemic features of our folk psychological practices, and contrary to what Turner and others assume, in attributing beliefs and desires to persons we describe features of persons, which they possess insofar as they are embedded in a larger natural and social environment. In a second step, I will briefly suggest how I differ in my reading of Weber from Turner's and why I regard my conception of our folk psychological practices to be fully in accord with Weber's complex manner of thinking about our grasp of the significance of human agency. Finally, I will directly discuss Turner's position and show why talk of mere patterns and of responses to affordances outside the realm circumscribed by our empathic capacities and folk psychological repertoire is explanatorily blind.

2 Thinking about Folk Psychology and the "Verstehen Bubble" Realistically and Empathically

Let me start my realistic defense of folk psychology with an admission. By no means do I deny that certain scientific ways of trying to utilize the folk psychological framework within the realm of the cognitive brain sciences seem to commit us to eventually finding some kind of neurological equivalent of folk psychological concepts. In my view such internalist conception of folk psychology indicates nothing more than a hangover from the days of Cartesian dualism. One is eager to declare one's rejection of dualism while still holding onto the thought that the mental realm is primarily constituted by a collection of internal properties, which belong to the very material, grey, and very bloody brain. Yet, if one holds onto such Cartesian assumptions within a materialist and scientific framework one is forced to think that folk psychological categories can be validated only if they are reducible to neurobiological ones or only if they are definable in a functional or computational manner. In this case, I would be inclined to agree with Churchland (1989) or Stich (1983) that the eliminativist conclusion is unavoidable. I am, however, enough of a

Davidsonion to think that within the folk psychological context we attribute mental states with a certain de dicto content (i)in an externalist manner, that is, by situating a speaker causally within his or her environment, (ii) that we thereby proceed holistically, since we can determine the content of one belief only in the context of determining the content of the speaker's other beliefs, and that (iii) we are guided by the principle of charity in that we can attribute a set of beliefs to persons only if they satisfy some norms of rationality. Furthermore, if one agrees that such commitments to externalism, holism, and normativity are in some sense constitutive for the folk psychological realm, then one has also to recognize that folk psychological categories and the categories of the physical sciences including the neurosciences are "not made for one another" and that we should not expect them to be reducible or grounded in any scientifically specifiable sense by the lower level sciences.[2] I do not view such insight as an unmitigated disaster for continuing to think that folk psychological accounts of human behavior possess real explanatory force rather than being merely "just so" stories. It is better understood as pointing us in a different direction, that is, towards thinking about the framework of folk psychology as providing us with a genuine and, at its core, autonomous explanatory domain. A fortiori, one is also liberated in thinking about the realm of the social sciences, particularly the explanatory framework of history, as being at least partially within this autonomous explanatory realm.

Here then is my way of trying to show the fly its way out of the Cartesian trap. To start, take the example of an ordinary action explanation such as that Lucas acquired an apartment because he believed that it makes economically more sense to buy rather than to rent and because he needed and desired a place to live in for the next few years.[3] In explaining Lucas's behavior in manner, we

---

[2] For my understanding of how the so-called principle of charity guides interpretation and how we should conceive of rationality within this context see the first two chapters of Stueber 2006. I would like to emphasize that I differ sharply from Davidson in accounting for the causal efficacy of mental properties, that is, I do not accept his position of anomalous monism. See particularly Stueber 2019. For Putnam's very similar argument of why functionalism cannot account for mental properties see his 1991.

[3] I regard such "ordinary" folk psychological explanations to be of primary importance for understanding rational agency, in contrast to formalized versions of rational choice theory. It is certainly interesting to consider the relationship between our commonsensical belief-desires explanations (which I mainly focus on in this context and which I regard as the framework we mainly use in the context of historical explanations) and a mathematically more formalized rational choice theory with its notions of preferences and expectations. Often it is regarded to be the scientifically more respectable version of folk psychology. At times, one gets the impression that Turner is thinking about rational choice theory when talking about the "Verstehen Bubble." Here I certainly do not have the space to fully address

intend to reveal him, as Davidson quite correctly pointed out, in his role as "rational animal," who has reasons for acting. From his perspective, something can be said for the action (Davidson [1963] 1980, 8–9) and we can "see for ourselves what it is about the action that appealed to the agent" (Davidson [1991] 2001, 216). The philosophical debate about the nature mental of content has strongly suggested that the fact that Lucas believes that it makes economically more sense to buy rather than to rent is a fact that supervenes only broadly on the physical and is thus a fact that is irreducible to internal states of the brain. Lucas can have such beliefs only if he is embedded in a complex social environment. Rather than characterizing a feature of his brain it is more appropriate to think of folk psychological concepts as identifying properties that persons with brains possess in light of their complex causal embeddedness in a larger environment (See in this respect also Baker 1995). Folk psychological states are thus best understood in analogy to properties such as being rich, being famous, or being the President of the United States, that is, properties, which an individual can only acquire as a member of a particular social and economic organization. Despite the fact that such properties are in some sense relational properties—one can possess them only in terms of one's relation to other persons, objects or institutions—such properties certainly should be regarded as characterizing an individual's causal powers within a certain social context. It is because one is rich or famous that one is able to get a table at a certain restaurant, can go to a certain college or can travel around the world. Similarly, it is because one is the President of the United States that one can order drone strikes killing people with impunity, even if they are high ranking officials of other countries and so on.

The notion of causation here presupposed is the one that has been rather popular in recent philosophical discussions and that has been articulated in

---

this rather complex question. I would like to make two quick points though. First, regardless of how exactly one conceives of this relationship, I do not think that either rational choice theory or ordinary folk psychology need to be validated from the bottom up or that its notions need to be brain ready. Second, I view our ordinary folk psychological practice of making sense of each other's behavior in terms of our reasons for acting as basic and primary for conceiving of others as rational agents. Moreover, in contrast to Davidson, I do not view rational choice theory as merely making explicit the notion of rationality already implicit in our folk psychological practices. Rational choice theory presupposes an idealized conception of rational agency that insufficiently takes into account our cognitive limitations. It is therefore legitimate to wonder whether rational choice theory provides us with genuine explanations of human behavior within the social realm. At most, rational choice theory can be viewed in analogy to Weber's ideal types. These issues need to be explored in greater detail in subsequent publications. For an accessible and brief survey, see Risjord 2014, chp. 5.

recent years by Woodward, particularly in order to account for the explanatory character of the special sciences (see particularly Woodward 2003). Roughly described, according to Woodward's so-called interventionist understanding of causation a variable x is a cause of y if and only if an intervention (I) on x—that is, changing its values—makes a difference to the value of y. Accordingly, causal knowledge and causal explanations require implicit reference only to knowledge of "counterfactual dependencies" among properties of a system that allows us to answer "what-if-things-had- been-different-questions" (Woodward and Hitchcock 2003, 4). Certainly, manipulating the value of being rich or being famous seems to have some effect on the behavior of the involved individuals, in the same manner that successfully impeaching a President would drastically curtail the causal powers of the relevant individual. Moreover, we do seem to also be able to manipulate the causal powers of a person by changing the kind of beliefs he or she holds or by changing the strength of those beliefs.

Equally important for our purpose, within Woodward's model (and it is exactly this aspect that makes it suitable for the social sciences) causal knowledge does not require reference to strict laws but only to invariant generalizations whose validity is restricted to a particular domain defined by certain boundary conditions. For instance, people's behavior in the US tends to conform to what the law requires such as driving on the right side of the road. Changing the law would thus also change their behavior. Without doubt, in formulating such generalizations, we presuppose the existence of certain social institutions (particular law enforcement institutions but also education in civics) whose existence circumscribes the domain within which these invariant generalizations hold. Even if these institutions constitute essential conditions of the social domain where we use such explanatory strategies we do not need to refer to them in our formulations of so-called invariant generalizations. This is so because knowledge of such features does not increase the explanatory force of an explanation within a specific domain. In order to manipulate the driving behavior of a population we only have to change and manipulate the relevant laws. Manipulating the domain itself would not necessarily change the particular behavior in the direction we are interested in. Rather, it would destroy the very realm within which we can manipulate lawful driving behavior and within which we explain such behavior based on our knowledge of such laws.

Woodward's distinction between a certain explanatory vocabulary—in terms of which such invariant generalizations are formulated—and the domain of application to which it can be validly applied is also helpful for thinking about the relation between our explanatory strategies formulated in the folk psychological idiom and the cognitive neurosciences, which Turner is so concerned about. Folk psychological explanations apply only to agents whose brain is functioning normally. Yet, to be told that the brain is functioning normally does not add to explaining his actions in terms of his reasons for acting. Being told that his brain does not function well only tells us that such explanatory strategies do not apply any longer. Accordingly, the cognitive neurosciences are not in competition with our ordinary folk psychological strategies.[4] Rather, they are complementing such strategies in providing us with a better and firmer understanding of the exact scope of the domain of folk psychology and allowing us to better grasp what exactly it means to have a "normally" functioning brain and how, for example, certain psychopathologies might affect such functioning. Accordingly, the cognitive neurosciences at most provide us with knowledge of the physical boundary conditions of folk psychological explanations.

However, folk psychology is not merely special because of the irreducibility of its conceptual repertoire. In that respect it might not differ from the conceptual framework of other special sciences. It is also unique because its practice is epistemically tied to our empathic abilities that alone allow us to appreciate the explanatory force of specific folk psychological explanations. As I said before, in attributing beliefs and desires to other people we want to reveal them in their role of rational agents who have their reasons for acting in the situation that they are facing. And as I have argued extensively elsewhere it is in this context that our empathic capacities, particularly what I call reenactive empathy, play an essential epistemic role in grasping another person's beliefs and desires as their reasons for acting (Stueber 2006 and 2008). Grasping the explanatory potential of folk psychological explanations requires us to adjust our own perspective in light of the mentioned beliefs and other relevant mental states in order to realize that we would have reasons for acting similarly. This is so because individual mental states constitute reasons for acting only insofar as they are holistically integrated in the appropriate manner with a whole set of other beliefs and background assumptions. Grasping them as reasons thus requires us to grasp how exactly they are fitting in with a whole range of other beliefs. In the case of Lucas, for example, we only understand his reasons for buying the apartment because we are somehow aware of his background assumptions about financial interactions. In ordinary circumstances—that is, in explaining behavior within a shared culture—such epistemic task proceeds

---

4   I have also argued elsewhere that the facts to be explained from the folk psychological perspective do not exist within the perspective of the vocabulary of the physical sciences. See Stueber 2005.

effortlessly since we share a vast set of background assumptions. I can see that Lucas has reasons for buying rather than renting, since I would have such reasons. The very fact that those shared assumptions are ordinarily in the background might also have contributed to the idea that grasping the explanatory power of folk psychological explanations depends merely on folk psychological generalizations that we implicitly appeal to. Yet, if this were so, we should have no difficulties in grasping the explanatory force of "unusual" belief/desire explanations such as somebody buying an apartment knowing that the housing bubble would burst soon just because he wanted to waste some money. Such an "explanation" is resisted precisely because we are stunned given that it violates our own values of how to deal with money. In order to grasp such a desire as a reason we would have to know a lot more of the person's beliefs and about his values and how they differ from our own assumptions. Only in this manner can we imaginatively adjust our perspective in order to grasp how somebody can view it as a consideration that speaks for his behavior. Only then can I grasp them as his reasons because I could grasp them as my reasons if I adopted his perspective by taking care of the relevant differences between us.

Once the information about relevant differences is provided (such as that he intended to avoid paying alimony to his divorced wife) we often grasp effortlessly how such a thought fits in with other thoughts and can be understood as his reason for acting.[5] In light of the additional information we now know how to think more specifically about the mental framework of the other person within which we have to integrate the mental attitude mentioned in the attempted explanation of his behavior. Nevertheless, we need to notice the potential magnitude of this task, that is, of how to appropriately integrate a mental state with all of our other mental attitudes. If we would indeed have to consider all of them in their totality for that very purpose it seems we would never be able to accomplish this task, or at least not very quickly, given our limited cognitive capacities. We have to somehow grasp which smaller subset among the vast set of our mental states is relevant to consider in a particular

---

5 Here I will not dwell on the difficulties that might arise in attempting to reenact another person's thought processes in case of great cultural and personal differences, when we encounter a variety of forms of imaginative resistance. I do acknowledge these difficulties and I also accept that there might be some real limits to empathic understanding. I do however take the existence of such difficulties as further evidence for the fact that folk psychological understanding is mediated by our empathic and imaginative capacities (see Stueber 2006, chp. 6; 2011). In those cases (such as in cases of severe depression), our only option consists in appealing to explanatory schemes that are backed up by mere statistical generalizations. Those strategies are however a mere second best, indicating that we are outside the domain of rational agency.

context; that, for instance, Lucas's religious beliefs might not be relevant to consider now (even if they are potentially relevant in different contexts or at different historical times). To solve the problem of relevance means to solve what is commonly referred to as the frame-problem. To use Fodor's terminology, to identify the relevant aspects of our belief set means to be able to put a frame around them. Yet where to put the "frame" seems to be an irreducibly open-ended and contextual affair, not an activity that can be conceived of as the application of a theory or a theoretical algorithm, and certainly not a theory articulated in folk-psychological terminology (See also Henderson and Horgan 2000 and Stueber 2017). Ordinarily we do possess the practical capacities and the cognitive know-how and solve such problems on an everyday basis in making up our mind of what to do in specific circumstances. Accordingly, we also have to rely on our own cognitive abilities in grasping how other people think, deliberate and decide by using them when empathically imagining their perspective.

Three additional points are worth emphasizing in this context. First, whether we adequately grasp another person's reasons for acting depends on us being correct in our assumptions about the relevant differences between the other person's outlook and our own. Second, particularly in case of greater cultural differences, information about such differences has at times to be provided in a more explicit manner so that we get to utilize our empathic imagination in the right manner, a fact that certainly has not be sufficiently emphasized by some of the contemporary simulation theorists. Third, reenactive empathy on its own cannot decide which one of two plausible folk psychological interpretations provides us with a true causal account of another person's actions. Reenactive empathy allows us only to assess the initial plausibility of folk psychological interpretation in that it enables us to empathically grasp a person's potential reasons for acting, allowing us to understand the conditions under which Lucas acted for reason of wanting to waste money or for sounder investment reasons. In order to decide between two plausible interpretive hypotheses we need additional information providing us with evidence about the likelihood which of the presupposed mental states, values and character traits the other person actually has. Such evidence consists in pointing to his past behavior, his explicit declarations of intentions, his upbringing, his social environment and so on. Most importantly, such information does not make the use of our reenactive capacities superfluous. Rather it merely guides their use and provides further evidential backing, since without them we cannot even grasp the primary condition for a folk psychological account to have any causal explanatory force, that is, that the thoughts mentioned are a person's reasons for acting.

So far, I have focused only on the cognitive complex form of empathy, that I refer to as reenactive empathy, a form of the imagination where we put ourselves in the situation of the other person. As Adam Smith expresses it, in those imaginative endeavors we do not merely perceive another person's passions, but are more concerned with "the situation which excites it." (Smith 1759/1982, 12). In addition to reenactive empathy, I also acknowledge a direct observational form of understanding that I refer to as basic empathy. Like Turner, I think it is plausible to think of it as being in some form linked to the activities of mirror neurons. In contrast to Turner, I regard its scope to be more limited. In my opinion we should think of basic empathy as a developmentally early capacity allowing us to grasp the like-mindedness of other people particularly in two respects: It allows us to recognize in a non-conceptual manner some emotions of other persons expressed in their faces, bodily gestures, or tone of voice and so on. In addition, it allows us to recognize the goal-directedness of another person's movement, that she is about to grasp a glass or runs towards another person, that is, it allows us to recognize the intentionality of another person's behavior in a de re manner, rather than the prior de dicto intentions (beliefs or desires) that made the other person intentionally grasp the glass. In this manner I regard basic empathy to provide us with the basic epistemic means of delineating the domain of skillful and emotionally expressive bodily movements to which we apply our folk psychological categories in order to explain such behavior in terms of an agent's reasons for acting.

However, I do not claim that folk psychological explanations constitute the sole explanatory strategy within the social realm. Certainly, human behavior is causally affected also by a variety of external factors, such as the structure of social institutions, class, race, and gender, which need to be studied in a rigorous manner in order to gain a proper understanding of the social realm. Moreover, we also appeal to our notion of social roles and mere cultural and personal habits (independent of attributing any mental states to particular individuals) when explaining and predicting behavior. And yet (or so I would maintain), while knowledge of structural regularities is important, the social realm is ultimately constituted, maintained, and mediated by the actions of individual agents acting alone or collectively and their intended, and importantly, also unintended consequences. And it is for this very reason, that I regard the cognitive neurosciences at most to complement our knowledge of the social realm by providing us insights about the physical conditions of the domain of folk psychology, rather than with a means for replacing or validating its categories.

For the purpose of this essay, these programmatic remarks have to suffice as an explication of my claim that our folk psychological practices constitute an autonomous explanatory domain. However, as I will show in the following, I regard my position to be fully consistent with Weber's conception of an interpretive sociology, which he outlined in his methodological remarks at the beginning of his reflections on *Wirtschaft und Gesellschaft* (*Economy and Society*) and which Turner also relies on in his attempt to hint at a naturalistically more acceptable conception of understanding in the social sciences. Afterwards will I discuss and raise some concerns about Turner's suggestions for liberating the social sciences from the folk psychological categories of the "Verstehen Bubble."

3 Weber on Understanding Significant Agency

In talking about Weber, I will focus my discussion on what he would refer to as historical explanations interested in "the causal analysis and explanation of individual actions, structures and personalities possessing cultural significance" rather than explanations being concerned with general types of social activities, which constitutes the proper focus of sociology (Weber 1968, 13). Accordingly, I will leave the discussion of the role of ideal types for Weber's conception of understanding mostly aside in order to maintain my focus of this essay on the status of folk psychological explanations.[6]

Weber understands sociology as the science "concerning itself with the interpretive understanding of social action and thereby with a causal explanation of its course and consequences," that is action with which the agents associates a subjective meaning (Weber 1968, 4). As every other science, understanding in the social sciences strives for what Weber calls "*Evidenz*" (Weber 2014, 2), a term that is best translated as indicating the obviousness, clarity, and evidential justification of the attribution of meaning to another person's actions from the perspective of interpreter. Weber further distinguishes between what he calls direct observational understanding (*aktuelles Verstehen*) and explanatory understanding (*erklärendes Verstehen*). As examples of direct observational understanding, Weber refers to our ability to immediately grasp the meaning of a sentence one reads or the emotions manifested in another person's facial expressions, to immediately understand what a woodcutter is doing (that is cutting wood), to perceive that somebody touches the door in order

---

[6] Mostly, the English translations of Weber's text are from the Roth and Wittich edition published in 1968. I have deviated from those translations only if absolutely necessary. My own translations are based on the German edition of *Wirtschaft and Gesellschaft* published in the *Max Weber-Studienausgabe* in 2014.

to close it, or to see that somebody aims the gun at an animal. Direct observational understanding thus grasps what one might call the elemental units of bodily behavior or aspects of such behavior, which express primary mental features of a person without situating them in a larger context of significance (*Sinnzuzammenhang*). Situating such directly observationally understood activity within a larger context of significance is the function of explanatory understanding since it is in this manner that we are able to grasp the underlying motivations for the woodcutter cutting wood. We then understand that he works in order to earn a living or that he cuts wood in order to heat his house and so on.[7] As I would be tempted to express it, explanatory understanding allows us to grasp a person's reasons for acting rather than merely understanding what he is doing or what emotions he expresses.

Importantly though, and here I might be deviating a bit from Turner's interpretation (see Turner 2019), direct observational and explanatory understanding does not necessarily differ in regard to its clarity and obviousness, what Weber refers to as *Evidenz*. Weber also claims that rational means/end relationships exemplified in somebody's behavior and grasped with the help of explanatory understanding are as obvious to us as grasping the meaning of somebody uttering 2 x 2 =4, a form of direct observational understanding (Weber 1968, 5; 2014, 2). Or to use my favorite conceptual scheme, recognizing that the other person is angry based on basic empathy is as obvious to us as grasping with the help of reenactive empathy that Lucas's thoughts about the economic viability of buying versus renting constitute reasons for buying the apartment. Both forms of empathic understanding are immediately obvious to us because both resonate with us, even if such resonance is mediated by different causal mechanisms, by the activities of mirror neurons on the one hand and by the activation of the reenactive imagination on the other.

It is important to recognize that Evidenz so far concerns only our grasp of the appropriateness of attributing meaning to an action (Weber 1968, 7; 2014, 11). Such *Evidenz* on its own does not automatically validate an interpretation as the causally adequate interpretation of that behavior. "Every interpretation

---

7 "'Erklären' bedeutet also für eine mit dem Sinn des Handelns befaßte Wissenschaft soviel wie: Erfassen des Sinn-*zusamnenhangs,* in den, seinem subjektiv gemeinten Sinn nach, ein aktuell verständliches Handeln hineingehört" (Weber 2014, 5). I translate the sentence as follows. "Explaining means for a science in the business of grasping sense: Grasping the larger context of meaning, to which an action, according to its subjectively intended meaning, understood in a directly observational manner belongs." The English translation of the Roth/Wittich 1968 edition does not appropriately indicate that "aktuell verständliches Handeln" are actions that are grasped by directly observational understanding (i.e., aktuelles Verstehen). It misleadingly refers to it as "an actual course of understandable action" (Weber 1968, 9).

attempts to attain *Evidenz*. Yet no matter how evident an interpretation is in regard to its attribution of meaning, merely based on its character of *Evidenz* in this respect, it cannot claim to be the causally valid interpretation" (Weber 2014, 5; my translation; 1968, 9). Validating a "meaning adequate" interpretation as being also causally adequate requires additional reference to statistical regularities, which we come to know based on experience. For Weber, interpretive understanding in the social realm aims ultimately at causal explanations of meaningful actions, that is, it is understanding that is both adequate in regard to our grasp of the significance of a behavior and that at the same time also illuminates its causes. Translated into my framework one might think of *Evidenz* in regard to it being meaning adequate ("*sinnhaft adäquat*") as having to do with grasping the potential reasons in virtue of which an agent might have acted. As a first step in our interpretive endeavor we thus order interpretive hypotheses in light of our ability to reenact thoughts as reasons. To take one of Weber's examples, to interpret the activity of the woodcutter as being motivated by either the desire to earn a living or to heat his house is in some sense equally obvious. Accordingly, in order to decide which one of the interpretive plausible hypotheses is also causally adequate further evidential considerations are necessary. The degree of evidential obviousness, *Evidenz* in Weber's sense, associated with our grasping the potential significance of an action is thus always to some degree higher than the *Evidenz* associated with an interpretation that is both meaning adequate and causally adequate.

Weber's account of our understanding of individual agency accords well with my conception of the causal explanatory character of action explanation, even if Weber does not use the empathy concept. Weber also does not deny that knowledge of mere causal regularities independent of attributing subjective meaning to an action (such as knowledge that the results of the SAT are generally correlated with income levels) can be important for the social sciences and our knowledge of the social realm. Yet while he acknowledges that knowledge of such regularities, independent of the attribution of meaning, can be of help in exploring the social realm, he, in my opinion correctly, points out that such knowledge can never constitute the core of the social sciences as it would deny the very existence of the foundation of the social realm, that is meaningful activity of individuals who in their actions are oriented towards others. Knowledge of mere regularities can only help us in understanding the conditions—the occasion, hindering and favoring circumstances—under which meaningful human action and interaction take place (Weber 1968, 7; 2014, 3f). That is, they make us more sensitive to the conditions that make it harder to be successful in taking the SAT. Yet such knowledge does not allow us to understand why it is that people take an SAT in the first place.

4 Turner's Suggestions: Patterns and Affordances Rather than the Cultural Relativity of Folk Psychology

So why then is Turner so worried about the scientific respectability of the explanatory schemes devised within the "Verstehen Bubble"? As far as I can understand his worries, they have to do with their cultural relativity. More specifically, Turner makes two very different claims in this respect. First, he points out that research has shown that theory of mind terms are not culturally universal (Turner 2019, 50). For the sake of the discussion here, I will grant these claims. Yet I am not committed (and as far as I can see no simulation theorist is) to assume that theory of mind terms are either innate or somehow provided by biological evolution and for that very reason culturally universal. It is indeed possible that we acquire such terms in a particular cultural context by learning a specific language. The very fact that our acquisition of mental terms happens to be culturally relative does in no way imply that they cannot be universally applied. "*Schadenfreude*" is a German term. Even though, people in other cultures certainly feel *Schadenfreude* and we can also explain their behavior using the concept of *Schadenfreude*. Moreover, none of this implies that people in other cultures cannot learn to apply the term appropriately. Similarly, I would suggest, even if not all cultures use the concepts of beliefs and desires this does not imply that we would incorrectly explain their behavior in terms of such concepts. Moreover, it does not show that such cultures are unable to learn to use these folk psychological concepts. My position only requires that humans possess basic and cognitively more complex empathic capacities, and I assume that such capacities tend to be culturally universal.

Second, in asserting the cultural relativity of folk psychology, Turner also points out that folk psychological interpretations depend on the standpoint of the interpreter and that they are therefore lacking the proper degree of scientific objectivity. Yet here I think one has to proceed very carefully. Without doubt, given the fact that folk psychological explanations depend essentially on our empathic capacities, we can properly access such explanations only in view of our own conceptual framework in thinking about the world. That is, in order to understand Lucas's behavior and in order to properly explain it causally we have to be able to utilize certain economic concepts or we somehow have to acquire such conceptual capacities for the purpose of being able to grasp explanations couched in such terminology. Yet such cultural relativity seems to have more to do with our ability to epistemically access and evaluate the appropriateness of such explanations rather than their objectivity. It certainly needs to be acknowledged that in understanding another person, even in empathically understanding another person, we do not become that person. As Weber quite correctly points out "one need not have been Caesar in order to understand Caesar"(Weber 1968, 5). In reenacting another person's thoughts as his reasons, we take into account relevant differences, cultural, conceptual, and social. In doing so, certain aspects of another person's "being in the world" will be moved into the foreground of our attention even if they normally are part of the background of that person's psychological structure (Goldie 2011). In reenacting the reasons of a generous person, we might have to remind ourselves of his generosity in a manner that does not seem to correspond to that generous person's outlook towards the world. Such a person normally does not think explicitly about his generosity. It is also for this very reason that Collingwood points out that reenactments of past thoughts, for example, essentially incapsulate them in a context of present thoughts, that is our mental outlook, which, by being different from the original context always "confine it to a plane different" from the original one (Collingwood [1939] 1978, 114). Yet this insight does not imply that understanding is somehow providing us with less objective explanations (and only cultural relative ones). It only implies that we have strictly to distinguish between understanding another person and being the other person. For that very reason, it would also be completely irrational to make becoming the other person a standard for judging understanding him. Moreover, I would argue that even from the first-person perspective being someone and understanding oneself to be that person have to be distinguished. One tends, for instance, to learn something about oneself when talking to one's financial advisor about the risks associated with various investment strategies, in that one starts learning something about one's own dispositions to accept risks. That is, even from the first-person perspective there is a difference between making choices and fully understanding one's choices.

Furthermore, given that successful reenactment depends on properly assessing the relevant differences between the interpreter and interpretee, we also should expect that the information needed to perform such reenactment differs based on the cultural background of the interpreter. Similarly, the information that the interpreter provides in this context so that others will be able to follow his particular explanation of another person's behavior will depend on his and his audiences' perspectives. In no way does this imply that empathic understanding is merely subjective and arbitrary or that we cannot assess the quality and validity of a particular interpretation. We need to remember that we are not only able to reenact other persons' thoughts in order to explain their behavior, we can also reenact another interpreter's thoughts trying to explicate that very behavior. And in doing so, we are able to compare it to our own interpretation and evaluate our own interpretation in light of the other interpreter's perspective on the same topic. Accordingly, the very fact that understanding is always situated, does not mean that its validity can only be evaluated from that very same cultural context. For that very reason, interpretation (even if it does not use the experimental method) is not that different from explanatory understanding in the sciences, which to a degree always presupposes a certain theoretical framework and paradigm. Nevertheless, the validity of such paradigms can also be evaluated from the perspective of another one.

Weber and Turner are, however, right that there is a lot to learn about human culture and the social realm outside the explanatory framework of folk psychology, and that certain questions about important social facts such as the distribution of wealth cannot be answered solely within this framework. Clearly, Jared Diamond, in his widely lauded *Guns, Germs, and Steel* (1997), has provided such large-scale survey of human history outside the conceptual framework of the "Verstehen Bubble." More specifically he points to environmental rather than biological factors such as the availability of species of wild plants and animals, which are relatively easy to domesticate, the development of immunity to certain germs, and the transfer of agricultural accomplishments along a much wider East-West axis at the same latitude in Eurasia in order to answer the question of why it is that wealth and power in the modern world is distributed in a manner that favors Eurasian people. Similarly, we are well advised to also take considerations of evolutionary psychologists and anthropologists seriously as there is much to learn about the psychological structure that might make humans predisposed towards morality or might hinder its universal aspiration because of an innate bias towards the in-group. It is also in light of such knowledge that we can further evaluate the evidence for attributing genuinely moral motivations in explaining the actions of specific persons or think about how widespread racism and implicit racist biases might be within a certain society.

Such explanatory schemes could further limit the scope of folk psychological explanations in suggesting that certain types of social facts are best explained by the activities of more impersonal forces. Yet with Weber, and if I understand it correctly, in contrast to Turner, I do not think that a full-scale replacement is possible or in light of the arguments in the last two sections even warranted. I am puzzled when Turner in his 2018 book appeals to the language of patterns and affordances since it is brain-ready and therefore scientifically more grounded. I do agree with Turner that in social explanations we have to situate the individual appropriately within the larger social context. Social explanations can indeed not focus merely on what is under the skin of an individual. From a biological point of view the world provides affordances, that is, properties that are, relative to the various capacities of specific organisms, directly actionable, such as a hammer being directly perceived as something to hammer with, to use Heidegger's example from the social world. Yet, as I have argued in the first section, the ascription of folk psychological properties to an individual already proceeds in an externalistic manner. It does not merely describe internal features of the individual. Moreover, reconstructing Weber's account in *Protestant Ethic* in terms of affordances, so that the printed vernacular Bible and the new theology (Turner 2018, 141–2) are both regarded as affordances that scaffold tremendous social change does not seem to constitute much of an epistemic advance compared to Weber's original explanations. In order to think of the Bible as an affordance provided by the world we have to properly understand the cognitive capacities and cognitive perspectives in light of which we can grasp why people are indeed sensitive and responsive to such external facts. Accordingly, we have to be able to understand and empathically reenact the perspective of people in the sixteenth century so that such fervent response to the new theology and the printed vernacular Bible appears reasonable. In order to understand the Reformation and the formation of capitalism, we indeed do have to understand the technological changes that allowed for the widespread distribution of the Bible and all kinds of theological pamphlets. But understanding them as affordances in Turner's sense is possible only in light of a thorough grasp of the sensitivities and mindset of the people at that historical time. And that is also why Bittner (2001) and others get it wrong in thinking that reasons are mere facts in the world (Stueber 2013). Reasons could indeed be regarded as facts to which it is reasonable to respond as rational agents. However, the reasonableness of such responses can be only understood in light of the mindset of the persons who respond to such facts. It is for this very reason that folk psychology and the Verstehen Bubble is here to stay. It should also be seen as providing us with real explanatory knowledge about the social world, even if the explanatory tool box of the social sciences contains a few supplementary strategies. So "a thousand years from now, Virginia (and Stephen), nay, ten times ten thousand years from now," folk psychology will still enlighten our thinking about the social realm.

References

Baker, L.R. 1995. *Explaining Attitudes*. Cambridge: Cambridge University Press.
Bittner, R. 2001. *Doing Things for Reasons*. Oxford: Oxford University Press.
Churchland, P. 1989. "Eliminativism and Propositional Attitudes." In *Neurocomputational Perspective: The Nature of Mind and the Structure of Science*, 1–22. Cambridge, Mass.: MIT Press.

Collingwood, R.G. [1939] 1978. *An Autobiography.* Oxford: Clarendon Press.
Davidson, D. [1963] 1980. "Actions, Reasons, and Causes." In Davidson, *Essays on Actions and Events*, 3–20. Oxford: Clarendon Press.
Davidson, D. [1991] 2001. "Three Varieties of Knowledge." In Davidson, *Subjective, Intersubjective, Objective*, 205–220. Oxford: Clarendon Press.
Diamond, Jared. 1997. *Guns, Germs, and Steel: The Fates of Human Societies.* New York: W.W. Norton.
Goldie, P. 2011. "Anti-Empathy." In A. Coplan and P. Goldie (eds.), *Empathy: Philosophical and Psychological Perspectives*, 302–317. Oxford: Oxford University Press.
Henderson, D. and T. Horgan (2000) "Simulation and Epistemic Competence." In H.H. Kögler and K. Stueber (eds.), *Empathy and Agency: The Problem of Understanding in the Human Sciences*, 119–143, Boulder: Westview Press.
Hutto, D. and E. Myin. 2012. *Radicalizing Enactivism. Basic Minds Without Content.* Cambridge, Mass.: MIT Press.
Putnam, H. 1991. *Representation and Reality.* Cambridge, Mass.: MIT Press.
Stich, S. 1983. *From Folk Psychology to Cognitive Science.* Cambridge, Mass.: MIT Press.
Stueber, K. 2005. "Mental Causation and the Paradox of Explanation." *Philosophical Studies* 122: 243–277.
Stueber, K. 2006. *Rediscovering Empathy: Agency, Folk Psychology, and the Human Sciences.* Cambridge, Mass.: MIT Press.
Stueber, K. 2008. "Reasons, Generalizations, Empathy, and Narratives: The Epistemic Structure of Action Explanation." *History and Theory* 47: 31–43.
Stueber, K. 2011. "Imagination, Empathy, and Moral Deliberation: The Case of Imaginative Resistance." *Southern Journal of Philosophy* 49, Spindel Supplement: 156–180.
Stueber, K. 2013. "Explaining Human Agency: Reasons, Causes and the First-Person Perspective." In *Reasons and Causes: Causalism and Anti-Causalism in the Philosophy of Action*, ed. by G. D'Oro and C. Sandis, 199–225. Basingstoke: Palgrave/Macmillan.
Stueber, K. 2017. "Empathy and Understanding Reasons." In *Routledge Handbook of Philosophy of Empathy*, ed. by Heidi Maibom), 137–147. New York and London: Routledge.
Stueber, K. 2018. "Understanding Individual Agency: How Empathy and Narrative Competence Cooperate." In *Philosophical Perspectives on Empathy: Theoretical Approaches and Emerging Challenges*, ed. by A. Waldow and D. Matravers, 129–143. New York and London: Routledge.
Stueber, K. 2019. "Davidson, Reasons, and Causes: A Plea for a little bit more Empathy." *Journal of the History of Analytic Philosophy* 7: 59–75.
Risjord, M. 2014. *Philosophy of Social Science: A Contemporary Introduction.* New York and London: Routledge.
Smith, A. (1982 [1759]). *The Theory of Moral Sentiments*, Liberty Classics.

Turner, S. 1994. *The Social Theory of Practices: Tradition, Tacit Knowledge, and Presuppositions.* Chicago: University of Chicago Press.

Turner, S. 2010. *Explaining the Normative.* Oxford: Polity Press.

Turner, S. 2018. *Cognitive Science and the Social.* New York and London: Routledge.

Turner, S. 2019. "Verstehen Naturalized." *Philosophy of the Social Sciences* 49: 243–264.

Weber, M. 1968. *Economy and Society,* ed. by G. Roth and C. Wittich. New York: Bedminster Press.

Weber, M. 2014. *Wirtschaft und Gesellschaft (Max Weber Studienausgabe).* Tübingen: J.C.B. Mohr (Paul Siebeck).

Woodward, J. 2003. *Making Things Happen: A Theory of Causal Explanation.* Oxford: Oxford University Press.

Woodward, J., and C. Hitchcock. 2003. "Explanatory Generalizations, Part I: A Counterfactual Account." *Nous* 37:1–24.

Individualistic and Holistic Models of Collective Beliefs and the Role of Rhetoric and Argumentation

The Example of Religious and Political Beliefs

Alban Bouvier

Abstract

This paper addresses the issue of the relevance of research programs focused on the role of argumentation and rhetoric in the emergence, transformation and disappearance of collective beliefs, an issue that has been recently tackled by Dan Sperber. Several alternative models based on methodologically individualist assumptions are briefly investigated from Alexis de Tocqueville, Max Weber and Vilfredo Pareto to James Coleman, Raymond Boudon, and Jon Elster. But I also argue that recent holistic models, such as Margaret Gilbert's, inspired by an original re-reading of Emile Durkheim, provide fruitful conceptual tools compatible with methodological individualism.

Keywords

Argumentation – Collective Beliefs – Holism – Methodological Individualism – Rhetoric

1   Introduction

The specific problem I address in this paper is the following: as numerous sociologists and anthropologists have noticed (notably Bourdieu), most people, in general, are not very much interested in the specific content of the collective beliefs of their group and do not spend much time evaluating the logical or empirical rationality of, or engaging in discussion about them. These data seem to limit the relevance of any research program focused either on the reconstruction of plausible reasons or on the effective role of reasoning, argumentation and rhetoric in the emergence, transformation and disappearance of collective beliefs (e.g., Raymond Boudon's and Jon Elster's programs). Of course, these latter programs have been adapted in order to grasp the complexity of collective beliefs. However, they remain individualistic: they may introduce relations of interaction (or of interdependence) among individuals as well as system of relations or social structures, but they do not take groups in themselves into account (except in cases groups can be viewed as acting as individual units of action).

Currently, new holistic and allegedly holistic models of collective beliefs are the center of many debates, especially in social philosophy but also increasingly in social psychology, political sciences and economics, in continuity, in particular, with the work of Raimo Tuomela, Philip Pettit, and Margaret Gilbert. I will argue a) that certain recent allegedly holistic models—distinct from the classical models of interiorized social pressure—provide fruitful hypotheses for the understanding of collective beliefs because they are focused on the specific properties of groups; and b) that they are nevertheless compatible with individualist assumptions in Max Weber's, or Vilfredo Pareto's, sense and that they should be used in conjunction with a range of various individualistic models. I will also argue that all these models make sense as long as one focuses on effective argumentative and rhetoric procedures as Vilfredo Pareto did one century ago.[1]

2 The Explanation of Collective Beliefs and the Role of Argumentation and Rhetoric.

The explanation of collective beliefs, and more precisely, the explanation of the formation, diffusion, transformation, and disappearance of collective beliefs are difficult issues. They have been addressed from many viewpoints in the social sciences with numerous models of explanation having been introduced over the past two centuries since the times of Marx and Tocqueville, Durkheim and Weber, Pareto and Tarde, Malinowski and Boas. Some of these scholars, such as Max Weber and, still more typically, Vilfredo Pareto and Lucien Lévy-Bruhl, had raised the issue of the rationality or irrationality of beliefs much

---

1 Previous versions of this paper were presented in several places, including the *6th Analytical Sociology Conference*, June 7 and 8, 2013, Stockholm and a special session of the *Philosophy of Social Science Seminar*, May 7, 2015, Simpson Center for the Humanities, Washington University, Seattle. In this new version which I have prepared for this "Homage to Stephen Turner," I have focused more on topics recently addressed by him in his remarkable exploration of the main issues raised by the encounter between cognitive and social sciences (Turner 2018). And still more specifically on how these issues were investigated in Dan Sperber's recent work, which is put forward by Turner in his own recent book as typical. I also briefly refer to a few of Turner's very numerous earlier publications, related either to the history of sociology or to the philosophy of the social sciences (in particular Weber and Durkheim). Turner's very impressive expertise in both fields—a rare feature within the US academic context—deserves to be noticed.

more centrally than the others: mainstream anthropology and sociology have been, from then onward, more focused on the interiorization of representations, norms, and values processes irrespective of whether they are rational or not, although some authors, such as Durkheim, were interested in both issues. One of the most typical representatives of the mainstream view remains Pierre Bourdieu's (1972, 1980), who brilliantly argued that people do not spend much time in thinking about the content and the rationality of their "beliefs" and that, moreover, the so-called collective "beliefs" are often tacitly incorporated in practices rather than being fully explicit.

However, as soon as the late 1930s, Evans-Pritchard (1937), wanted to explicitly address Lévy-Bruhl's (1923 [1922]) and Pareto's (1935 [1916]) issues more empirically than the two scholars did (as it appears in Evans-Pritchard 1965), and played a significant role in the first re-emergence of the issue of rationality in cultural anthropology at a time when cognitive studies in social science had not arisen yet (see, in particular, for a still relevant survey, Horton, 1982).[2] Later and independently, the historian of sciences, Alexandre Koyre (1970)—one of Thomas Kuhn's main sources of inspiration (Kuhn, 1970)—supported a view similar to Evans-Pritchard's regarding alchemy and magic in the medieval ages.[3] Both Evans-Pritchard and Koyre dealt with the idea of a contextual rationality of beliefs (close to what Popper (1957) called "situational analysis"): although the collective beliefs of a particular group, past or present, may appear irrational in comparison to ours, their understanding of the world can be considered rational given the limited information said group has or had.[4] Still more recently, in the context of strong relativism in epistemology, and of increasing doubts about the heuristic value of structuralism, especially when closely linked to mainstream anthropology and sociology (as in Lévi-Strauss' work), the importance of Evans-Pritchard's framework regarding the issue of

---

2   Pareto's main specificity in comparison to Lévy-Bruhl according to Evans-Pritchard (1965) was to state that what Lévy-Bruhl called "pre-logical" thought can be encountered in every society. Pareto took a lot of examples in Western culture. In line with J. S. Mill's *System of Logic* (1974 [1843]), he anticipated the recognition of the role of cognitive biases in the formation of collective beliefs.

3   Koyré also referred positively to Lévy-Bruhl.

4   Furthermore, for Evans-Pritchard (1937), people such as the Azande (a population now living mainly in South Sudan) who believe in magic might be hyper-rational in the sense that they want to find specific causes even for occurrences that seem to be completely random from a scientific perspective (with regard to the scientific process). Lévy-Bruhl, initially an historian of philosophy, suggested that Malebranche's rationalism in the seventeenth century might also have been a kind of hyper-rationalism: like in the Zande world, nothing is random in the Malebranchist world; every event is an effect of God's will.

the rationality of collective beliefs has been rediscovered itself (Hollis and Lukes 1982).

Strikingly, some of the most recent scholars who have addressed the issue of understanding collective beliefs outside the Durkheimian mainstream (typically Dawkins and Krebbs 1978; Boyer, 1994; Sperber 2001a, 2001b; Atran, 2010, 2014; Mercier and Sperber 2011, 2017) have not taken their seminal ideas from the other founders of sociology or of anthropology but from Darwin's or neo-Darwinian theories, which however regard all the living being's (and not only the human ones), even those who cannot be expected to have any beliefs.[5] They have the daring ambition to fill the gap between our ancestral phylogenetic origins and our contemporary world. This means that they focus on the "distal" mechanisms of our cognitive processes involved in collective beliefs, at the risk of constructing mere speculative paleontology since we do not have any access to the cognitive dispositions of our earlier ancestors (while primatologists have direct access to living chimpanzees and bonobos).

Without rejecting this program as such, one may prefer to be more modest and more cautious, think that it is more reasonable to go step after step and, as a consequence, prefer to investigate more "proximal" causes instead of jumping to the oldest ones. This methodologically cautious attitude is typical of Elster's (as it was Pareto's, too, one century ago while he was already evaluating the heuristic value of evolutionary theories).

Whatever anthropologists and sociologists think of the relevance of the specifically neo-Darwinian programs in their domain, many have re-investigated the issue of the rationality or irrationality of collective beliefs, especially religious beliefs, after the anti-relativist shift and a few the still more specific issue of the role of argumentation and rhetoric in the formation, transformation and disappearance of collective beliefs, sometimes referring explicitly to Pareto's tradition and sometimes rediscovering its core ideas unawares. I will take a few examples.

Thus, Raymond Boudon—one of the leading figures of methodological individualism (MI) in sociology, along with James Coleman and Jon Elster, and also one of the precursors of "analytical sociology" (Hedström and Bearman 2009a)—referred to Pareto very favorably in several articles and books (see, e.g. Boudon, 1981 [1979]); mainly because Pareto's *Treatise* includes a lengthy

---

5 However, Sperber (1997) has sometimes mentioned Tarde favorably before mentioning Darwinism as his main source of inspiration. Many of the neo-Darwinist authors follow the very influent Barkow, Cosmides, and Tooby's (1992) work, which criticized and rejected what they labelled "the Social Sciences Standard Model (SSSM)," viewed as continuing the Durkheimian heritage.

investigation of argumentative, rhetoric and sometimes fallacious procedures involved in the emergence and diffusion of collective beliefs (in religion, ethics, politics and pseudo-science). In later works, Boudon (1994, 2001) turned away from Pareto, whom he did not find sufficiently rationalist, in favor of Weber and Simmel. Actually, Boudon himself might have slightly misjudged the specific approach introduced by Pareto, whose specificity, in comparison of Weber and Simmel, who were rationalist too, was to focus on effective argumentation procedures and rhetoric devices used to support religious, political, moral or pseudo-scientific views. Boudon, on the contrary, generally preferred to reconstruct plausible reasons like Weber and Simmel often did or suggested to be done (Bouvier, 2002, 2007, 2016).[6]

Still more recently, Jon Elster, whose research tradition is the same as Boudon's (the modeling of mechanisms that generate social facts, see, e.g., Boudon 1998; Elster 1998), has devoted many publications to the detailed study of effective deliberations in political life, especially in the writing of Constitutions (see especially Elster). And, in this part of his work, Elster has often turned to one of Pareto's primary influences, Bentham (see especially Elster 2013).

Entirely independently of these methodologically individualist programs, Mercier and Sperber (2011, 2017; preceded by Sperber 2002), have argued in favor of an "argumentative" theory regarding the phylogenetic origin of reasoning. In a nutshell, they contend that the faculty of reasoning has a "Machiavellian" origin (in the sense of Byrne and Whiten 1988),[7] and that this feature is still at work in human interactions: humans argue for winning more than for knowing and in order to aim at that end, they try to manipulate others. Happily, Sperber and Mercier said, a faculty of epistemic vigilance has emerged to counter everyone's propensity to mislead others. Sperber emphasized this Machiavellian dimension within the framework of a criticism of

---

6 Pareto has been alternatively forgotten and re-discovered many times in various ways. Apart from Edward Evans-Pritchard, one should of course, in the same period, mention George Homans (Homans and Curtis 1934) and Talcott Parsons (1937). Among many other more recent re-readings, see Boudon 1981 [1979]; Powers 1987; Bouvier 1999; Femia and Marshall 2012.

7 The hypothesis (actually often rather a thesis, strongly claimed without being nevertheless supported by epistemologically compelling arguments) of a "Machiavellian" origin of intelligence is the following one: "The intelligence is an adaptation to deal with the complexity of living in semi-permanent groups of conspecifics, a situation that involves the potentially tricky balance of competition and cooperation with the same individuals" (Byrne 1996, 172). This idea was forged initially to explain the behavior of certain apes, which seem able to cheat their conspecifics.

Alvin Goldman's (1999) too "rosy" vision of the social world: "I would like to slightly redress the balance and put a touch of grey in Goldman's rosy picture by considering testimony and argumentation in the light of some evolutionary considerations" (Sperber 2012). Sperber added: "My main claim will be that a significant proportion of socially acquired beliefs are likely to be false beliefs, and this is not just as a result of the malfunctioning, but also of the proper functioning of social communication. I will argue in particular that the cognitive manipulation of others is one of the effects that makes the practices of testimony and argumentation adaptive."

Ironically, Goldman already wanted to "redress the balance" (but in the other direction, that is against the widespread explanations in term of the narrow versions of Rational Choice Theory, according to which people always search to maximize their utilities and of which Sperber's theory is a supplementary version) and found reasons to think that we have cognitive natural dispositions to truth apart from our propensity to look for our immediate material self-interest, possibly by transmitting wrong information.[8] It is within this context that Goldman quoted Thomas Reid, who argued that such dispositions or principles are necessary, especially for children, to fast acquire knowledge: "The first of these principles is a propensity to speak truth [... The second principle] is a disposition to confide in the veracity of others, and to believe what they tell us (Reid 1970 [1764]: 238–40)" (Goldman 1999). Sperber's comments on these quotations are the following ones: "In stark contrast to this view, Dawkins and Krebs, in their famous article "Animal Signals: Information or Manipulation" (Dawkins and Krebs 1978) have argued that the prime function of communication is not information but manipulation of others."

If one sets aside Sperber's phylogenetic concerns, what remains is the idea that people first argue in order to defend their interest (Mercier and Sperber add: especially their reputation) and to veil their genuine motivations either consciously or unconsciously: "The implicit psychology—the presumption that people's beliefs and actions are motivated by reasons—is empirically wrong. Giving reasons to justify oneself and reacting to the reasons given by others are first and foremost, a way to establish reputations and coordinate expectations" (Mercier and Sperber 2017, 143).[9]

---

8 Moreover Goldman's concern was not descriptive but normative (his aim was to formulate the dialogical norms of argumentation that could permit us the acquisition and the transmission of reliable information and true knowledge): this was not at all a description—either "rosy" or grey—of reality.

9 Turner elaborates on this specific passage (2018, 189) as an expression of a typical position in the contemporary social sciences depreciating "comprehensive sociology" in Max Weber's sense.

This idea is very close to what Pareto (1935 [1916] expressed at length and in details in his theory of "residues" and "derivations" although Sperber does not seem to be aware of that precedent (which weakens the claim of introducing a really new idea). Moreover, what is often ignored in introductions to Pareto's sociology is that Pareto, in his general theory of human motivations, always suspected that each propensity is more or less compensated by another (e.g., the strong propensity to self-interest might be compensated for by a certain propensity to altruism, the tendency to conservatism by a tendency to innovation, etc.). Besides, Pareto did not consider only emotional tendencies, as it is often assumed, but cognitive tendencies too, such as the propensity to always reason, even "out of fuel" (at the risk of ratiocinating), and the propensity to incessantly find analogies between phenomena (at the risk of finding false analogies), tendencies that are arguably the psychological sources of both myths and sciences. However Pareto did not mention Thomas Reid's specific ones. But is seems clear that these Reid-Pareto hypotheses about the cognitive mechanisms would deserve further empirical investigations as much as those on which Sperber and Mercier focus.[10]

What is still more important is that, contrarily to what Mercier and Sperber contend, the empirical observations and experimentations do not demonstrate that "the presumption that people's beliefs and actions are motivated by reasons [...] is empirically wrong." These observations and experimentations only show that sometimes this presumption is wrong. Thus, Mercier and Sperber support a claim much stronger than they epistemologically should, presumably to "attract" reader's attention—a little cynical strategy given their understanding of the Machiavellian feature of intelligence. Moreover, Mercier and Sperber (2017) use other fallacious rhetorical strategies (such as the use of a "straw man"; see Walton 1996; Van Eemeren et al. 2014, 550) when they criticized alternative theories.[11] Sperber (1997) used to be more rigorous and much fairer in recognizing the relevance of other theories, in this case of what he called "strong methodological individualism" "combined with "weak cognitivism," which could be Coleman's, Boudon's, and Elster's views, in parallel with "strong cognitivism" combined with "weak methodological individualism" (Sperber's, Boyer's, and Atran's views), depending on the social facts or events to explain.[12]

---

10   See Habermas (1968) also, in the entirely distinct post-Marxist tradition.
11   See Sampson (2009) for similar comments on Barkow, Tooby, and Cosmides's own use of "strawmen" within the same general context of investigation.
12   Reciprocally, a "weakly cognitivist" methodological individualist could easily accept that certain cognitive categories have an innate and universal origin and that an infra-individualist cognitivist program is fully relevant here—on condition, of course, that it

In the following sections, I do not continue to tackle the issue of the relevance of phylogenetic and infra-individualistic programs. I start by examining three distinct individualistic models of collective beliefs. The first two models are quite clearly individualistic and also entirely micro-sociological, although the second does make room for interactions, and, more precisely, cognitive interactions. Both date back to Tocqueville and have been reintroduced by several contemporary social scientists and in particular by Jon Elster (quite independently, actually, from his reference to Bentham)[13]. The third model is still individualist but it also introduces institutions and social structures, and thus contains meso- or macro-sociological levels of explanation. It dates back to Weber's relatively underappreciated work on American religion, and has been used more or less implicitly by many social scientists, especially James Coleman, who worked to clarify its implications, and even by Pareto and Boudon (Bouvier 2011, 2020). Finally, the fourth model, which is often considered to be holistic because it takes groups into account, is arguably both holistic and individualistic. Although it dates back to Durkheim and Simmel, is has been refined more recently by Margaret Gilbert (1989, 1994, 2000).

I will outline and briefly illustrate these four models, indicating in each case the role they allow for argumentation and rhetoric (as I said, outside of a neo-Darwinian framework such as Sperber's).[14]

3   Two Interactionist-Individualist Models of Collective Beliefs: The Tocqueville-Elster Models of Collective Beliefs

In *Political Psychology* (1993), *Explaining Social Behavior* (2007), and other works, Jon Elster frequently emphasized Tocqueville's intuitions. According to Elster, one can find at least two distinct models of collective beliefs in Tocqueville's work: the model of the "culture of hypocrisy" and the model

---

does not use fallacious arguments. My only reservation regarding Turner (2018) is that Turner does not give explicit room for these weakly cognitivist programs combined with strong individualism. I have tried to show that, within this perspective, one can address the issue of sub-intentional phenomena (located at the boundary of what Turner (2018) calls the Weberian "bubble"—the domain of intentional phenomena—which should be therefore understood as "permeable" to a certain extent) (Bouvier 2018a).

13   See above; Elster 2013.

14   Another limitation of Sperber and Mercier's "argumentative theory" is that it does not provide the scholar with any case study demonstrating its heuristic value in the understanding of collective beliefs. This makes another important difference with the theories I will consider here.

of "pluralistic ignorance" (a label first used by Katz and Allport 1931; a model greatly specified and experimentally tested by Miller and McFarland, 1987). In the first model "everybody publicly professes a certain belief while knowing that nobody actually holds it in private" (Elster 2007, 377), while in the second, "most people do not believe [a certain proposition] but believe that most people do" (377). This second model is more interesting because of its greater subtlety; cognitive interactions play a major role, in that people's beliefs depend on the misrepresentation of others' beliefs, and also because the entire process leads to a self-reinforcing phenomenon of pluralistic ignorance. However, the first model, the culture of hypocrisy model, may be particularly relevant in conjunction with other models, a possibility that I will explore at a later point.

Tocqueville claimed that when he visited the US in the mid-nineteenth century most people did not genuinely believe in God or in Christian dogmas. However, as most people also believed that atheists and agnostics were small minorities, and consequently did not want to pay the social price of non-conformity (namely probable ostracism), most professed publicly that they believed in God and behaved as if they were true believers (for example, by regularly attending church or temple). Tocqueville also suggested that some groups might be entirely hypocritical, in the sense that, in these specific social contexts everybody knew that everybody was no longer a true believer. However, due to the social stigma attached to atheism, conformity to the general norm persisted.

Drawing from Timur Kuran (1995), one could add that, although they were conceived in relation to a liberal society, the first model (the social hypocrisy model) could also account for Russian communism, and the second one (the pluralistic ignorance model) for East German communism, before their respective collapses between 1989 and 1991. In the Russian case, people were chronically scared and intimidated by policy security agents, but they could trust their friends and relatives. In the German case, people suspected that even certain relatives and certain friends could be secret policy security agents. In the Russian case, people dared to express their intimate opinions in private; in the German case, they dared not and, as a result, everyone was quite possibly mistaken about the nature of the intimate beliefs of everyone else.

Similarly, with regard to contemporary Islamic countries, observers have noticed more and more frequently that the people's relationships to Islam are far more diverse than is often thought. As early as the beginning of the twentieth century, the Egyptian winner of the Nobel Prize for Literature, Naguib Mafouz (1990–2), often compared to Balzac or Dickens for his outstanding ethnographical skills, described the social hypocrisy of many Muslims in Cairo, especially in high society. The same people who professed intransigent Islamic beliefs in public, even before their own families, sometimes would lead entirely different lifestyles with their intimate friends, in a manner similar to that of Western hedonist cynicism. One could probably easily find cases of pluralistic ignorance in other Islamic countries where, as in Egypt, Western culture and scientific worldviews had already deeply penetrated high society, but political constraints and controls on private life were more invasive.

What could be the role of argumentation in the transformation or disappearance of these collective beliefs? Several scholars (e.g., Elster, 1993, 2007; Bicchieri and Fukui 1999) have observed that the pluralistic model resembled Andersen's famous tale about the Emperor's clothes, in which a child states the truth: "the king is naked." In this story, the child's statement acts as an argument, or a piece of factual evidence, at everyone's disposal, against the collective belief. But the tale's more important lesson is that the reason it was a child who formulated the (obvious) argument, was that the child could not identify the potential danger that such a revelation implied. The tale does not specify whether the child's parents were imprisoned or killed, but this is probably what would have happened in a real dictatorship.

In the US and the Islamic cases, the religious collective beliefs have yet not disappeared, although pluralistic ignorance might have plausibly changed into hypocrisy in many contexts. However, in the case of Eastern Germany, there was a sudden collapse of the pluralistic ignorance phenomenon in 1989. Unlike Andersen's story, this did not occur after someone (or a few people) dared to say the truth, like the child. Instead, it was the "Emperor" himself, Gorbachev, who initiated the change, when he declared "Glasnost" (meaning openness and more freedom to express one's own ideas) and clearly stated that Warsaw Pact troops would not enter Eastern Germany even in case of social trouble. People did not react by expressing their intimate opinions through speech, but rather by acting, either by leaving for Hungary or by destroying the Berlin wall. (Threshold effects played a major role in these processes). Arguments, in the form of the myriad criticisms of the communist system, had played a role in the collapse of Eastern Germany, but this occurred much earlier, and they were formulated primarily in Western media; they were seldom discussed and exchanged among East Germans themselves.

In conclusion, these first two models, while useful, also have their limits. In particular, the Tocqueville model does not account for the enormous differences in political restrictions between the American, Russian, Eastern European, and Islamic contexts: stated simply, the "tyranny of the majority" in a democracy is not the equivalent of actual imprisonment and threats on life. Finally, in all these cases, there is strong evidence of revivals, which sometimes appear genuine. The two following models will account for these two issues.

4 A Structural-Individualist Model of Collective Beliefs: The Weber-Coleman Model of Collective Beliefs

The pluralistic ignorance model, however sophisticated it may be, is, along with the social hypocrisy model, a typically *individualistic* model of collective beliefs as methodological individualism is generally understood, namely purely micro-sociological. However, one must notice that it is not an "atomistic" model since interactions play a major role in the mechanism of pluralistic ignorance, which rests on beliefs about others' beliefs. This is why it is better to label it interactionnist-individualist model.

A less typically individualistic model is the one implicitly introduced by Weber in his analysis of American religious beliefs, as outlined in a small work on what he described as the "sects" in the US (1904b). This model fits in well with the *structural-individualist* model (as Wippler, 1978, labeled it) that Boudon (1982) and, still more clearly, Coleman (1990) set up and on which Mario Bunge (1996, 1998) has focused attention.[15] It provides some additional conceptual tools for the explanation of the permanence of collective beliefs in societies where true believers are less and less numerous, whether these beliefs are religious or political.

Like Tocqueville half a century earlier, Weber was struck by how many Americans, especially businessmen, declared belief in God and behaved ethically as Christians, but nevertheless did not seem to be genuine in their beliefs. Weber claimed that the reason American businessmen were often affiliated with very demanding "sects" (Weber's wordings), such as the Baptists, Anabaptists, and Quakers, was that these affiliations were seen as guarantees of trustworthiness, a priceless quality in business. Thus many members of these sects were arguably not motivated by ethical rationality (what Weber would have called Wertrationalität) in their affiliation but by pragmatic or means-end rationality (Zweckrationalität). But this is not what I want to emphasize here. I would like to show that the implicit model used by Weber in this opuscule was both more complex and more interesting.

When Coleman set up the structure of opportunity and constraint model in his *Foundations* (1990), he did not refer to Weber or to religious beliefs (as he did when he was aiming at explaining the relationships between macro-level and micro-level phenomena at the very beginning of the Foundations). He introduced this model to account for the choices of voters between distinct

---

[15] The structural-individualist model is far less recent than Lars Udehn (2001, 2002) seems to think.

political options, but the model also can be applied to Weber's analysis of religious affiliations in the US. According to Weber, businessmen could choose among a large variety of religious options (they were almost certainly hypocritical regarding their genuine beliefs; see the Tocqueville model above), which acted as a "structure of opportunity and constraints" in Coleman's wording.[16] These included a) the more or less informal social networks which characterized "sects" (with several sub-options: Baptists, Anabaptists, etc.), b) the more institutionalized larger churches (with several sub-options again) and also, of course, c) the absence of affiliation.[17]

This individualist and structural-institutional model is also well suited to certain aspects of Eastern Europe and Russia before the collapse of the Soviet system. Certain people who declared to be communists were not only hypocritical but also pragmatic and opportunistic (under constraint, indeed, because there were not many other options offered by the "social structure"). They saw positive economic advantages in declaring that they were communist instead of simply remaining silent on this issue. The relationship to Christianity in Eastern Europe could have been also a matter of both social hypocrisy and opportunity (under constraint) in certain countries. In Poland, when Catholic hierarchy often supported Solidarnosc, choosing to maintain affiliation to the Catholic Church—a macro-social structure rather than a simple social network in this case—it could be justified for pragmatic reasons (means-end rationality). The affiliation of many leading political figures all over the world, through loose social networks between states (even in Islamic countries) with communism when the USSR was a world political power, also fits in well with this model.

---

16   In his *Foundations,* Coleman (1990) gave several versions of what is now usually called "the Coleman model" (or "Coleman's boat," or "Coleman's bathtub" because of the global shape of the diagram illustrating this conceptual model). Bunge (1998) prefers to call it "the Boudon-Coleman Model". Each of them has a distinct meaning. Most scholars often mention only the first version (*Foundations*, 28) without seeming even aware of the other versions. A further one (set up in Coleman, 1990, 400–1) is much more relevant here.

17   Of course, I do not contend that the model Weber used in this small and often neglected work on the Protestant *Sects* (Weber, 2002b [1904]), often confused with his well-known work on the Protestant *Ethic* (Weber, 2002a [1904]), is the only or even the most important model that Weber built. But this one can be easily reconstructed as an illustration of the structural-individualist model which I am setting forth. Turner has devoted one of his first works on Weber (Turner and Factor 1994) on the juridical background of Weber's sociology, a characteristic that greatly enlightens the kind of methodological individualism Weber supported and in particular why he was so suspicious of collective concepts (*Kollective Begriffen*) such as "the State," "the nation," "the people" (das *Volk*), or "the spirit of capitalism." See also Turner (1986).

Regarding Islam, a similar analysis could probably be applied in a variety of contexts. For a long time, for example, it might have been advantageous for businessmen to profess Islam in countries where Islam had dominated everyday life, whatever their real beliefs actually were. More recently, and more obviously, it is surely also the case of the many smugglers acting in sub-Saharan Africa since the Arabic spring and the Libyan revolution despite claiming to be Islamic.

However, the constraints in the American case described by Weber were only economic: it was wiser to be affiliated to a "sect" if one wanted to be successful. There were no political risks as there were in Eastern Europe, in Russia or in many Islamic countries, where there were or there are still daily threats on freedom and life.

Argumentation could have played a role in the collapse of these kinds of "collective beliefs" in a variety of ways. For example, argumentation could have been used to prove that a particular affiliation or sect was not sufficiently demanding with regards to morality, that evolution in legislation had made personal trustworthiness far less valuable, or that the structure of opportunity and constraint had changed (e.g., closed clubs such as the Rotary Club have replaced religious affiliations, see Coleman 1990). However, argumentation could probably have played a role earlier in criticizing religious worldviews with regard to rival worldviews. The same could probably also be said regarding communism and Islam.

5   A Holistic-Model of Collective Beliefs: The Durkheim-Gilbert Model

The Tocqueville-Elster and Weber-Coleman models of collective beliefs only deal with conformist collective beliefs—albeit in various ways. I would like to focus now on collective beliefs that are plausibly not conformist beliefs, but, on the contrary, sincere strong beliefs, such as the revival of Christianism in the US since the 1980s (Berger 1999), or the revival of Islam in many countries since the Iranian revolution in 1979 (e.g., Khosrokhavar 2002; Atran and Norenzayan 2014).[18]

My claim is that a fourth model, inspired by Durkheim and often seen as holistic, might be relevant, at least for the Christian and Islamic cases.[19] As

---

18   I do not know enough on the communist case under this respect to be able to extend comparisons.
19   The word "holism" is often reputed to be pejorative within a methodologically individualist framework. However, the real target within this framework, is only what Hayek (1952),

it is well known, according to Durkheim, collective beliefs, or rather "collective representations" in his terminology, are distinct from individual beliefs or individual representations—meaning that groups themselves are supposed to have beliefs distinct from those of their members. This thesis is puzzling because, as groups do not have their own brains, it is difficult to think how they can have their own ideas. Many interpretations and reconstructions have been given and could be still given of Durkheim's intuitions.[20]

A simple individualist reconstruction is that the collective beliefs are beliefs dating back to earlier periods of a society when they were not distinct from individual beliefs; they were subsequently transmitted from individual to individual and from generation to generation without much reflection on their specific content, only being adopted through an unconscious process of interiorization. Even if these beliefs can hardly be said to be genuine beliefs in a strong sense, since "believers" are not really aware of the foundation of their beliefs, they are not hypocritical either.

Margaret Gilbert (1994) provided an entirely different reconstruction of Durkheim's intuitions, and suggested a return to an author who greatly inspired Durkheim, namely Rousseau. She interprets genuine collective beliefs as the result of a tacit general will or of more or less tacit, although conscious, contracts. In these tacit contracts, which she calls "joint commitments," certain individuals commit with other individuals to publicly support a common view, even if this is distinct from their own personal views or deals with issues they consider unimportant. In this circumstance, their primary motivation is not individual pragmatic reasons, but rather simply because they want to feel like

---

in line with Schumpeter (1998 [1908]), called the "fallacy of misplaced concreteness," based on the tendency to think that every concept, especially collective concepts, such as nation, social class, capitalism, Protestantism, matches a real entity (see previous footnote), a cognitive tendency—or what we would now call a "cognitive bias"—examined by Pareto (1935 [1916]) too. Ontological vigilance does not exclude at all the recognition of the specificity of collective entities as such when it has been demonstrated that they were ontologically dependent on individuals. Tthis is what Weber (2002a [1904]), brilliantly illustrated on the case of Protestantism. Thus, from a methodological individualist viewpoint fully understood, one may say that there is both "bad" holism and "good" holism (Bouvier, 2020).

20 Turner (2007) mentions that there has been a re-discovery of Durkheimian intuitions on this matter and refers to Gilbert (1989), among others (see below). Quite rightly he specifies that even before Gilbert, at least one author, Wilfred Sellars introduced similar ideas. Moreover, on the basis of his amazing erudition, Turner adds that Wilfred's father, Roy Wood Sellars, an outsider in the US, and an almost unknown scholar in Europe already had similar ideas. See also Olen and Turner (2015) on the *two* Sellars and their common interest in one of Durkheim's most famous followers, Celestin Bouglé.

members of a group and consequently to aim for a collective goal, possibly whatever this goal may be.

The interiorization model works best with cases where membership is neither recent nor the result of a conscious choice, as is the case for suicide-bombers (Japanese kamikazes during WW II, Palestinians more recently). The joint commitment model best describes other circumstances, particularly for nascent groups lacking institution foundations, including social networks. Certain bombing attacks, such as September 11, 2001 in the US and more recent attacks committed by young Muslims, long uprooted from their social origins and not really connected to other Islamic groups (Khosrokhavar 2002; Gambetta 2005), could be characterized as joint commitments among a very small number of individuals acting as members of a new community (a new "Umma" in case of Islamic activists) (Bouvier 2018b).

Joint commitments are not necessarily related to extremist activities. Christian revivals in the US might also deal with joint commitments among a very limited number of people wanting to found new communities. The issue is more complicated regarding Russia and Eastern Europe. In the 1980s in Eastern Europe, there were apparently still many genuine communists, according to reliable surveys (Kuran 1995). These people were able to make a distinction between communist ideals and the reality they knew, and could criticize daily life without abandoning the core principles of their belief. But it seems difficult, at least on the basis of my own knowledge of these cases, to determine to what extent interiorization processes, on the one hand, and new joint commitments, on the other hand, played a major role.[21]

In the case of interiorization, one cannot expect arguments to be effective, since people are not even aware of this unconscious process nor of the basis of their beliefs. On the contrary, in the case of joint commitments, argumentation could play a role in the disaggregation of collective beliefs since the joint commitment is common knowledge. However, to be successful, argumentation would have to be applied not to the content of the beliefs, which is unimportant here, but rather to the joint commitment itself. It would, for example, have to persuade members of a given group that the joint commitment has been violated by some other members of the group. The disappearance of

---

21 On the relevance of Gilbert's model of joint commitment in other domains, see, e.g., Gold and Sugden (2006); Carassa, Colombetti, and Morgandi (2008). On other holistic models compatible with methodological individualism, see, e.g., Tuomela (2002), Pettit (2003), and List and Pettit (2011).

collective beliefs based on joint commitments occurs more plausibly when violations are self-evident. In these cases, they did not need any external argumentation.[22]

6 Conclusion

To conclude, I would like to emphasize a few points. First, that argumentation and rhetoric may play a distinct role in every case that I have discussed, although this role is variable and sometimes secondary. Secondly, holistic models, reformulated on clear contractualist bases, and therefore reducible to individualist foundations, are relevant and useful tools for the understanding of collective beliefs.[23] Thirdly, these models have to be used in connection with individualist models that leave room for complex cognitive interactions or for the structural role of social institutions (at the meso- and the macro-levels). And lastly, these programs are not based on speculative hypotheses regarding the phylogenetic emergence of rationality, especially on the role of any Machiavellian intention. But, taken as a large set of hypotheses, they seem to have a refined heuristic value in the understanding of collective beliefs[24].

References

Atran, S., 1990. *Cognitive Foundations of Natural History: Towards an Anthropology of Science.* Cambridge, Cambridge University Press.

Atran, S., 2010. *Talking to the Enemy: Faith, Brotherhood, and the (Un)Making of Terrorists.* New York, Harper Collins.

Atran, S. and A. Norenzayan. 2014. "Religion's Evolutionary Landscape: Counterintuition, Commitment, Compassion, Communion." *Behavioral and Brain Sciences* 27: 1–18.

Barkow, J., L. Cosmides, and J. Tooby. 1992. *The Adapted Mind: Evolutionary Psychology and the Generation of Culture.* Oxford: Oxford University Press.

Bentham, J. 1999 [1791]. *Political Tactics.* Oxford: Clarendon Press.

---

22 A famous case was the German-Soviet Pact of August 1939, which was viewed by many communists of Western Europe as itself violating implicit commitments with them.

23 I have elaborated much longer on the empirical relevance of Gilbert's model of collective beliefs (with comparison to alternative models) in papers addressing various kinds of examples: on religious matters: Bouvier, 2018b; on scientific matters: Bouvier 2004.

24 I thank ANR-17-EURE-0017 FrontCog & ANR-10-IDEX-0001-02 PSL for their financial support.

Berger, P. (Ed.) 1999. *The Desecularization of the World: Resurgent Religion and World Politics*. Grand Rapids, MI: Eerdmans Publishing.

Bicchieri, C. and Y. Fukui. 1999. The Great Illusion: Ignorance, Informational Cascades, and the Persistence of Unpopular Norms. In *Experience, Reality and Scientific Explanation: Workshop in Honour of Merrilee and Wesley Salmon*. Edited by M.C. Galavotti and A. Paganini. Dordrecht: Kluwer, 89–121.

Boudon, R. 1981 [1979]. *The Logic of Social Action. An Introduction to Sociological Analysis*. London: Routledge & Kegan Paul.

Boudon, R. 1982 [1977]. *The Unintended Consequences of Social Action*. London: Palgrave McMillan.

Boudon, R. 1994 [1990]. *The Art of Self-Persuasion*. London: Polity Press.

Boudon, R. 1998, Social Mechanisms without Black Boxes. In *Social Mechanisms. An Analytical Approach to Social Theory*. Edited by P. Hedström and R. Swedberg. Cambridge: Cambridge University Press, 172–203.

Boudon, R. 2001. *The Origins of Values*. New Brunswick, NJ: Transaction Publishers.

Bourdieu, P. 1972. *Esquisse d'une théorie de la pratique, précédé de Trois études d'ethnologie kabyle*. Geneva, Switzerland: Librairie Droz.

Bourdieu, P. 1980. *Le Sens pratique*. Paris: Les Éditions de Minuit.

Bouvier, A. (Ed.). 1999. *Pareto aujourd'hui*. Paris: Presses Universitaires de France.

Bouvier, A, 2002, "An Epistemological Plea for Methodological Individualism and Rational Choice Theory in Cognitive Rhetoric", *Philosophy of the Social Sciences*, 32(1) : p. 51–70

Bouvier, A. 2004. "Individual and Collective Beliefs in Sciences and Philosophy. The Plural Subject and the Polyphonic Subject Accounts. Case Studies." *Philosophy of the Social* Sciences 34(3): 382–407.

Bouvier, A. 2007. "An Argumentativist Point of View in Cognitive Sociology." New Trends in Cognitive Sociology, special issue *European Journal of Sociological Theory* 10: 465–480.

Bouvier, A. 2011. Individualism, Collective Agency and the 'Micro-macro relation. In *Handbook of the Philosophy of Social Sciences*. Edited by I. Jarvie and J. Zamora. Thousand Oaks, CA: Sage Publications, 198–215 (Chapter 8).

Bouvier, A. 2016, "Analytical Sociology, Argumentation and Rhetoric. Large Scale Social Phenomena Significantly Influenced by Apparently Innocuous Rhetorical Devices." *Proceedings of the European Conference on Argumentation, Lisbon,* 2015.

Bouvier, A. 2018a. Intentional, Unintentional and Sub-Intentional Aspects of Social Mechanisms and Rationality. The Example of Commitments in Political Life. In *The Mystery of Rationality: Mind, Beliefs and the Social Sciences*. Edited by Gérald Bronner and Francesco Di Iorio. Cham, Switzerland: Springer, 17–36.

Bouvier, A. 2018b. "The Empirical Relevance of the Joint Commitment Model of Collective Beliefs in the Social Sciences: Strength and Weakness." *Protosociology* 35, *Critical Essays on the Philosophy of Margaret Gilbert*: 41–59.

Bouvier, A. 2020. Individualism versus Holism. In *Research Methods Foundations*. Edited by P. A. Atkinson, S. Delamont, M. Hardy, and M. Williams. Sage Publications. *Research Methods Foundations.* doi: 10.4135/9781526421036803102.

Boyer, P. 1994. *The Naturalness of Religious Ideas. A Cognitive Theory of Religion*. Berkeley: University of California Press.

Byrne R.W, and A. Whiten. 1988. *Machiavellian Intelligence: Social Expertise and the Evolution of Intellect in Monkeys, Apes, and Humans*, Oxford: Clarendon.

Byrne, R.W. 1996. "Machiavellian Intelligence." *Evolutionary Anthropology* 5: 172–180.

Bunge, M. 1996. *Finding Philosophy in Social Science*. New Haven: Yale University Press.

Bunge, M. 1998. *Social Science under Debate. A Philosophical Perspective*. Toronto: University of Toronto Press.

Carassa, A., M. Colombetti, and F. Morgandi. 2008. The Role of Joint Commitment in Intersubjectivity. In *Emerging Communication: Studies in New Technologies and Practices in Communication* 10. The Netherlands: IOS Press, 187–201. http://ebooks.iospress.nl/publication/22372.

Coleman, J. 1990. Foundations of Social Theory. Cambridge: Harvard Belknap Press.

Dawkins, R. and J. R. Krebs. 1978. Animal signals: Information or Manipulation. In *Behavioural Ecology: An Evolutionary Approach*. Edited by J. R. Krebs, Davies N. B. Sutherland, MA: Sinauer Associates, Inc., 282–309.

Eemeren, van, F.-H, B. Garssen, E. C.W. Krabbe, F.A. Snoeck [should be written like Henkemans, since this is a part of the family name] Henkemans, B. Verheij, and J.H.M. Wagemans. 2014. *Handbook of Argumentation Theory*. Dordrecht: Springer.

Elster, J. 1982. Belief, Bias and Ideology. In *Rationalism and Relativism*. Edited by M. Hollis and S. Lukes. Boston: MIT Press, 123–148.

Elster, J. 1991. "Constitutionalism in Eastern Europe: An Introduction." In *The University of Chicago Law Review* 58(2), Approaching Democracy: A New Legal Order for Eastern Europe: 447–482.

Elster, J. 1993 [1990]. *Political Psychology*. Cambridge: Cambridge University Press.

Elster, J. 1998. A Plea for Mechanisms. In *Handbook of Analytical Sociology*. Edited by P. Hedström and R. Swedberg. Oxford: Oxford University Press, 45–73.

Elster, J. 2007. *Explaining Social Behavior: More Nuts and Bolts for the Social Sciences*. Cambridge: Cambridge University Press.

Elster, J. 2013. *Securities against Misrules. Juries, Assemblies, Elections*. Cambridge: Cambridge University Press.

Evans-Pritchard, E. 1937, *Witchcraft, Oracles and Magic among the Azande*. Oxford: Oxford University Press.

Evans-Pritchard, E. 1965. *Theories of Primitive Religion*. Oxford: Oxford University Press.

Femia, J. and A. Marshall. 2012. *Beyond Disciplinary Boundaries: Essays on Pareto*. Gower House: Ashgate.

Gambetta, D. 2005. *Making Sense of Suicide Missions*. Oxford: Oxford University Press.

Gilbert, M. 1989. *On Social Facts*. London, New York: Routledge.
Gilbert, M. 1994. Durkheim and Social Facts. In *Debating Durkheim* Edited by W. Pickering and H. Martins. London: Routledge.
Gilbert, M. 2000. *Sociality and Responsibility*. Lanham, MD: Rowman & Littlefield.
Gold, N. and R. Sugden. 2006. Michel Bacharach. Beyond Individual Choice: Teams and Frames in Game Theory. Princeton: Princeton University Press.
Goldman, A. 1999. *Knowledge in a Social World.* Oxford: Oxford University Press.
Habermas, J. 1968. *Erkenntnis und Interesse*. Frankfurt: Surkhamp Verlag.
Hayek (von), F.A. 1952. *Scientism and the Study of Society*. Glencoe, Illinois: The Free Press.
Hedström, P. and R. Swedberg (Eds). 1998. *Social Mechanisms. An Analytical Approach to Social Theory.* Cambridge: Cambridge University Press.
Hedström, P. and P. Bearman. 2009a. *Handbook of Analytical Sociology*. Oxford: Oxford University Press.
Hedström, P. and P. Bearman. 2009b. What is Analytical Sociology All About? An Introductory Essay. In *Handbook of Analytical Sociology*. Edited by P. Hedström and P. Bearman. Oxford: Oxford University Press, 3–24.
Hollis, M. and S. Lukes (Eds). 1982. *Rationalism and Relativism*. Boston: MIT Press.
Homans, G. C., and C. P, Jr. 1934. An Introduction to Pareto: His Sociology. New York: Alfred A. Knopf.
Horton, R. 1982. Tradition and Modernity Revisited. In *Rationalism and Relativism*. Edited by M. Hollis and S. Lukes. Boston: MIT Press.
Katz, D., and F. H. Allport. 1931. Student Attitudes. Syracuse, NY: Craftsman.
Khosrokhavar, F. 2002. *Les nouveaux martyrs d'Allah*. Paris:Flammarion.
Koyre, A. 1970. *Mystiques, spirituels, alchimistes du XVIe siècle allemand*. Paris: Gallimard.
Kuhn, T. 1970. *The Structure of Scientific Revolutions*. Chicago: The University of Chicago Press.
Kuran, T. 1995. *Private Truths, Public Lies: The Social Consequences of Preference Falsification*. Cambridge: Harvard University Press.
Levy-Bruhl, L. 1923 [1922]. *Primitive Mentality*. London: Allen & Unwin.
List, C. and P. Pettit. 2011 *Group Agency: The Possibility, Design, and Status of Corporate Agents*. Oxford: Oxford University Press. doi:10.1093/acprof:oso/9780199591565.001.0001.
Mahfouz, N. 1990–2 [1956–7]. *Cairo Trilogy.* New York: Doubleday.
Mercier, H. and D. Sperber. 2011. "Why Do Humans Reason? Arguments for an Argumentative Theory." *Behavioral and Brain Sciences* 34: 57–111.
Mercier, H. and D. Sperber. 2017. *The Enigma of Reason*. Cambridge: Cambridge University Press.
Mill, J.S. 1974 [1843]. *A System of Logic, Ratiocinative and Inductive* in *Collected Works of John Stuart Mill.* Toronto: University of Toronto Press.

Miller, D. T and C. McFarland. 1987. "Pluralistic Ignorance: When Similarity is Interpreted as Dissimilarity." *Journal of Personality and Social Psychology* 53(2): 298–305.

Olen, P. and S. Turner. 2015. "Durkheim, Sellars, and the Origins of Collective Intentionality. *British Journal for the History of Philosophy* 23(5): 954–975.

Pareto, V. 1935 [1916], *The Mind and Society.* New York: Harcourt, Brace and Company.

Parsons, Talcott. 1937. *The Structure of Social Action.* Glencoe, Illinois: The Free Press.

Pettit, P. 2003. Groups with Minds of Their Own. In *Socializing Metaphysics.* Edited by F. Schmitt. New York: Rowman and Littlefield.

Popper, K. 1957. *The Poverty of Historicism.* London: Routledge Classics.

Powers, Ch., 1987. *Vilfredo Pareto.* Beverly Hills: Sage Publications.

Reid, Th., 1970 1764], *An Inquiry into the Human Mind*, Chicago: University of Chicago Press.

Richardson, R. C. 2007. *Evolutionary Psychology as Maladapted Psychology.* Cambridge, Mass.: MIT Press.

Sampson, Geoffrey. 2009. *The "Language Instinct" Debate*, rev. edn. London: Continuum, 134–5.

Schumpeter, J., 1998 [1908]. *Das Wesen und der Hauptinhalt der theoretischen Nationalökonomie.* Berlin: Duncker & Humblot.

Sperber, D. 1975. *Rethinking Symbolism.* Cambridge: Cambridge University Press.

Sperber, D. 1982. Apparently Irrational Beliefs. In *Rationalism and Relativism.* Edited by M. Hollis and S. Lukes. Boston: MIT Press, 149–180.

Sperber, D. 1997. Methodological Individualism and Cognitivism in the Social Sciences. Unpublished English version of "Individualisme méthodologique et cognitivisme." In *Cognition et sciences sociales.* Edited by R. Boudon, A. Bouvier and F. Chazel. Paris: Presses Universitaires de France. http://www.dan.sperber.fr/?p=33.

Sperber, D. 2001a. "Conceptual Tools for a Natural Science of Society and Culture (Radcliffe-Brown Lecture in Social Anthropology 1999)." *Proceedings of the British Academy* III: 297–317.

Sperber, D. 2001b. "An Evolutionary Perspective on Testimony and Argumentation." *Philosophical Topics* 29: 401–413.

Tocqueville (de), A. 2000 [1835–1840]. *Democracy in America.* Chicago: University of Chicago Press.

Tuomela, R. 2002. *The Philosophy of Social Practices. A Collective Acceptance View*, C. U.P.

Turner, Stephen. 1986. *The Search for a Methodology of Social Science: Durkheim, Weber, and the Nineteenth Century Problem of Cause, Probability, and Action.* Boston Studies in the Philosophy of Science, 92. Dordrecht, Holland: Reidel.

Turner, Stephen. 2007. Defining a Discipline: Sociology and Its Philosophical Problems, from Its Classics to 1945. In *Philosophy of Anthropology and Sociology.* Edited by S. Turner and M. Risjord, M. Amsterdam: Elsevier, 3–70.

Turner, Stephen. 2018. *Cognitive Science and the Social. A Primer*. New York and London: Routledge.

Turner, S. and R. A. Factor. 1994. *Max Weber, The lawyer as Social Thinker*. London and New York: Routledge.

Udehn L. 2001. *Methodological Individualism. Background, History and Meaning*. London: Routledge.

Udehn L. 2002. "The Changing Face of Methodological Individualism." *Annual Review of Sociology* 28: 479–507.

Walton, D. 1996. The Straw Man Fallacy. In Logic and Argumentation. Edited by Johan van Bentham, Frans H. van Eemeren, Rob Grootendorst and Frank Veltman. Amsterdam: Royal Netherlands Academy of Arts and Sciences, 115–128.

Weber, M., 2002 a [1904]. *The Protestant Ethic and the Spirit of Capitalism.* Max Weber (2002), *The Protestant Ethic and the "Spirit" of Capitalism and Other Writings*. London: Penguin Classics.

Weber, M. 2002 b [1904]. *The Protestant Sects and the Spirit of Capitalism.* Max Weber (2002) *The Protestant Ethic and the "Spirit" of Capitalism and Other Writings*. London: Penguin Classics.

Wippler, R. 1978. "The Structural-Individualistic Approach in Dutch Sociology." *Netherlands Journal of Sociology* 4: 135–155.

PART 3

Intentions and Norms

What Does Normativity "Explain"?

Peter Olen

Abstract

Stephen Turner's Normaitivity is an under-discussed challenge to dominant conceptions of normativity. I explore main themes in Turner's work while entertaining possible challenges and objections to his arguments about Wilfrid Sellars's philosophy. My central focus is Turner's rejection of normativity as explanatorily necessary in accounts of persons and behavior, especially as it pertains to more recent defenses of Sellars's philosophy (as found in the work of Willem deVries and Jim O'Shea). I conclude by arguing that so-called normativist and anti-normativists positions on explanation must both concede parts of their position in order to count as adequate explanations of human behavior.

Keywords

Normativity – Wilfrid Sellars – Explanation – Social Science

1 Introduction

I was fortunate to be in Stephen Turner's graduate seminar on normativity just as his book on the same topic was nearing completion. Throughout the first half of the seminar we explored Martin Kusch's *A Sceptical Guide to Meaning and Rules* in an effort to discern broad, unifying theses that underpinned what Turner called the 'normativist' position. Not surprisingly, what Turner described throughout the course as a typical argument in support of the normativist position found its way into his book: defenders of the *sui generis* and necessary character of normativity pick some phenomenon that is in need of further explanation, description, or elaboration, stipulate that said explanation,description,or elaboration would be incomplete without being couched in normative terms, and then insist on the necessity of the normative for understanding the phenomenon in question.[1] If understood as an acceptable

---

[1] This can be found most directly in Turner 2013, 192–3.

argumentative strategy, this leaves critics of normativity at a distinct disadvantage: How could one reject the need to include normative considerations in one's account of some concept if they are—from the very beginning—asserted as requirements for any adequate explanation of a given concept?

Turning against this specific argumentative strategy motivates, so far as I can tell, much of Turner's objections to normativist accounts. The exact issue between Turner's anti-normativist stance and normativist accounts is muddled by what initially appears to be terminological confusions. What is the difference between *explaining* and *analyzing* a given concept? When must we look for *descriptions* or *explanations* of a given phenomenon, instead of *characterizations*? Are normative concepts in the [theoretical] business of describing and explaining our practices, or do they fulfill some other function? These questions, while addressed in piecemeal fashion throughout the literature, tend to be answered by simply *assuming* that normative concepts are either integral for understanding our place in the world, that normative concepts are involved in practices distinct from describing and explaining, or that some phenomenon would be unrecognizable outside of an account of their existence that includes normative concepts.

Although I do not agree with Turner in every aspect of his arguments against normativism, we have jointly developed a reading of Wilfrid Sellars's work.[2] And even though some of this joint work presupposes Turner's own arguments about normativity, I have not been able to explore his views on this issue in writing until now. In what follows I will offer some criticisms of Turner's depiction of the normativist/anti-normativist split, while still remaining sympathetic to his overall conclusions. I neither advocate for any particular interpretation of Sellars's philosophy here, nor do I endorse any of the challenges found in various interpretations discussed below, but I think interpretations of Sellars's work function as a serious threat to Turner's understanding of normativity. This challenge is most clearly embodied in Willem deVries' and James O'Shea's conception of how the natural and the normative fit together.

2 Turner on Normativity

One way of reconciling the clash between competing descriptions or explanations is to simply deny they are in the same business. Instead of characterizing

---

[2] See Olen and Turner 2015; Olen and Turner 2016.

scientific (or causal) and normative discourse[3] as describing or explaining linguistic practices, we might argue that while broadly scientific accounts of language (i.e., those found in the fields of anthropology or linguistics) clearly *describe* or *explain* our practices, accounts that stress the role of normative concepts 'implicit' in our linguistic acts and actions do not. Sellars and, more recently, Allan Gibbard,[4] have argued that no descriptive account of meaning can capture the conditions behind the acceptance or rejection of particulars words or sentences 'meaning' something. Instead, normative accounts of language are either *required* to account for linguistic practices (e.g., are implicit in, presupposed by, or necessary for the possibility of specifically human language) or they are doing something altogether different (i.e., they are 'characterizing', 'analyzing', or 'classifying' a piece of language or behavior) than simply explaining those practices. Thus, while potentially reconcilable, descriptions or explanations of language and normative accounts of language are both necessary to account for uniquely human linguistic practices.

As it stands, this simply won't do. The assumption that normativity (or the very idea of implicit or presupposed standards of correctness) is irreducible, a required aspect in the explanation of agency and action, yet somehow not describing or explaining phenomena, leaves the issue obscured. What we want out of debates over normativity is, in part, an answer to the question of whether a 'complete' account of the world—specifically, *our* descriptions and explanations of the world, as well as our place in it—would need to account for normativity in a way that would not eventually collapse into scientific description or explanation. That is, whether a 'final' understanding of humanity's place in the world could [exhaustively] be described or explained in purely scientific terms.

In *Explaining the Normative*, Turner attempts to untangle this central tension between normativist and anti-normativists positions as found throughout the philosophical and social science literature. By "normativity" or the "normative," Turner means "a special realm of fact that validates, justifies, makes possible, and regulates normative talk, as well as rules, meanings, the symbolic and reasoning" (Turner 2010, 1). Normativity is taken as indicative of "non-natural,

---

[3] One issue throughout the debate between normativists and anti-normativists (as Turner frames it) is just how to frame the two positions. For example, not all scientific explanations are causal and, not surprisingly, not all causal explanations are scientific. Nonetheless, the distinction intends to capture a difference between descriptions or explanations that—all things considered—can be classified as fitting solely within a scientific or causal framework and those that require something 'above and beyond' said framework.

[4] See Gibbard 2013.

non-empirical stuff that is claimed to be necessarily, intrinsically there, and in some sense to account for the actual" phenomenon in question (Turner 2010, 5). This conception of the normative is generally framed *against* social science and flat-footed naturalistic explanations of the same phenomenon in an attempt to stave off, or re-take, conceptual land philosophy lost to encroaching scientism. The "specialness" of normativity is indicative of the oddness (i.e., non-natural) of the concept, as arguably found in its resistance to straightforward naturalization (Turner 2010, 14).

The central point of Turner's criticism tracks the narrative I began with: accounts of normativity (semantic, moral, legal, or otherwise) are not localized or instrumental accounts of norms, but claim universality as to the scope and presence of norms. It is not just that norms are depicted as pervasive throughout human practices, but that they are also assumed as *requirements* for any adequate explanation of said practices.[5] Thus, one finds Turner arguing that the term 'normativity' itself "purports to explain" a variety of phenomena: from the genuineness of social norms, the rationality of theories, the meaning of words, and the source of 'genuine' legality or morality (Turner 2013, 192). Normativists argue for the conceptual necessity of normative concepts or language for a given subject by denying that description of causal explanations can adequately account for a given phenomenon "without reference to normative considerations" (Turner 2010, 8). In these cases, referencing normative considerations entails the recognition of normative facts, such that there are distinct facts about normative concepts or properties that are required for explanations, but yet are [somehow] inaccessible through description or causal explanation.[6] Attempts to reduce or eliminate normative concepts or terms results in either inadequate explanations or the re-introduction of such terms.[7] As Turner points out, this is a crucial move in the normativist's argument:

---

5 Brandom's scorekeeping model of language, for example, is not one possible accounting of language, but a claim to account for *all* human linguistic practices. But, as Turner points out, there are numerous cross-cultural considerations that should give pause when embracing such a seemingly universal theory about linguistic practices. See Turner 2010, 31–36.

6 I am somewhat puzzled by Turner's emphasis on 'normative facts' as a distinction in kind. My assumption is that a belief in 'normative facts' is, from Turner's standpoint, presupposed by any commitment to a concept or property that is not captured in description or causal explanation. This seems to eliminate any possible consideration of a non-factualist understanding of normativity (such as the Sellarsian option discussed in part III), which arguably avoids the need to posit a realm of facts seemingly unexplainable by the natural sciences.

7 The re-introduction of normative terms need not entail that such terms be taken literally (i.e., as if talk of norms automatically demands their existence). Turner makes this point,

> Scientists may be unable to talk about their theories without using normative terms like "good" or "elegant" or event "must." But this normative language does not, in any simple or direct way, require us to believe in normativities. It would be a different matter if we could not *explain* their ways of talking about their theories without appealing to the notion of normativity, and this is what the normativist needs to claim: that a special fact of normativity is presupposed or required in some sense by this talk or to make this talk intelligible.
>
> TURNER 2010, 13

This leads to what appears to be a genuine issue about necessity and explanation: normativists must argue that normative facts or terms are already part of the phenomena in need of explanation (and thus ineliminable from the start) or required in order to explain some given phenomena. Either way, what explanations of certain phenomena require just are normative concepts or terms in order to adequately explain the subject in question.[8] Thus, normative concepts or discourse cannot be replaced or eliminated in the course of explaining specific phenomena.

Of course, much of this depends on what we mean by "necessary" or "required" for explanation. While it is surely true that arguments for the binding character of normativity are usually presented as required in order to 'adequately' account for some phenomenon, there is a sense in which this might be looking through the right lens, but from the wrong angle. While it might be correct to deny the universality of normative concepts as 'in' the world (and, therefore, deny the existence of so-called normative facts), that does not mean such concepts are not required in explanations from our human perspective. Normative explanations, while possibly not required in all instances, might simply be the kinds of explanations we invoke in our effort to explain our world in recognizably human terms. This, of course, does not make such explanations required in the fullest sense (or, more so, make normative concepts or terms required in all explanations), but it might mean that such explanations are required when explaining human practices from a specifically humanistic standpoint.

---

but see Olen 2016 (chp. 6) for a clear example of this kind of argument in Rudolf Carnap's critique of Sellars.

8   What constitutes an 'adequate' explanation is never clear. From my perspective this issue is not fully addressed by either the normativist or anti-normativist. Turner does take a stab at the question elsewhere. See Turner 2013a.

The potential error when overlooking this point is a confusion between discussing concepts as necessary in all instances and discussing them as necessary in or for certain kinds of explanations.[9] The broader scope of claiming that normative concepts are required for understanding linguistic practices from all perspectives requires normativity to play a substantially inflated role. For example, O'Shea claims that even in the final stereoscopic image of humanity's place in the world, specifically human practices would still need to invoke norms and principles (as generated by shared intentions) in order to construct a shared, knowable world (O'Shea 2007, 189). Our explanations of such practices would need to mention, instead of use, such norms and shared intentions, but the result of this is that our explanations themselves would confirm Turner's fear of being required to contain normative concepts and terms in order to constitute adequate explanations of human practices.

Yet, it is not clear why we cannot have a localized sense of normativity as a requirement in certain kinds of explanations that, while in-principle eliminable, is required when using said explanations. This is mimicking, in part, Turner's conception of a "Good Bad Theory":

> Using "theory" here is merely extending our folk language to talk about our folk language. With that qualification, we may describe these various folk conceptions as "Good Bad Theories", meaning that they are good theories for a particular, unspecified set of purposes in a particular setting, but bad theories if we are thinking of them as adequate explanations of anything, or as proto-explanations that can be turned into genuine explanations with a little empirical vetting and some minor revision.
>
> TURNER 2010, 43

The difference between Turner's articulation of this and my own is simply the concession that 'Good Bad Theories' might be necessary for certain explanations. Turner might recognize this, as he comments in his discussion of intentions: "If we could grasp the point of the actions directly, we would not need to invent intentional explanations" (Turner 2010, 44). Extending Turner's reasoning here, it is not clear that we could ever get to a point where we always directly grasp the point of actions, so it stands to reason we might always need explanations that invoke normative concepts or terms. Echoing O'Shea's point above, we might think a world recognizably knowable to ourselves, while

---

9   O'Shea makes a similar point in discussing the use and mention of concepts. See O'Shea 2010, 461.

perhaps only idealistically conceivable without such normative concepts, simply demands such explanations in order to function as recognizably human. Those explanations would not be necessary in the sense that we are required to fuse them to our scientific understanding of the world, but they might be necessary for explanations of *our* world from *our* standpoint.

Another way Turner attempts to problematize the move towards universality is to explore the diversity problem (i.e., the diversity of our linguistic practices) as a response to normativsts' claims of universality. Turner argues that normativist models of linguistic practices insist on a single model of norms and terms in order to cover all kinds of practices in numerous cultures. Thus, one should read Brandom's inferentialist score-keeping model of language as applicable across cultural differences. Yet Turner argues that such scope is not possible in normativists' explanations of practices, mainly because the concrete, differing experiences of individuals protests against the idea of a universal set of norms for language or rationality (Turner 2010, 35).

Yet, I think this is a mistake on Turner's part. Brandom, for example, has no problem accounting for the diversity of practices within different communities.[10] Insofar as a given community has different practices, they will find different actions acceptable, other actions unintelligible, etc ... It is, at least in some cases, a theoretical stretch to argue that normativists' claims to universality make it impossible to account for localized differences – even extremely localized differences between sub-groups and individuals within the same community. The claim to universality turns on the idea that whatever norms may be found in a given community (and whatever concepts, consequently, may be applicable to understanding that community) are dictated by the community themselves. Thus, the normativist can account for differing concepts in differing communities without thereby committing themselves to the universality of a specific set of concepts. Granted, such an argument deflates the idea of having a universal conception of linguistic rules or rationality, but this would play directly into the idea that normative explanations have no problem functioning along the lines of Turner's Good Bad Theories.

---

10   Even in its classic formulation, Brandom's normativism can accommodate this kind of view. The distinction I draw above is clearly reflected in Brandom's claim that "classifying the behavior of a community in this way into social practices according to complexly criterioned responses is something that *we* do from the outside, as part of an attempt to understand them. The members of the community need not explicitly split up their activities in the ways we do, though they must do so implicitly, in the sense of responding as we have postulated" (Brandom 1979, 188).

What stands in the way of accepting this line of reasoning is the idea that normative concepts and terms would need to be something more than instrumentally useful; they need to be, in some sense, true. But this is where some of Turner's initial objections come back into play: that normativist insists on a non-natural, 'special' ideal that cannot be naturalized, that norms are required parts of explanations (not just useful explanations, but correct ones), and that explanations without such concepts or terms would essentially fail to function as explanations. These objections amount to a difference between normativity as a phenomenon to be explained (which seems to be the target for most of Turner's objections) and normativity as an ineliminable, albeit somewhat empty, aspect of one kind of explanation.

What this alternative proposal does not address, though, is exactly why such normatively-laden explanations are needed in the first place. Even if we can avoid many of the problems above by construing normativity as an instrumental aspect of explanation, we still have not addressed the issue of exactly when or why normative concepts are required to explain anything—even in a conditional or pragmatic sense of 'required'. Turning to think about the issue from the standpoint of Sellars's philosophy, the pressing part of Turner's objection isn't the main narrative developed throughout his book, but a contested point about whether normative concepts purport to explain at all. Insofar as Turner is correct, Sellars's philosophy shows up as just as mysterious as other normativists' positions. Yet, I do not think this is necessarily fair to both Sellars and the tradition that arises out of interpreting his work.[11] Sellars does not insist on the existence of normative *facts* nor does he explicitly argue that normative concepts or discourse are required for *explanation*. This is, perhaps, because thinking of normative concepts or discourse as explaining our practices is a misunderstanding of what normative concepts or discourse do. And this is exactly what Sellarsian accounts of normativity argue when responding to the kind of criticism's found in Turner's conception of normativity.

3 Competing Moves

There are various responses Sellars might make to what Turner considers the pressing issue of explanation here, but I want to consider two responses that directly pertain to Turner's work. Willem deVries and James O'Shea offer

---

[11] That being said, Turner does recognizes a wide-variety of approaches to understanding normativity, See Turner 2010, 14–15.

interpretations of Sellars's philosophy that aim at reconciling Sellars's scientific realism with his well-known commitment to the 'logically irreducible' nature of normativity. Additionally, Griffin Klemick has offered an observant discussion of the differences between his and our accounts of Sellars's understanding of ethics that sheds substantial light on where we depart from normativist accounts of ethics and agency. These approaches to Sellars, while beginning at different starting points, converge on the claims that 1) there is a meaningful difference between analysis and explanation, 2) that normative concepts or discourse require analysis (or, itself, analyzes behavior) as opposed to explanation, and 3) normative concepts or discourse do not explain, but in fact analyze, characterize, or express various concepts or principles. This amounts to what I previously mentioned as a non-factualist, non-explanatory account of normativity that could arguably avoid most of Turner's objections. Part of the genesis for this reading of Sellars is found in his dual endorsements of the idea that normative discourse and concepts are logically irreducible, but "in the dimension of describing and explaining the world, science is the measure of all things" (Sellars [1956] 2000, 253). This combination of claims is, *prima facie*, confusing. One would think, especially following Turner's line of reasoning about normativity, that it would be impossible to be jointly committed to these two claims. Yet, such a joint commitment is conceptually impossibly only if we operate under the assumption that the only legitimate way of thinking about normativity itself is as an aspect of explanation.

DeVries and O'Shea have readings of Sellars that ostensibly reconcile these issues. Both offer arguments, pulling from different aspects of Sellars's work, which stress the necessity of the normative while reconciling the seeming gap between the casual and the normative. DeVries draws a distinction between empirical and practical reality, where to claim a conceptual framework or object are "practically real" is to claim that there are "categorical prescriptive truths" concerning that framework or object, such that the framework contains intentions that are "warrantably assertible" (deVries 2005, 272). That is, "practical reality is a matter of the truth of prescriptive and normative claims, and that, in turn, is a matter of recognized, intersubjectively held, intersubjectively applicable, shared intentions" (deVries 2005, 277). The practical reality of normative discourse, while distinct from its empirical reality, need not be considered any less real or legitimate. Normative concepts and terms, while not carving the world at its joints, can be seen as operating along guidelines of truth and justification—they are not mere shadow puppets of 'more real' concepts that track the world or ourselves.

This understanding of conceptual frameworks, especially keeping in mind Sellars's conception of the manifest image, points to the essentially constitutive role norms play in determining the semantic and pragmatic conditions within a given framework. In these cases, norms function as a priori constraints on what can and cannot be said, what behavior is or is not sanctioned. And clearly none of those actions are attempts to explain behavior. The conceptual frameworks through which we function as moral agents, perceive and navigate the world, and engage in scientific practices are all constrained and guided by norms. This is, as mentioned in section 2, the inflated sense of normativity that would be required in order to demand a robust role for norms, but notice nowhere does it appear as if such norms are explaining behavior. To argue that norms are, in effect, practically real is to argue that because we are the kind of beings who perceive and act through norms, we take such frameworks and conceptual objects to be real (despite the empirical facts that may underlie such conceptual frameworks).[12] This relies on the intersubjective and practical nature of norms to guide our actions and inferences, constrain our linguistic practices, or ground our moral obligations. Yet, in none of these cases would we claim that norms explain said actions or practices.

Persons, as the basic object of the manifest image, are shot through with normativity. But here is where deVries' conception of practical reality is most important. In order to avoid conflating the description of persons found within the scientific image with the normative conception of persons in the manifest image (as well as collapsing the latter into the former), deVries constructs a classification or analysis of persons in the manifest image as being essentially norm-governed beings. This is a vision of humanity from a specific perspective, but one that stretches beyond subjective impressions and is seemingly practically indispensable:

> Does Sellars's treatment of persons and intentionality demote them to subjective illusions like ghosts or poltergeists? No. It does mean that persons and intentional states are phenomena available only to a certain point of view, the point of view of a self-conscious, rational, logic-using agent who is a member of a community that is, individually and collectively, engaged in pursuing various ends in a world it did not make.
> DEVRIES 2005, 278

---

12   DeVries is clear that such the scientific image derives its practical reality form the manifest image – a conceptual articulation of the way in which we 'connect' scientific concepts and terms with their pragmatic upshots, while the scientific image functions as more empirically real because it is "more determinate more complete, and better supported." See deVries 2005, 272.

Returning to deVries' discussion of practical reality, from the perspective of persons as self-conscious beings, normative concepts and discourse appear as simply ineliminable. Insofar as we are concerned with understanding persons as persons, then we are somewhat forced to recognize the role of norms in understanding that which is essentially norm-governed behavior.

What does this mean in the context of Turner's argument? DeVries' reading of Sellars provides us with an understanding of norms that sharply turns away from the idea that normativity only or primarily fulfills an explanatory role. The sciences, as discussed above, do all of the describing and explaining necessary to understand a mind-independent world. Yet, I imagine Turner's reply would simply be that such scientific descriptions of persons—once pushed to their logical conclusions – would simply replace these norm-governed view of persons. While it may be true that such concepts make sense from a given perspective, there is little reason to think that perspective (Sellars's manifest image) is a necessary one for understanding our place in the world. From Turner's standpoint, the argument is about whether such a perspective must eventually be used to explain our practices and place in the world. If such conceptual frameworks are playing no ultimate role in explaining our actions, then in what sense must we buy what they are offering? Why think we need an explication of conceptual frameworks that, in fact, do not fulfill the role of explaining our actions?

O'Shea argues that understanding normative concepts as those through which we live allows us to draw a distinction between our ontological commitments (as described by science) and those that are required to see the world through human eyes. The latter sort of concepts need not be reduced to scientific description or explanation, but can maintain coherence within a scientific picture by conceding ontological status to the sciences, while claiming some logically independent role for themselves. This argument is embodied in Sellars's claim that normative concepts should be considered "causally reducible, yet logically irreducible." By this, Sellars meant that such concepts can be described or explained from a scientific perspective, but their ability to characterize behavior itself is not collapsible into descriptions or explanations of behavior. Sellars's *scientia mensura* idea quoted above—that, when it comes to description and explanation, science is the measure of all things—can explain our behavior, but it fails to characterize or analyze human behavior as such. And without recognizing the role normative concepts play in characterizing and guiding uniquely human behavior, we have misunderstood the very nature of normativity itself.

O'Shea explicitly draws a distinction between what it is for Sellars to follow the analytic, as opposed to explanatory, task in his overall project: the analytic task is one of that begins "with socially instituted norms of linguistic practice" and attempts to flesh out the complex relationship between the norms that constitute and guide our behavior, and the uniformities in behavior that embody those norms (O'Shea 2010, 466). The analytic task characterizes the conceptual relationships between norms and behavior without explaining the behavior itself. The explanatory task, on the other hand, is "to show that the essentially normatively characterized intensional conceptual activities of persons, while conceptually irreducible and pragmatically ineliminable, can in principle be given an ideal explanatory account in purely extensional, naturalistic terms" (O'Shea 2010, 465). If convinced of this distinction, one can see how Turner's objections towards normativity might seem initially off-base. The analytic task of philosophy, in its effort to characterize and classify uniformities of behavior as fulfilling various functional/conceptual roles (and, thus, account for the conceptual understanding of human agency), does not attempt to explain human practices, but, instead, articulates how the conceptual order through which we live is embodied in practical uniformities of behavior. This provides a role for normativity to play that is involved in explanations of behavior (insofar as we are concerned with finding a specifically conceptual understanding of human practices), that is itself not an explanation of said behavior. As noted in O'Shea's original distinction, the explanatory task is the process through which the sciences will attempt to explain such conceptual activity in naturalistic terms (O'Shea 2010, 465).

While Klemick's disagreement with us (as found in his "quasi-realist" reading of Sellars) turns on how to read Sellars's metaethics, I take it the larger issue is just how to understand the relationship between normative and non-normative discourse. So, the particulars of our disagreement over Sellars is, I think, less relevant than the issues Klemick's critique highlights. Specifically, the idea that a defender of Sellars can retain a gap between the normative and non-normative, yet also argue that normative discourse (while *sui generis*) fits perfectly well within a completed scientific picture of humanity encapsulates Turner's own confusion over normativists' dual commitments to naturalism and normativism. Why does this confusion arise? Klemick argues the root of our misreading of Sellars is due to the fact that we start with the assumption that various aspects of Sellars's normative picture of humanity's place in the world exist in order to explain (Klemick 2018, 22). Instead, one should read Sellars as advocating for an understanding of the normative-laden manifest image as supplementing "the ideal scientific description with purely practical language for purely practical reasons" (Klemick 2018, 22). Even if our thoughts and obligations explain our behavior from within a scientific framework, normative terms themselves would only be mentioned (not used) in these explanations, ergo even when normative terms appear in said explanations, their role is not to explain the actions themselves.[13]

Arguing that normative concepts and terms themselves do not explain turns on the same distinction between analysis and explanation one finds in O'Shea; the "lynchpin" of Klemick's argument turns on the idea that once properly analyzed, we would see ought-statements (as one example of normative discourse) as expressions of intentions and, therefore, "fundamentally non-descriptive" (Klemick 2018, 23). Where deVries, O'Shea, and Klemick converge is on the idea that normativity (as it is necessarily found in conceptual frameworks or linguistic rules) is a requirement for an intelligible, humanistic conception of knowing and being in the world. While normativity and normative discourse itself may not purport to explain anything, explanations that are missing the normative dimension of human practices (ostensibly the dimension captured in normative accounts of human behavior) overlook a fundamentally practical and necessary aspect of our experience and conceptual articulation of our world.

Can these theoretical moves avoid Turner's objections to normativist accounts of persons? I take it the argument between explanation and analysis goes back to the question of what, exactly, these concepts are doing. And pointing out that they are 'characterizing behavior' and, thus, are not explaining behavior, does not necessarily avoid the explanatory aspects of the issue. From the anti-normativist standpoint, the argument is about just why we need to invoke these concepts in the first place (outside of placeholders for more complicated explanations of human behavior). And this is where we become repeatedly stuck on the same issue: if normative concepts are not explaining behavior, then what are they doing? Why must we use such concepts to characterize or analyze human behavior? Why cannot we use other concepts (such as the ones available through the social sciences) to account for human behavior? More so, why can't we treat normative concepts as mislabeled pieces in a fictional puzzle of how human behavior is really grounded? There is an impulse to deny this conclusion – to argue, instead, that concepts so practically embedded in our lives cannot, at bottom, be false or misleading (even

---

13   This echoes O'Shea's argument that even in a completed scientific image of humanity, norms would retain their conceptually ineliminable role in characterizing our practices: "Is anyone *saying* anything in this ideal, stereoscopically integrated image of persons-in-the-world? If so, then their sayings and doings about and amongst the microphysical phenomena will be normatively governed by whatever shared intentions will have generated the implicit principles that have given them a *knowable world* for their sayings and doings to be about in the first place" (O'Shea 2007, 189).

though the normativists can accept the fact that concepts are not carving the world at its joints).[14] Thus, there are good motivations for drawing a distinction between empirical and practical reality, one which saves such concepts from being *completely* in error by providing a perspective through which they get to count as [intersubjectively] true (in the sense that we are, all things considered, warranted in asserting said concept). Thus, the existential crisis of seeing our day-to-day concepts as—at their core—utter fabrications is avoided.

More directly to the explanatory point, it surely seems as if normative concepts and terms are being used in order to explain behavior. Pushing the conceptual goal posts back in order to show how normative concepts or terms characterize behavior, or how such concepts are necessary for our practical engagement with the world, does not squarely deny the explanatory role such concepts may play. What are these characterizations of behavior doing? What is the point of invoking such a practice if it does not, in some sense, factor into our explanations of practices as a whole? The Sellarsian tradition has an answer to these question: normative concepts or terms arise out of analyzing our behavior, which in turn gives us a non-descriptive or non-explanatory account of concepts. Yet, even if explanation is not the primary reason for using such concepts, it would seem that an analysis of some human practice is, at bottom, helping explain the behavior in question. Otherwise, what is the point of invoking an analysis of normative concepts or discourse?

Frequently, what seems to be missing in these arguments are not claims to the effect that we ought to distinguish between normative and descriptive discourse, or that different kinds of discourse are amenable to different kinds of treatments (e.g., description, explanation, analysis), but an answer to the question of exactly why we are required to do so. I imagine this will be Turner's response to the Sellarsian tradition: even if one is claiming there is a substantive distinction between analyzing normative discourse and explaining it, it is not clear these different approaches do not bottom out in explanation.

4   Conclusion

What I take to be the challenges and possible responses to Turner's rejection of normativism (from a Sellarsian standpoint) can be encapsulated in two main points: 1) Many of Turner's objections to normativism are not applicable to a Sellarsian variant of the position because 2) normative concepts or discourse

---

14   See deVries 2005, 271–272.

are not in the business of explaining, but instead express, characterize, or otherwise analyze human practices (as opposed to explaining them). That being said, Sellarsian defenses of normativity are not clearly correct that normative concepts or discourse are not—in the end—invoked in order to explain some aspect of behavior. I have offered some reasons to doubt the Sellarsian response to these concerns (hopefully in the spirit of what I think would be Turner's objections to the various positions). Even if Turner is correct about the explanatory inertness of normativity (as least as it is formulated by the normativist—Sellarsian or otherwise), we are still left with the issue about how to think through the practical concepts through which we live in the world.

And here, perhaps, is where the Sellarsian has a leg up on Turner's position. If we are willing to accept normativity as something akin to Turner's idea of a "Good Bad Theory," then we might have good reason to think that normative concepts and discourse are, in a practical sense, ineliminable and play a role in explanation (albeit one that could eventually be eclipsed by the sciences). Turner would be right that such concepts are not required to explain human behavior per se, but they might be practically ineliminable for our interactions with the world (actions which, in part, encompass explanation itself). Turner might also be right that this kind of practical stance need not exhibit the 'necessity of the normative', but it would go some distance in showing how it might be difficult to explain our practical interactions without them. While not required in the universal sense that was discussed at the beginning of this chapter, they might simply be too useful for any account of human behavior to be eliminated.

Like any good compromise, this would make both sides of the debate wildly unhappy. One imagines Turner would see this as simply sneaking normativity through the backdoor once again, while many Sellarsians would see this as essentially abandoning Sellars's project of constructing a stereoscopic image of humanity's place in the world.[15] The main way this differs from O'Shea's or deVries' suggestions above is in the idea that such concepts are always understood—in the end—as eliminable. I read O'Shea and deVries as arguing

---

15   In terms of Turner's complaint here, you can see this in his concluding remarks about lustral rites: "Even if we construe Zande witchcraft beliefs as a Good Bad Theory, it is still a theory. The connections between the elements are still rational. Even the account given here assumes some kind of rationality. Rationality is a normative concept, indeed the normative concept par excellence. So this line of argument is no escape from normativity" (Turner 2010, 117). Yet I do not think such localized conceptions of normativity would need to be seen as theories in any strong sense, which would avoid the need for a rational connection in the sense discussed by Turner.

any instance that demands our conceptual frameworks be used simply cannot allow for these concepts to be [eventually] eliminated. This is just a disagreement on one point, but it is clearly one that holds significant ramifications for one's conception of normativity. But the point that has to be reconciled—and I leave this for Turner to address—is whether the anti-normativist can show why conceptions of normativity that hold a non-factualist, non-explanatory role for normative concepts or terms cannot work.[16]

References

Brandom, R. 1979. "Freedom and Constraint by Norms." *American Philosophical Quarterly* 16: 187–196.
deVries, W. 2005. *Wilfrid Sellars*. Montreal: McGill-Queen's University Press.
Gibbard, A. 2013. *Meaning and Normativity*. Oxford: Oxford University Press.
Klemick, G. 2018. "Sellars Metaehitcal Quasi-Realism." *Synthese*, https://doi.org/10.1007/s11229-018-1804-x.
Kusch, M. 2006. *A Sceptical Guide to Meaning and Rules*. Montreal: McGill-Queen's University Press.
O'Shea, J. 2007. *Wilfrid Sellars*. Cambridge: Polity Press.
O'Shea, J. 2010. "Normativity and Scientific Naturalism in Sellars' 'Janus-Faced' Space of Reasons." *International Journal of Philosophical Studies* 18: 459–471.
Olen, P. 2016. *Wilfrid Sellars and the Foundations of Normativity*. London: Palgrave Macmillan.
Olen P. and Turner, S. 2015. "Durkheim, Sellars, and the Origins of Collective Intentionality." *British Journal for the History of Philosophy* 23: 954–975.
Olen, P. and Turner, S. 2016. "Was Sellars an Error Theorist?" *Synthese* 193: 2053–2075.
Sellars, W. [1956] 2000. Empiricism and the Philosophy of Mind. In *Knowledge, Mind, and the Given: Reading Wilfrid Sellars's "Empiricism and the Philosophy of Mind,"* eds.

---

16 A final way to look at the difference in viewpoints is to ask whether the *thought* of normative concepts or rules is enough to explain human practices, or whether the explanation of such practices requires concepts or rules that somehow reach 'above and beyond' such thoughts. While it would be fair to characterize the Sellarsian view as thinking the social, or more so shared, nature of intentions and claims demands an idea of concepts or rules to exist beyond our mere thoughts of them (thus securing the intersubjective nature of norms), Turner thinks the belief in such shared concepts (pragmatically coordinated and settled) is enough to get the explanatory job done. What matters from an explanatory standpoint is not whether such concepts or norms are 'genuinely' issued by collective intentions, but whether one *thinks that* such concepts or norms are shared.

Willem deVries and Timm Triplett. Indianapolis: Hackett Publishing Company, 205–276.

Turner, S. 2010. *Explaining the Normative*. Cambridge: Polity Press.

Turner, S. 2013. "The Argument of Explaining the Normative." *Revista Internacional de Sociología* 71: 192–194.

Turner, S. 2013a. "Where Explanation Ends: Understanding as the Place the Spade Turns in the Social Sciences." *Studies in the History and Philosophy of Science* 44: 532–538.

Norms

You Can't Always Get What You Want … but You Can Get What You Need

David Henderson and Terence Horgan

Abstract

In Cognitive Science and the Social: A Primer (2018), Stephen Turner provides a head-spinning catalog of difficulties confronting those working within a wide range of disciplines. The difficulties arise from the ways in which what is emerging from thinking about what is really going on at the level of underlying cognitive (or cognitive-ish) processes seems not to mesh with much that has been supposed in a standard (dominant and venerable) framework for work in the social sciences (or with much that has gone on in standard cognitive science). The picture Turner provides is, admittedly, murky—as the recent work Turner surveys is diverse and developing, having cross-cutting currents. In this paper, we focus on a narrow range of work in the social sciences—work on social norms. This would seem a fitting focus, as it deploys intentional psychology in ways that Turner argues are crucially problematic: invoking shared rules and expectations within communities. We take to heart some of the trends in cognitive science to which Turner rightly calls attention. We argue that, properly understood, many important themes in work such as Bicchieri's (and Guala's, and Pettit's) can be recast in ways that are not problematic in light of emerging cognitive science. When it comes to understanding social norms, we likely will not get what one might have traditionally wanted, but we will get what we need—social norms.

Keywords

Norms – Explanation – Rules – Verstehen – Representation – Turner – Bicchieri

1   Plan

In *Cognitive Science and the Social: A Primer* (2018), Stephen Turner argues that there are deep tensions in the concepts that are central to what should be mutually supporting, integratable, domains: the concepts at home in the various human sciences (such as anthropology, sociology, economics, and much psychology) seem undercut by the concepts and results emerging in cognitive science. Turner believes that these tensions are very likely not to be mitigated by ongoing work in the various fields—the problems are ineliminable. Reminiscent of Davidson, and perhaps for related reasons, Turner insists that it is unlikely that there will be a breakthrough at the level of the cognitive sciences that ultimately allows us to make good on the entities and processes imagined in the human sciences. The human sciences—the social sciences and much psychology—are said to be wedded to an essentially dramatic idiom of beliefs and desires—a conceptual framework tied to a what can be gotten by mirroring others in simulation. What is grasped in this way is understood to be shared. Of particular concern to us here is that agents in communities are said to share rules or norms and to share expectations for conformity to the norms, which supposedly accounts for how humans come to coordinate and cooperate. But, Turner insists, cognitive science finds variation and difference where the human sciences see sharing and sameness.

This kind of pessimism remains jarring—despite some variant of this idea being around at least since Davidson. Many of us suspect that there are greater prospects for an integrated understanding of human social and cognitive life than is projected—we hold out for greater commensurability between work and results across scientific disciplines. One supposes that work in the human sciences and work in cognitive science might at some remove bear a relation to each other like that between biology and chemistry, or between chemistry and physics. Our understanding of physics allows us to account for chemical phenomena, vindicating, perhaps with some refinement, the generalizations afforded by chemistry. These, in turn, allow us to understand what is going on in biological phenomena—and to refine our generalizations about classes of biological systems and processes. In the bargain, the understanding of processes at the "lower level" affords some support for our understanding of processes at the "higher levels." Of course, it may be granted that this comes with refinements that acknowledge some roughness in generalizations thereby supported. Acknowledging such refinements, we thereby arrive at an epistemically enhanced confidence in those generalizations. Associated with all this, one commonly witnesses a kind of conceptual development—commonly treated as a matter of refinement in conceptions associated with concepts. Famously, conceptions associated with some concepts have seen deep refinements. For example, concepts such as GENE and SPECIES have undergone such fragmentation that one is inclined to say that earlier concepts have been replaced—with multiple concepts being recognized as descendents of those in use earlier. Still, there is a kind of recognizable continuity in the concepts in play in biology, and with the changes come a form of commensuration of the concepts across the related sciences.

Can one expect, or at least reasonably look for, a parallel commensuration and integration between the human sciences trafficking in intentional idiom and cognitive science? Turner (perhaps with relish) worries that there are good reasons to think that no such reassuring relationship will (could) emerge with further work in and across these disciplines. As we read him, a central issue concerns the extent to which the human sciences (with their intentional idiom/concepts) could be conceptually plastic in a way that is analogous to conceptual plasticity evinced in the biological sciences. Such plasticity has allowed for the conceptual and epistemic integration of work focused on biological domains with work on relatable physical domains.

After getting clear on Turner's nay-sayings, we focus on one body of theoretical work in the human sciences—work on social norms of various stripes. This work deploys intentional psychology in ways that Turner argues are crucially problematic: invoking rules and expectations that are supposedly shared across agents. We argue that such work may be better off than Turner suggests.

2 Stephen Turner's Guide to a Livable Morass

The preponderance of work in the human science involves the attribution of intentional states—beliefs and desires, and related events or states (perceptual recognition, moods, representations of rules, and so on). Agents are understood to respond to these by making decisions and inferences, thereby coming to have yet further beliefs and desires, and to undertake actions. Of course, to correctly identify such antecedents and consequences—one must, under interpretation, attribute contents which are, in some sense, shared across the agents whose beliefs, desires, and actions are thereby accounted for. What concerns Turner (2018), and us in this paper, is the idea that the attribution of such intentional states constrains the human and social sciences within conceptual boxes that foreclose the kind of conceptual refinements and realignments that would be needed to engage fruitfully with work in the cognitive sciences. Turner argues that the human sciences are thereby stuck in the conceptual mud. We argue that they need not be.

As Turner develops his misgivings in *Cognitive Science and the Social* the problems that arise when attributing mental/intentional states revolve around two aspects of the state-concepts with which the human sciences are heavily invested: (1) the states are supposedly internal states that are at the same time shared across agents, and (2) the states are paradigmatically of a sort grasped by an interpretive practice (Weber's narrow *verstehen*) in which one deploys one's own cognitive processes on feigned intentional states to model the thinking of agents.

2.1   *The Internal External Distinction—and the Idea of Sharing Internal States*

The vast preponderance of work within the human sciences trades in states that are in an important sense, internal. In calling these states "internal" Turner is not saying that (social scientists are committed to the idea that) all important features of intentional states turn on, or supervene on, features internal to the agent—on skin-in-states of the agent with or in such a state. Much of the work attributing beliefs and desires to agents seems to be in no tension with the idea that there may be a dimension to their meaning that turns upon wider relations to a world beyond the agent. Thinking about atoms, genes, and the like, may turn on the things in the world with which a community of agents have antecedently interacted. Similarly for thinking about classes and institutional positions—about poppers and presidents; and for thinking about individuals—Popper or Wittgenstein. The sense in which beliefs and desires, as the bread and butter of much work in the human sciences, are internal need not be in any tension with a view about whether content or semantics is at least partially externalist. Rather, the sense in which a given agent's belief and desires are thought to be internal is something on this order: the agent's having that belief at a time is a matter of something—a representational state, perhaps, or some pattern of activation across neurons--where (a) that state is itself internal to that agent as a biological system, and (b) such states causally interact with other such states in a way that is characteristic of beliefs, desires, and intentions. But, what way is that? Well, there is little reason to suppose that this is subject to precise a priori specification. Some would propose that it is a matter of some minimal degree of "rationality." We will return to such ideas below, for now, we note that it seems plausible that the range of ways in which such states can and do interact (and the range of states with which they interact) may be both (a) subject to empirical discovery by disciplines such as cognitive psychology (including perceptual psychology, the psychology of reasoning, and decision-making, and related social psychology), and (b) such as to have room for some diversity across agents.

Turner does not suppose that the human sciences are stuck in conceptual mud simply by virtue of pursuing issues in terms of internal states. Rather, his misgivings have to do with an additional thesis regarding those internal states to which the human sciences are wedded: the idea that these internal states—beliefs, desires, and the like—can be (and indeed, commonly are) "shared."

As Turner emphasizes, the commonsensical ways of talking within much of the human sciences supposes that you and we can share various beliefs and desires—and that our sharing these can account for our undertaking parallel or coordinated actions. When coordinating or cooperating, you and we can have many of the same beliefs and desires. For example, when playing an economic game, we can each have many internal representations that are the same in that they characterize the payoff structure of the choice situation.

But, to make Turner's misgiving vivid, suppose for a starting place that beliefs are representations realized in patterns of activation in one's neural net—that at least occurrent beliefs are. Standing beliefs would be realized in standing connections within an agent's neural net. Is it then at all plausible that folk really share beliefs as such internal states? For concreteness, think of an illustrative occurrent belief—say the belief that there is likely to be (continuing) significant anthropogenic climate change within the next 50 years. It should be immediately obvious that the relevant pattern of activation within any one of our embodied neural nets is likely different from the corresponding pattern of activation making for the relevant belief in any other of us. (Indeed, it seems that the pattern of activation representing this content in one of us today, just now, is likely to be somewhat different than the pattern of activation in that same agent representing that content a year ago.) Parallel points apply to patterns of connectivity that would make for the standing belief in question. In view of such variation and diversity, one might wonder: in what sense do we (you and I) share a belief? Do we really share an internal state? Insofar as we can reconstruct Turner's worry, it is that, by virtue of positing internal states of the sort they do, the human sciences are stuck in a kind of conceptual mud that will not mesh with work in cognitive science. The fine clay of the mud seems to turn on the idea of internal states that are shared—that they are or can be the same across each of a set of agents. Yet is would seem that the relevant internal states of agents will not be the same across agents who supposedly share the same state. (At the very least, sharing the same belief or desire—in the cases on which we later focus, sharing the same rule or normative sensibility—will need to allow for multiple realizability.)

2.2   *The Verstehen Bubble and a Kind of Interpretivist Anchor Around the Neck of the Social Sciences.*

Turner pursues a second line of thought, reinforcing the above misgivings about social scientific commitments to shared representation. The idea is to provide a diagnosis of a sort—accounting for why the human sciences (and social sciences in particular) are wedded to accounts in terms of such shared representations—and are thus stuck in a conceptual mud. The idea is that there is a particularly ready to hand interpretive practice—one likely rooted in some deep tendencies of homo sapiens as species—that makes intentional psychology almost unescapably epistemically attractive to us (including us in the human sciences). The practice can be understood broadly or narrowly, but it is the narrowly drawn practice—one rooted in the ease with which we humans deploy our own cognitive machinery on what we imagine are the intentional contents of others, simulating them empathetically—that accounts for the inescapability of the narrow practice and the related attraction of the broader interpretive practice. To continue the metaphor above: as an easy and available interpretive/explanatory practice, empathetic simulation constitutes roots by which the human sciences become stuck in the conceptual mud of supposedly shared internal states. Turner finds a reflections on these matters in Max Weber's understanding of sociological methods. Here is one pertinent passage:

> Weber defined sociology restrictively as the study of meaningful social action, which he described as *verstehende Soziologie*, or understanding sociology. He avoided philosophical language, including terms like intention. His account of Verstehen, or understanding, was not hermeneutic in any traditional sense. It focused instead on the capacity for employing empathy and achieving *Evidenz* with it that distinguished sociology, and by extension other sciences of action, from natural science. His thought was that for some kinds of action we have empathic understanding that is evident, that is to say requires no further grounding and is perhaps – this is one contemporary meaning of *Evidenz*, found in Brentano ... — evident to anyone observing the same action.
> TURNER 2018: 100-01

Roughly, the idea may be put in the form of twist on an old aphorism regarding the blandishments of Paris to simple farm folk:

> How can you keep [human scientists] down [toiling in the needed more revisionary cognitive science fields] when they have seen [the *Evidenz* of simple empathetic understanding]?

Turner notes that one can, of course, give the beginnings of a cognitive science account of empathetic *Evidenz*—an account of how, in certain contexts, what folk are doing can seem to be a matter of "directly accessible joint attention"(Turner 2018: 186). This account would appeal to mirror neurons as a basis for a form of "mind reading." But, what must be appreciated is that the attributions of intentional states delivered by such processes seem is so compelling as to make for an irresistible anchor—or so Turner suggests. The practice of simulation and its results give rise to what he terms the Verstehen bubble—a realm of intentional interpretation beyond which we humans are loathe to venture far or for long:

> This notion of meaning can be restated in cognitive science terms, more or less as follows: meaning, and the boundaries of the Verstehen bubble as the term has been used here, is the property of objects of joint attention. Joint attention makes the action "social" in Weber's sense because joint attention is inherently other-regarding. Moreover it directly links to neuronal processes – joint attention in primates involves mirror neurons.
> TURNER 2018: 186

We should hasten to clarify: Turner is not suggesting that all intentional states are directly accessible by empathetic *Evidenz*. Rather, the suggestion is that one needs to distinguish between a narrower Verstehen bubble—the domain of the empathetic Evidenz, itself—and a broader Verstehen bubble—the domain of what is interpretable in intentional terms. The idea is that the narrower form is such a cognitive attractor for us humans that we find the less evident form of hermeneutic interpretation (which deploys the same concepts and takes its departure from much that is Evidenz) irresistible itself. Given simulation as Evidenz—which spots such a compelling beginning in the form of an apparently *grasped/shared* intentional state--one cannot help but continue to fill in the hermeneutic puzzle. Here is Turner on the narrow Verstehen bubble:

> I have used the term "Verstehen bubble" without defining it, and there is a reason for this: the term is best understood in the narrow sense that Weber had in mind – the realm of the meaningful or intelligible, to which he added, for sociology, the qualifier of social, or oriented to other people. This is a definition within the Verstehen bubble: it uses more or less ordinary language of the sort we use in normal human communication. But we can reformulate this qualifier in cognitive science terms by reference to the concept of joint attention: something is in the Verstehen bubble if it is the object of joint attention, and potentially in the bubble if it is a potential object of joint attention. Joint attention can be defined as it is for monkeys – it involves the mirror neurons or the equivalent human system. But it is also accessible to consciousness: to be jointly attentive is to be conscious of the attention of the other.
> TURNER 2018: 207

Here, joint attention in the form of mirroring is understood as a matter of sharing an internal representation (or some constellation of representations, as it includes some shared awareness of the sharing).

Further passages that do not reflect only this narrow usage then point to a verstehen bubble in a broader sense: a bubble of interpretation—arising out of what is Evidenz, but involving also the hermeneutic understanding in intentional psychological terms that arises in a less direct and immediate interpretive back and forth. This broader verstehen bubble is spawned by the project of filling in the picture in extended intentional terms. Here again, it might be suggested, such accounts allow one to (apparently) "think with" or "think along" with the other—albeit with less "*evidenz*."

For example, perhaps one has with direct joint attention "thought along with" certain others as they have slit the throat of a farm animal, say a goat. Then, on what is "evidently" a solemn occasion, one finds them engaging in behavior that closely mirrors the earlier slaughter, but now with a large pumpkin! One does not need to "bleed out" a pumpkin—and one simply cannot get blood out of a pumpkin (or turnip, or other vetetable). Strange? Now, one notes that the agents also use words that were previously used in the earlier episode of joint attention involving the goat. What the hell is going on? Why do they treat the pumpkin as if they are slaughtering an animal for a feast? Pretty hard to resist inquiring—and doing so in a framework connected to what is and had been evident! With some work—via a hermeneutic back and forth—perhaps it may be possible to think along in this new context.

This makes for a pretty neat account of being stuck in the mud of intentional psychology and related interpretive practices! It affords the plausible beginnings of an account of a cognitive attractor of a sort. But, let us pursue some clarification.

3 A Needed Qualification: The Plasticity of the Broad Verstehen Bubble

There is reason to think that the verstehen bubble in Turner's broad sense may not be as constraining as the above would seem to suggest. The reason for so thinking revolves around this point: interpretive understanding, and thus the broader verstehen bubble, is cognitively penetrable by wide ranges of information about the ways in which people think—and such information can include results from cognitive science and psychology. Plausibly, much that is inside the broad verstehen bubble—much that is attributed to others under interpretation—is grasped in a way that already draws on much cognitive psychology. For example, recently, when walking across a general-purpose public space on a university campus, one of us, DH, encountered a man with a big sign, who was expressing a concern for immortal souls. As DH walked on, the man said that, if DH did not acquire some beliefs regarding an earlier human sacrifice, DH would end in a very bad place ... (apparently even worse than the Trump Whitehouse)! When he sensed (from DH's expression, using his mirror neuron system) a misgiving regarding these beliefs, the man doubled down to motivate DH: "the time is short, these are the final times." DH gathered that that this was to motivate, but it turns on a way of thinking to which DH is moderately resistant. It bears a striking resemblance to a marketing move: "act now while supplies last." As we understand the gambit, when it works, it does so by way of a cognitive heuristic related to framed loss—here the loss of an opportunity. Now, we ourselves do not find the ideas invoked easy to "think along with"—although the transitions are not difficult to follow and explain in light of our theoretical understanding of human cognitive processes. To think this way, one would have to buy the story about a way of avoiding impending hell in order to suppose that the clock was ticking, and thus to feel the looming loss of opportunities, which would motivate believing the story. (A strained circularity, we sense.) Still, one can diagnose the attempt to overuse a kind of heuristic without "thinking along with the agent" by way of an automatic triggering of one's own cognitive tendencies. One's "thinking along with" the other can be tutored by background understandings of cognitive psychology. As one of us argued at length elsewhere, not all interpretation is a matter of an empirically uninformed simulating those one seeks to understand (Henderson 2011). Much of it remains on the rails, not by virtue of a coincidence of cognitive processes in those one seeks to understand, but rather by being informed by rough invariant generalizations.

Based on other of Turner's writings, we believe that he would acknowledge that information of a descriptive psychological sort can indeed commonly inform the hermeneutic back and forth by one pursues interpretive understanding.[1] Even when one is thinking about one's subjects in light of generalizations regarding human cognitive processes, one can still be engaged in a familiar kind of interpretation, and arguably, one remains in the "verstehen bubble." We mention such interpretive contexts largely to say that Turner has not given a principled basis for thinking that the wide verstehen bubble need be narrowly constraining in a way that requires interpretation to mesh

---

1 Indeed, the point is reflected in Turner's *Sociological Explanation as Translation* (1980). Henderson gratefully recalls the influence that that discussion had on him as a graduate student and in developing the line of thought in David Henderson 1987, 1990, 1993.

poorly with cognitive science. It might mesh with cognitive psychology and cognitive science as it itself comes to be informed by the results in those disciplines.

Now, Turner doubtless would concede that the broad verstehen bubble has not been well delimited. Still, he would presumably insist that nothing we have said responds to what is central to his misgivings above: a range of human sciences, from the various interpretive social sciences to much work in cognitive psychology, proceed in terms of intentional states understood as internal states that are shared across agents—shared beliefs, shared desires, and the like. In all this, it is supposed that what got into you can be the same as what got into me. Doubts about this seem to be the pivot on which all issues turn for Turner. In subsequent sections of this paper, we want to focus on what we take to an exemplary bit of work in philosophically sensitive social science—good and promising work—which would seem on the face of it to be open for critique in light of Turner's concerns: work on social norms (of various stripes) that is informed by a range of ideas from economics, evolutionary psychology, and anthropology. In particular, we will focus on an account of norms advanced by Cristina Bicchieri (2006, 2017), although we could have focused on any of a range of related accounts. Our question is whether, and if so how, can a framework such as Bicchieri's be understood in a way that renders it unproblematic in light of Turner's misgivings.

4 Opulence vs. Austerity about Inter-Level Connections

Turner raises doubts about whether putative intentional psychological states really are instantiated in humans—and, in particular, whether such states really are shared across individuals (as is so often presupposed in the explanatory uses of folk-psychological concepts). His concerns can be usefully situated within a wider dialectical context: the familiar debate in philosophy of mind between three kinds of materialism, often called "reductive materialism," "nonreductive materialism," and "eliminative materialism." Each of these broad positions makes claims (i) about how putative psychological properties of a creature must be related to underlying neurophysical properties, in order for those putative psychological properties to be instantiated by the creature, and (ii) about whether or not the instantiation-conditions for such properties are likely to obtain in humans or other earthly creatures. (The three positions, in turn, each have a generalized version, pertaining to all putative inter-level relations between lower-level and higher-level scientific disciplines—with fundamental physics at the bottom level.)

Reductive materialism (e.g., Kim (1993) typically demands, as a condition for the instantiation of psychological properties, either identities or nomic coextensions between such properties and underlying neurophysical properties; it also typically requires the pertinent neurophysical properties to be "natural kinds" within neuroscience, rather than (say) being highly disjunctive. This position also affirms, optimistically, that in the case of humans and other creatures that are normally considered to have mentality, there really exist such inter-level identities or nomic coextensions between intentional psychological properties and certain natural-kind neurophysical properties.

Eliminative materialism (e.g., Churchland 1981; Stich 1983) typically affirms the same instantiation-requirements on psychological properties as does reductive materialism. Also, advocates of this position often suppose that such demands are probably met for *some* kinds of psychological properties, such as sensory-experiential properties like pain, itchiness, and visual color-experience. But with respect to the paradigmatically intentional mental properties posited by folk psychology—belief, desire, intention, expectation, and the like—eliminative materialism contends, pessimistically, that the (putatively) requisite mental-to-physical property identities or nomic coextensions do not obtain. Eliminative materialists conclude that folk-psychological intentional mental properties are not really instantiated by humans, and should be banished from mature scientific theorizing.

Reductive materialism and eliminative materialism share a construal of folk-psychological concepts that is *opulent,* in the following respect: given the background materialist assumption that humans are complex physico-chemical systems, the construal presumes that folk-psychological concepts require that the properties they express are instantiable in humans only if they are reductively correlated in humans with natural-kind neurophysical properties.

Nonreductive materialism (e.g., Fodor 1974), on the other hand, instead construes folk-psychological concepts as *austere* about the requisite inter-level relation between folk-psychological and neurophysical properties. Given the same materialist background assumption, this alternative conception only presumes that the folk-psychological concepts require that the properties they express must be *neurophysically realized* whenever they are instantiated in humans. This allows for the possibility that one and the same intentional mental property can be neurophysically realized in multiple different ways across individual humans—and indeed within a single human at different times. Moreover, nonreductive materialism allows for the possibility that neurophysical realizer-properties often are extremely complex, rather than constituting natural kinds at the neurophysical level of description and explanation;

it is enough that realized properties are themselves natural-kind properties at higher, psychological, level of description and explanation.

Turner's worries about the scientific legitimacy of the intentional concepts of folk psychology seem to us to be similar in spirit to the worries of the eliminative materialists. We ourselves, however, advocate nonreductive materialism. (Pertinent texts whose arguments we endorse include Fodor 1974; G. Graham and Horgan 1991; Henderson and Horgan 2005; Horgan and Woodward 1985; Horgan 1993a, 1993b) We will not rehearse here the case for nonreductive materialism, apart from the following observation. The opulent construal of the ideology of folk psychology, shared in common by reductive and eliminative materialists, imposes demands on inter-level connections between psychological properties and neurophysical properties that are not motivated in any clear or obvious way by the explanatory and predictive purposes for which folk psychology is normally employed. This fact imposes a heavy burden of proof on advocates of the opulent conception, a burden which we doubt they can successfully bear.

Our discussion in the remainder of this paper should be understood as emanating from our own affinity for nonreductive materialism, together with our sense that Turner's worries about intentional psychological concepts reflect a mistaken affinity on his part for eliminative materialism. Before proceeding, however, let us briefly elaborate upon our own favored version of nonreductive materialism, in ways that will prove useful below.

The elaboration concerns the relation of realization, between a mental property M and a neurophysical property P that realizes M in an agent (on a given occasion of M's instantiation). In order for P to qualify as a realizer of M, we suggest, P must subserve a pattern D of dispositions that *functionally conforms* (as we will put it) to M. Functional conformity is a somewhat flexible matter. Normally, various different specific disposition patterns, in different individuals or in a single individual at different times, can all functionally conform to a single intentional mental property M. It is enough that these differing patterns be *sufficiently similar* to one another. They need not be exactly alike.[2]

The underlying thought here is that one and the same intentional mental property—say, *believing that Donald Trump is not a stable genius*—can be

---

2   An important reason why the disposition patterns need not be exactly alike, as between two individuals each of whom instantiates mental property M, is that these individuals differ in some of the other mental properties they respectively instantiate. They might have somewhat different background beliefs from one another, for example, or somewhat different desires. The specific pattern of dispositions that an M-realizing property subserves, in a particular individual, typically depends in part upon other mental properties that the individual instantiates.

instantiated respectively in two different agents by two respective neurophysical states P and P′ even if P subserves in the first agent a pattern D of psychological and behavioral dispositions that differs somewhat from the corresponding disposition-pattern D′ that P′ subserves in the second agent. There is no single, unique, pattern of dispositions that one must possess in order to rightly qualify as believing that Donald is not a stable genius; multiple different patterns will all suffice, provided that they are sufficiently similar to one another.

An additional important point, by way of further elaboration of the notion of multiple realization, is that there can be horizontal "levels" even within a single field of inquiry—with higher-level properties in the given field being multiply realizable by lower-level properties in that same field. In particular, this can happen within the field of psychology, especially insofar as one construes psychology as encompassing both common-sense folk psychology and also those aspects of cognitive science that go beyond the conceptual framework of pre-scientific common sense.

This being so, higher-level psychological properties might well be multiply realizable by lower-level psychological properties.[3] Distinct lower-level psychological properties Q_1, ..., Q_n will realize a single higher-level psychological property M if the following conditions obtain: first, Q_1, ..., Q_n, when successively instantiated in distinct agents a_1, ..., a_n, successively subserve disposition patterns D_1, ..., D_n in those successive agents; and second, each of these disposition patterns functionally conforms to the property M. The disposition patterns need not be identical to one another; it is enough that they are sufficiently similar that they all qualify as functionally conforming to M.

5   Norms? Rules? Shared?

Social norms have been the focus of much recent cross-disciplinary work by sociologists, anthropologists, and economists—and by several philosophers. To a first approximation, social norms are rules that serve to coordinate

---

3   Indeed, this could happen iteratively within psychology, via a hierarchy of levels: a high-level psychological property could be multiply realizable by psychological properties at a lower level, each of these latter properties could be multiply realizable by psychological properties at a still-lower level, and (potentially) so on. An analogous situation is familiar in computer science, involving implementational hierarchies. ("Implementation" is the computer-science word for what philosophers call realization.) A computer program written in a high-level programming language is multiply implementable by programs written in llower-level programming languages, which themselves are implementable by programs written in yet-lower level programming languages, ..., etc. on down to so-called "machine language."

humans as members of social groups—social norms (partly) explain the coordinated and cooperative behavior one finds among humans within their various social groups. Social norms are not necessarily explicitly represented or clearly stated rules; followers may only become consciously aware of them when they are broken, if then. (Think of the norm for conversational speaking distance.)

The concept of a Social Norm would seem to be cast from the conceptual mud of which Turner cautions. There are several philosophical analyses one might consult, but *all ultimately involve the idea that some rule-like content comes to be shared among interacting agents*, and many of those agents having preferences for acting accordingly, at least provided enough others do so as well.

Some think of social norms themselves as the regularities in behavior, but ultimately talk of something on the order of shared rules will enter their account. Thus, Pettit sees social norms as regularities in behavior caused or sustained by normative attitudes. Peter Graham reconstructs Philip Pettit's account as follows:

> A regularity R in the behavior of members of a population P, when they are agents in a recurrent situation S, is a social norm to the extent that, in any instance of S among members of P:
> (i) Members of P conform to R (and this is common knowledge)
> (ii) Members of P prescribe conforming to R (believe each of us ought to do R) and disapprove of failures (and this is common knowledge).
> (iii) The fact that nearly everyone approves (believes one ought to conform) and disapproves (believes it is wrong not to conform) helps to insure that nearly everyone conforms. (2015: 250–1).

According to Pettit (1990), a social norm is socially *normal* (in the statistical sense)—and it is a regularity in behavior that results from *a (commonly held) normative prescription* for the actions undertaken. As reflected above, this seems to require (enough) folk to *share* some representation of a way of acting—and to *share* expectations for conformity to *R* within the group, and to *share* expectations for common reactions to conforming and deviating actions.

Geoffrey Brennan, Lina Eriksson, Robert Goodin, and Nicholas Southwood (2013) see social norms as socially *shared* normative attitudes, whether they influence behavior or not. So they reject Pettit's idea that social norms *as such* are regularities in behavior (though they agree that norms *typically* cause or sustain regularities in behavior). Thus they key upon what are the latter clauses of Pettit's definition. For Brennan et al, the social "norms of a group are the rules or normative principles that are accepted by the group" (Brennan et al. 2013: 18). Again, shared "rules or normative principles" are in view.

We here focus on Cristina Bicchieri's account, which understands norms as involving *shared* rules—and *shared or similar expectations and preferences* for conformity to those rules. Bicchieri's approach is rooted in economic thinking regarding cooperation and coordination in social games—in situations in which the consequences of an individual's choice will turn on the choices made by others. Of course, all this turns on the set of agents understanding outcomes in shared ways (*mutatis mutandis*).

Bicchieri (2006, see also 2017) distinguishes three kinds of broadly social norms: social norms in her narrow usage (to be explicated below), descriptive norms, and conventions (where conventions are a subset of descriptive norms). She uses the following ideas to define these categories: *conditional preferences, empirical expectations, normative expectations,* and *normative expectations with sanctions.*

A *conditional preference* is a preference to do something conditional on something else obtaining. One prefers to drive on the right-hand side of the street, provided that is what others in the community are doing. An *empirical expectation* is an empirical belief that people in a population will act a certain way in a recurrent kind of situation—for example, the expectation that others will drive on the right-hand side of the street. A *normative expectation* is a belief that many or most of the people in a population expect such behavior and also think that folk ought to act a certain way in a certain recurrent kind of situation.

Each of Bicchieri's three differing kinds of norms arise in response to a specific kind of social choice situation. Kinds of choice situations are understood in terms of classes of decision-theoretic social games. We focus here on social norms (on Bicchieri's restrictive usage). These are norms dealing with mixed-motive games—and such games themselves require that agents share the ordering of preferences regarding payoffs. A social norm is then understood as a shared rule, specifying coordinated choices that make for an equilibrium (within such a choice situation) (Bicchieri, 2006, pp. 33–4). Obviously, the picture involves a range of internal states—intentional states—that must be instanced across a preponderance of agents in the social group. Here is the account in a nutshell:

> SOCIAL NORM: Let R be a behavior rule for situations of type S, where S can be represented as a mixed-motive game. We say that R is a social norm in a population P if there exists a sufficiently large subset P of conditional followers of R in the population P such that for each individual i in the population of conditional followers:

1. *Contingency:* i knows that rule R exists and applies to situations of type S;
2. *Conditional Preference:* i prefers to conform to R in situations of type S on the condition that:
   a. (*Empirical Expectations*) i believes that a sufficiently large subset of P conforms to R in situations of type S; AND
   b. either
      - (Normative Expectations) i believes that a sufficiently large subset of P "normatively" expects i to conform to R in situations of type S, or
      - (Normative Expectations with Sanctions) i believes that a sufficiently large subset of P expects i to conform to R in situations of type S, prefers i to so conform, and may award i for compliance or punish i for non-compliance.

On this account, there can be a social norm without it being followed—this explication of the notion of a social norm only requires that the members of *Pcf*, the sufficiently large subset of the population, have a conditional preference for following R. On the other hand, "A social norm R is followed by a population P if there exists a sufficiently large subset $Pf \subseteq Pcf$ such that for each individual $i \in Pf$, conditions 2(a) and either 2(b) or 2(b') are met for i." (Bicchieri 2006, 11).[4]

One can highlight the range of intentional states supposed here to be shared across many of the relevant agents: Many members *of the population* each *want/prefer* to act a certain way (follow a *rule R* in S), conditional on the *belief* that a sufficiently large subset of the population conforms to R in S, and the *belief* that a sufficiently large subset of the population expects them to do R in S. They *don't want* to do R in S regardless of what they *believe* other people do

---

4 *Descriptive norms*, in Bicchieri's taxonomy, have to do with situations that can be characterized as coordination games (rather than mixed motive games).
　Let R be a behavioral rule for situations of type S, where S is a coordination game. We say that R is a descriptive norm in a population P, if there exists a sufficiently large subset $Pcf \subseteq P$, such that for each individual $i \in Pcf$:
　[1] Contingency—i knows that R exists and applies to the situations of type S,
　[2] Conditional Preferences—i prefers to conform to R in situations of type S, given that [the empirical and normative expectations below are jointly satisfied]:
　　a. Empirical Expectations—i believes that some sufficiently large subset of the population conforms to R in S (Bicchieri 2006, 31-2)
　On Bicchieri's account, conventions are a special class of descriptive norms (Bicchieri 2006, 38).

or what they *believe* other people normatively expect of them. All else being equal, they may not want to do R in S. They are motivated to do R in S because they *believe* that's what other people do in S, and they *believe* they are expected by others to do R in S. They are motivated to do what they *believe* other people do and normatively expect them to do. In all this they are responsive to some shared sense for some public good that results.

Bicchieri's account seems thus to be the kind of account that, by Turner's lights, is firmly stuck in the conceptual mud—it seems to posit internal representations (the kind of internal states featuring in desiring and cognitive states) that are shared across agents. Even more centrally, the account requires that folk each grasp or share the rule around which they come to be coordinated. But in just what ways must agents be understood to share representations for the account to explain social goings ons?

6 The Representation of Rules

Bicchieri's norms-as-rules approach seems on its face to demand psychological realism concerning the elements involved—the rules, the preferences, the expectations, how these might be formed or conditioned, how these might feature in agents' cognition, and how these might be acquired and distributed in a population. In exemplary fashion, Bicchieri is attentive to psychological work regarding how local environmental factors can provide individuals with information about what people do, or about peoples' evaluations of others' actions, and can thus make salient matters on which norm adherence depends (Bicchieri 2006, 63–70, 152–175). She recognizes the significance of issues regarding *just how* "norms are represented in memory" and how the situational salience of competing (previously learned) normative models or rules would depend on the dynamics of memory (2006, 70–3). She is interested in the way in which situations are interpreted so as to prime the application of a rule. With an openness to developments in cognitive psychology, evolutionary psychology, and cognitive science, such an approach seeks to avoid the pitfall of offering merely some convenient just-so story about coordination at the social level. It provides the promise of significant integration with work in cognitive psychology and experimental economics. As pursued by Bicchieri, it allows one to engage in a range of informed experimental manipulations to test ideas about social and descriptive norms.

For our purposes here, one question warrants special attention: *how to best understand talk of shared "rules" or "behavioral rules."* What is it to "know that some rule exists"? What is it to have learned some rule, the same rule as many others, so that (with related expectations and preferences) many in the relevant community come to follow the same rule? One can find some tantalizing hints scattered about Bicchieri's discussions. We will mention three discussions that seem particularly noteworthy: (1) her discussion of what she terms "local norms," (2) her discussion of conversational speaking distance, and (3) her drawing on ideas about prototypes and similarity judgments. These discussions point in a similar direction: *that one should be cautious, and not overly demanding, about how similar different agents need to be in order for talk of shared rules to be correctly applicable to them.*

We pursue a constructive project: clarifying in outline what the relevant internal states would need to be like, drawing on hints one finds in Bicchieri's writing.

To understand and explain folk, one must pay attention to their "local norms." Bicchieri explains that norms are *local* when their "interpretation" and the "expectations and prescriptions that surround them vary with the objects, people, and situations to which they apply" (Bicchieri 2006, 83). This seems to involve a distinction between a rule as some linguistic formulation ("divide resources fairly," or "don't litter") and a rule as interpreted. The rule-as-interpreted is associated with a more fleshed out understanding of what is fair, or of what counts as littering. Agents might hold or share the same rule in the sense of embracing the same general formulation—"divide resources fairly"—while not sharing the same local norm of fairness. Thus, some cultures would allow one to take family ties into account in awarding jobs, others would account that unfair. It seems reasonable to put the point thus: what is learned—*the norm as rule that directs behavior*, the rule around which folk supposedly attain coordination or a cooperative equilibrium, the rule that features in accounts of the behavior observed—*is the local norm*. The two cultural groups just envisioned learn and have different rules or norms. Within each group, agents supposedly share a local norm.

Of course, folk in the two groups might use the same words to characterize what they are doing as they follow their respective rules—saying that they are being fair, and following the norm of fairness. They might even argue about what it is to be fair. But, insofar as one seeks to account for the cooperative or coordinated choices of the relevant agents, it seems that one should see agents within the two groups as responding to different norms/rules. We here can get some perspective on the problematic that is central to Turner's misgivings over the idea of shared internal representations. What really is shared? Or what would sharing need to be in order for the envisioned approach to social norms to explain patterns of choices in a community? One way of bringing out the issue might be to think about a distinction one finds in the semantic literature on the individuation of concepts. There it is said that *concepts* are semantic entities—they determine extensions, the things of which the concept can be truly predicated. Thus, the concept of BIRD determines what things are truly said to be birds, the concept of ATOM determines what can be said to be truly said to be atoms, the concept of FAIR determines what actions/policies/distributions can be said to be fair, and so on. Of course, it is noted that at any given time, folk can have a *conception* of any of these matters that ill accords with that the concept dictates: famously, the conceptions had by historical state-of-the-art scientists positing atoms (for example, Dalton and fellow atomists) led them to mistake molecules for atoms—the community's conception did not, it is said, define or accord with the relevant concept. Similarly for the concept of HEAT. And similarly for concepts of BIRD or FISH.

We noted above that *norms-as-rules are best understood as local rules, and it seems that local rules are best understood as something on the order of shared (or relevantly similar?) conceptions.* Two examples. Perhaps the two communities envisioned above are using one concept—*the* concept FAIR—and differ in their conceptions of fairness. But, it is their conceptions that account for their respective practices. Their rule—insofar as it affords an account for cooperation in the respective groups—turns upon sharing) in conceptions. Perhaps two communities differ in their conception of food, or of a feast. What one can expect to find on the table when joining them in a meal or feast will depend on their conceptions—and not on some functional kind satisfying a biologist's concept of FOOD (if there were such a concept).

On Bicchieri's account, conventional or descriptive norms regulate choices in situations that amount to coordination games rather than cooperation games. But, in parallel fashion, there are said to be shared local rules and expectations in play. One can learn from these discussions, as they certainly make it strained to talk uncritically of "rules." For example, she discusses those normative sensibilities apparently at work regulating conversational speaking distances in a culture. Here, folk need not have some rule-statement or rule-formulation, and thus there is no need for them to do anything that would count as literally "interpreting" their "rule" so that they can apply it to the situation at hand. It is not as though folk start with a rule—thought of as some expression of a prescription: "maintain fitting conversational speaking distances"—then seek to figure out how it applies in a given setting. Rather, in a cultural context, whatever it is that they have learned (and is shared), whatever goes into the application would seem to constitute the rule, something on the order of a shared sense for appropriate distance in various conversational contexts.

It would seem fitting to say that what has been learned is some *normative sensibility*. There should be no suggestion that agent even have a term for behavior conforming to the sensibility. In the case of speaking distance, they might be relatively comfortable or uncomfortable in parallel situations, but not readily talk of "conversational distance" or the like. Further, even were they to have a simple formulation for marking conformity or violations, there should be no suggestion that agents could readily verbally articulate what the simple formulation requires.

In many cases, including local norms of fairness or of not littering, the capacity to judge cases will far outstrip what can be articulated in verbal interpretation. Commonly, something has been learned by agents that would be difficult for them to systematically articulate. Apparently, what is learned in acquiring a norm normally involves sensibilities that are more subtle than any associated linguistic expressions. It often involves a fair bit of what Henderson and Horgan (2000) term "morphological content." Such are some reasons for our preferring to write of "normative sensibilities" rather than of "rules" being shared.

Biccheiri (2006) clearly aspires to the integration of a cognitive science of concepts and conceptualization within an account of rules. Thus, in the third discussion we want to flag, she draws on a psychology of concepts that understands concepts as being encoded somewhat differently across agents who yet can share the same concept. She thinks of each agent who has learned not only a shared concept, but also a shared conception, as having learned a set of prototypes plus a sense for the similarity of instances to these prototypes. In a recent discussion (Bicchieri and McNally 2018), what is protypical for a given agent is represented in a set of schemas involving scripts for interactions or exchanges. These make for social expectations, both empirical and normative. Different agents sharing a rule will do so by virtue of have learned constellations of similar schemas. It is perhaps worth noting that Bicchieri and McNally (2018, 27) also understand these schemas as being realized in connectionist terms—their learning turns on formation of connections in an agent's neural net as a result of exposure to common actions and interactions encountered in that agent's trajectories through their social environment.

Different trajectories would result in some difference in agents' precise constellation of schemas, and differences in which scripts shine the brightest within their respective constellations. In effect, Bicchieri is construing the shared higher-order psychological property—the conception that each agent has learned—as being multiply realizable by various different-yet-similar lower-level psychological properties, with each such lower-level property constituting a specific set of prototypes together with a specific sense for the similarity of instances to these prototypes. This approach is deliberately, and aptly, tolerant of some variation across individuals in these lower-level properties.

Different folk who share the same conception of fairness, for example, can have somewhat different prototypes and similarity senses, while still having each internalized the very same conception (local norm) of fairness. So, agents can share a norm—a normative sensibility (or "rule")—while having learned somewhat different prototypes and similarity senses.

That said, shared rules or normative sensibilities will not do the work envisioned in Bicchieri's account of norms (and cooperation and coordination) if one individuates rules tolerantly as would be fitting were one individuating concepts in common externalist semantical ways. Again, this is because it is common to say that folk across in divergent ethical/political communities can be deploying the same concept of FAIR while having very dissimilar conceptions of fairness—and, as we have seen, significant similarity of conception is what matters on the approach to norms of concern here. If what really must be shared in a given norm are conceptions, then in order to share the relevant local norm of fairness, each member must have acquired some complex lower-level psychological property, consisting of specific prototypes and a specific sense for similarity of instances to these prototypes, subserving a disposition-pattern that conforms to the very same conception. The acquired conception thereby will be the same across the members of the population, even though this conception is psychologically multiply realized within the population.

We ourselves are not committed to thinking that norms, or local norms, clearly are best understood as being psychologically realized in terms of prototypes and similarity senses. The psychological study of concepts and conceptualization continues to evolve. Clearly the data that supported prototype theory must be accommodated—and the approach is heuristically quite useful. Indeed, as reflected below, we find it particularly heuristicallty useful when thinking of the kind of variation and similarity of internal processing that is really required for an account such as Bicchieri's to work.

More generally, we think that Bicchieri is right in thinking that the theory of norms ultimately must have as a component an account of the normative sensibilities—what goes into their learning, and their application. To succeed here it will need to be an interfield theory. Mendelian genetics became a richer theory, one with more empirical anchors, and one subject to greater refinement, and one consequently with greater explanatory power, when an integrated interfield account was given of its central posits (genes). In parallel fashion, talk of rules becomes a richer theory, one with more empirical anchors and one subject to more empirical elaboration, when its posits (viz., psychologically internalized rules) come to be understood in part in terms of more or less determinate cognitive phenomena.

We have now seen that, on accounts such as Biccheiri's, local norms—the rules or normative sensibilities around which folk coordinate or cooperate must be individuated so as to turn on *something on the order of conceptions* rather than concepts. More fully, we can say something substantive about what would be needed in that way of shared conceptions. A reasonable starting place is to reflect on the general theoretical demands of the norms-as-rules approach. One is not looking for an a priori account of what norms (or behavioral rules) necessarily are. Instead, one seeks an orienting articulation of theoretical commitments of this general approach. These are theoretical commitments that, if the theoretical approach is ultimately to prove empirically adequate, can be elaborated in ongoing empirical investigation. The theoretical approach has us positing certain entities—rules or (better) normative sensibilities—that play certain causal roles in folk's cognitive processes. What one is looking for is, in effect, a kind of minimal characterization of the normative sensibilities posited in terms of what these do in the production of coordinated behavior.[5] In light of one's sense for many apparent instances and noninstances of norms, and in light of this crude understanding of how these entities perform their signature causal roles in the production of coordinated social action, one could reasonably insist on an openness to letting empirical inquiry fill out the understanding of how these sensibilities are realized in human cognitive agents and in human society so as to yield coordinated and cooperative behavior. In this way, one would look to ongoing work in psychology, cognitive science, and related disciplines to sort out more determinately what manner of psychological/cognitive things these rules are, and what

---

5   Cummins (1983) elaborates an understanding of "functional analysis" in which functions are causal roles in a system. One can analyze the relatively sophisticated capacity of a complex system—a computer, a radio receiver, a cognitive agent—into the organized workings of a set of simpler capacities. These simpler capacities are "functions" or causal roles performed by system components. The norms-as-rules approach posits entities—something learned when learning behavioral rules—that have characteristic causal roles in the cognitive systems (agents) that manage to coordinate their actions in ways that allow for social life (which otherwise might deteriorate into narrowly selfish free riding). In articulating one's theoretical commitments in terms of such "functions" or causal roles, one is engaged in a mid-stream theoretical engagement that ultimately looks towards an empirically refineable interfield theory in which one would have a refined or elaborated understanding of the causal roles performed and of the entities performing these roles in human cognitive systems. Cummins (1975) discusses how functions as causal roles in a system have a place in the explanation of the sophisticated capacity of the system. The resulting explanatory understanding is distinct from an explanation of why there is a system (or a component) with such capacities—analysis of how a system works is distinct from an explanation of why there are such systems, although it can often contribute to such explanations.

knowledge of them amounts to. If the approach bears out under this empirical elaboration, one will have achieved a richer understanding of the entities or states that perform the causal role envisioned in the norms-as-rules approach.

However the details might ultimately go in light of further scientific developments, the crucial point is the following, as regards Turner's misgivings about the positing of internal psychological features that are shared across different individuals. A shared *higher-order* psychological feature, such as a specific normative sensibility that constitutes an internalized social norm, can perfectly well be multiply realizable within different individuals who share it. Indeed, it can perfectly well be multiply realizable twice over: first, by different lower-level psychological features; and second, because each of these distinct lower-level psychological features can itself be multiply realizable by different neurophysical features. Identity of higher-level psychological features is subserved by sufficient similarity—rather than identity—of lower-level psychological and neurophysical features. Moreover, the pertinent kind of commonality among realizing-properties is not a matter of how intrinsically similar or different they are, but rather a matter of the respective disposition patterns they subserve; the crucial thing is that each disposition pattern should conform to the same higher-order psychological feature. The spirit of this reply to Turner is aptly captured by the topiary metaphor that Quine famously articulated this way:

Different persons growing up in the same language are like different bushes trimmed and trained to take the shape of identical elephants. The anatomical details of twigs and branches will fulfill the elephantine form differently from bush to bush, but the overall outward results are alike. (Quine 1960, 8)

References

Bicchieri, Cristina. 2006. *The Grammar of Society: The Nature and Dynamics of Social Norms*. New York: Cambridge University Press.

Bicchieri, Cristina. 2017. *Norms in the Wild: How to Diagnose, Measure, and Change Social Norms*. New York: Oxford University Press.

Bicchieri, Cristina and Peter McNally. 2018. '"hrieking Sirens: Schemata, Scripts, and Social Norms: How Change Occurs." *Social Philosophy & Policy*, 36 (1): 23–53.

Brennan, Geoffrey, Lina Eriksson, Robert Goodin, and Nicholas Southwood. 2013. *Explaining Norms*. Oxford: Oxford University Press.

Churchland, Paul M. 1981. "Eliminative Materialism and Propositional Attitudes." *Journal of Philosophy* 78: 67–90.

Cummins, R. (1975) "Functional Analysis." *Journal of Philosophy* 72, 741–765.

Cummins, R. (1983) *The nature of psychological explanation*. Cambridge, Mass.: MIT Press.

Fodor, Jerry A. 1974. "Special Sciences (or the Disunity of Science as a Working Hypothesis)." *Synthese*, 28: 97–115.

Graham, George and Terence Horgan. 1991. "In Defense of Southern Fundamentalism." *Philosophical Studies: An International Journal for Philosophy in the Analytic Tradition* 62 (2): 107–34.

Graham, Peter. 2015. Epistemic Normativity and Social Norms. In *Epistemic Evaluation*. Edited by David Henderson and John Greco. Oxford: Oxford University Press, 247–273.

Henderson, David. 1987. "The Principle of Charity and the Problem of Irrationality." *Synthese: An International Journal for Epistemology, Methodology and Philosophy of Science* 73: 225–252.

Henderson, David. 1990. "An Empirical Basis for Charity in Interpretation." *Erkenntnis: An International Journal of Analytic Philosophy* 32 (1): 83–103.

Henderson, David. 1993. *Interpretation and Explanation in the Human Sciences*. Albany: State University of New York Press.

Henderson, David. 2011. "Let's be Flexible." *Journal of the Philosophy of History* 5: 261–299.

Henderson, David and Terence Horgan. 2000. "Iceberg Epistemology." *Philosophy and Phenomenological Research* 61 (3): 497–535.

Henderson, David and Terence Horgan. 2005. What Does it Take to be a True Believer? Against the Opulent Ideology of Eliminative Materialism. In *Mind as a Scientific Object: Between Brain and Culture*. Edited by C. Erneling and D Johnson. Oxford: Oxford University Press.

Horgan, Terence. 1993a. "The Austere Ideology of Folk Psychology.", *Mind and Language* 8 (2): 282–297.

Horgan, Terence and James Woodward. 1985. "Folk Psychology is Here to Stay." *Philosophical Review* 94: 197–226.

Horgan, Terence and James Woodward. 1993b. "Nonreductive Materialism and the Explanatory Autonomy of Psychology." *Mind and Language* 8: 282–297.

Kim, Jaegwon. 1993. *Supervenience and Mind: Selected Philosophical Essays*. Cambridge: Cambridge University Press.

Pettit, Philip. 1990. "Virtus Normativa: Rational Choice Perspectives." *Ethics: An International Journal of Social, Political, and Legal Philosophy* 100 (4): 725–755.

Quine, W.V.O. 1960. *Word and Object*. Cambridge, MA: MIT Press.

Stich, Stephen. 1983. *From Folk Psychology to Cognitive Science: The Case Against Belief*. Cambridge, MA: MIT Press.

Turner, Stephen P. 1980. *Sociological Explanation as Translation*. Cambridge: Cambridge University Press.

Turner, Stephen P. 2018. *Cognitive science and the Social: A Primer*. New York: Routledge, Taylor & Francis Group.

PART 4

Social Science

Cognitive Theories and Economic Science

Sam Whimster

Abstract

When economic models—here marginalist models of the Austrian school: Menger, Hayek, Lachmann and rational expectations—are superimposed on the standard theory of mind, a computing engine, we are able to distinguish between an evolutionary constant (goal-directed rationality) and additional rationality claims which on examination turn out to be loosely justified and extend to the ideological. Conversely, we can ask what parts of rationality explanations are exogenous to the mind and belong to the realm of culture and civilization. With the financialization of economic life, computing machines perform a large part of economic decision-making with the effect of hijacking the cognitive core of rationality and separating it from its civilizational surroundings. Economics as a discipline needs to reflect on the directions in which they drive their theories of rationality and whether these are compatible with human flourishing.

Keywords

Carl Menger – Friedrich Hayek – Ludwig Lachmann – rational expectations model – theories of mind – cognition – Alan Turing – human flourishing

1   Introduction*

There is an elective affinity between the science of economics and theories of cognition. Economics is concerned with the meeting of human needs for survival and flourishing, and individuals and social group are compelled to think how best to meet those needs. Survival and goal directedness is a constant in human evolution. This chapter follows a thread of Austrian economists—Carl Menger, Friedrich Hayek, Ludwig Lachmann, and the current theory of rational expectations—and examines how they treat the cognitive aspect of

---

* My thanks to Peter Ayton who gave me valuable advice in the area of cognitive decision-making.

goal-directedness. Respectively, in regard to the above four theorists/theories we encounter a civilizational, an epistemological, a *Verstehen*, and a Leibnizian approach. All four are interrogated through Theories of Mind and raise two main critiques: (1) how do civilizational and cultural explanations of economic behavior stand in relation to the philosophy of mind? (2) do attributions of beliefs and motives to individual economic agents fall foul of what theorists of mind call "folk psychology." My provisional answers are that Menger's stance defends the stance of culture; and that the attribution of motives to economic individuals fails hopelessly; indeed catastrophically, because those bogus attributions are used to justify ideologies that deny human flourishing.

Because of the elective affinity (of economizing and cognition), which is widely understood in folk psychology terms, economists can get away with standards well below those stipulated by philosophers of science and of language. One radical remedy is to remove and externalize the routinized and computational elements of economizing, on the lines Alan Turing proposed for arithmetic. Computing machines can, and increasingly do, much of the everyday work of economic decision-making. This would allow economists to think more carefully about species survival and how the mind of economizing citizens operates and is formed. It would take away economists' license to opine freely on politics and society on the basis of an assumed rationality, and consider the wider issues of social theory.

The chapter starts, and assumes throughout, that contemporary economies are highly financialized and are moving in an ever more machine-enabled direction.

2   Experimenting with National Economies

The science of monetary policy is esoteric but no minor thing in its effects upon the world. Financialization has invaded the lifeworld of citizens across the globe. From the viewpoint of economic policy, the Bretton Woods agreement of 1944, which lasted to 1971, has been uprooted and replaced with the primacy of monetary policy "liberating" the free flow of capital across borders. This has been accompanied by the replacement of nation-state economic regulation within a "Westphalian" Bretton Woods system with the creation of market exchanges that process and price monetary flows and their derivative financial instruments. From a citizen perspective, life course decisions on education, career choice, savings, investment in housing, partner choices and family, and retirement and pensions have been disrupted and upended by the primacy given to the dynamics of financial flows and financial markets.

Consider this snippet from the financial press, in which Peter Malmqvist who is Chief Equity Analyst at The Association of Swedish Shareholders writes in response to a *Financial Times* article on the new President of the European Central Bank:

> Your Big Read article "Lagarde plots new ECB course" (October 28 [2019]) is on the spot. Negative interest rates are no long-term solution. The toolbox must be expanded. Look no further than the eurozone's neighbouring Sweden. After aggressively lowered policy rates in 2014, the Riksbank entered into negative territory in early 2015, a level it has kept ever since. Not surprisingly, house prices exploded in 2015 by 15 per cent, in 2016 by 9 per cent and by August 2017 another 7 per cent. A surge in construction followed, in 2015 by 31 per cent and by another 27 per cent in 2016. The same with car sales, which expanded to a record of 400,000 units in June 2018 (the previous record was 300,000 in 2006). And inflation? A success! In July it broke the important level of 2 per cent for the first time since late 2011 and it has stayed at around that level ever since.
>
> Now, here is the thing: Sweden still has negative interest rates. The Riksbank stretched the experiment. It wanted to be sure inflation stayed on the targeted level, but in August 2017 the music stopped. House prices collapsed by 10 per cent in four months, construction declined by 30 per cent and car sales by 20 per cent. Also, the inflation rate declined from 2 to 1.5 per cent and the policy rate is still negative.
>
> Obviously, there is no such thing as a long-term interest rate stimulus. It's a shot in the arm, a sugar rush, but something else must kick-in long-term. That is what the Swedish experiment shows with a horrifying precision.
>
> MALMQVIST 2019

The Swedish Riksbank has an illustrious history. It was founded in 1668 and constitutionally it was under the control of Parliament, though during wars it became a credit bank to the ruler. In the nineteenth century it was firmly part of bourgeois parliamentary rule and this property-owning phase lasted until the 1950s when it fell in line with democratic state control of economic policy (Fregert and Jonung 1996, 448–50). The Riksbank was one of the first central banks to embrace the post 1971 world. As the letter above makes clear, it has the arbitrary power to disrupt citizens' life course decisions as a merely experimental move. By comparison with the record of other central banks (the Federal Reserve and the Bank of England) this is but a minor blip within the volatility that has characterized the era of "financial liberation." Central bankers across the world, who in fact meet in consilium on a regular basis at the Bank of International Settlements, look upon such experiments with equanimity, considering similar moves in their own territories.

The obvious remark at this point is to say this is both a technocratic dream - switching sectors of the economy off and on—and a lifeworld nightmare. Central bankers are openly discussing reducing interest rates to minus 4% or 5% and replacing bank account currency with digital currency solely controlled by central banks. This capacity to control the economy through infinitely extensible forms of money and the control over them takes us on to a new page of the social sciences.

It is analogous to the digital transformation of media and human communication, which of course is a huge topic. Social media—tweets, YouTube, internet, mobile phones—have a transformative effect on humans' states of mind. In analyzing networks of inter-human relations and memed messages communicated through social media, the cognitive sciences have much to say—to think of perception, neurons, reaction processes etc. Our comprehension of the digital transformation in many ways was held back by the standard theory of communication where transmission was subaltern to the intention and meaning of the message and its semantic receipt. Internet communication technology truly realizes the McCluhan adage the medium is the message, downgrading meaning and intentionality and its receipt (Whimster 2018). Economics, as a science, is in a curious situation in this respect. At various stages in its disciplinary formation it has depended on the conception of *homo œconomicus*, which implicitly involves a theory of mind even though the issue has been treated as an epistemological one. Working out the boundaries—the cognitive, the epistemological, intentionality, machine intelligence—is one way of refreshing and bringing up to date the Enlightenment project.

3   Carl Menger. *Kultur* over Cognitive Capacities

Dr. Carl Menger inaugurated the Austrian school of economics with the publication of his *Grundsätze der Volkswirtschaftslehre* (Menger, 1871; translation, *Principles of Economics*, 1981). For most economists, Menger's book stood as the turning point from classical economics—the tradition of Adam Smith, David Ricardo, J. S. Mill, and Karl Marx—to that of marginalist analysis, in which the economic subject calculates the utility an additional purchase over and beyond his existing expenditures. (The point holds for manufacturers buying factors of production or for consumers of final produced goods.) Menger provided some arithmetic tables showing when a farmer might choose to exchange, say, five of his sheep with a cow from a neighboring farmer. The calculation of usefulness (*Nützlichkeit*) is made from the marginal advantage obtained. In the standard model of cognitive theory "all cognition is computational" (Eck and Turner 2019, 162). This also applies to the classical school where the holders of the means of production—land, capital, and labor—each try to maximize their interest. The latter is crude political economy of the pursuit of interests, though unified to an extent through the theory of utility (the term used by English political economy). Each party was trying to maximize their overall utility. Menger fine-tuned this as a calculation made at the marginal unit and made it a universal model, *once* a level of society and civilization had been reached that permitted complex exchanges, in that any individual as an economizer (*wirtschaftendes Subject*) had the capacity to perform the arithmetic of additional advantage.

Where does Menger's economizing subject stand in relation to recent cognitive science? Cognitive theories seek to place and investigate rational faculties within the mind, arguing that they "must" be located somewhere therein. David Hume it will be remembered dismissed such speculation as metaphysics. The explosion in cognitive science shows no such inhibition. There are deep mind theorists, led by the philosopher Jerry Fodor; the decomposition of human abilities into mini engines—homunculi—as argued by Dennett et alia, and the experimentalists who take an instrumentalist approach to science. In the previous scientific Enlightenment, Adam Smith held that the propensity of men to truck, barter, and exchange was rooted in human nature. Menger was far more focused stating that individuals exchanging goods will only happen under certain specified circumstances. Three conditions must be satisfied which he spells out—and here we have to stay with the details. The "benefits of a mutual transfer of goods depend ... on three conditions: (a) one economizing individual must have command of quantities of goods which have a smaller value to him than other quantities of goods at the disposal of another economizing individual who evaluates the goods in reverse fashion, (b) the two economizing individuals must have recognized this relationship, and (c) they must have the power actually to perform the exchange of goods." Without these three essential prerequisites "an exchange of goods between two economizing individuals is impossible" (Menger 1981, 180). The first prerequisite involves computation but also a *sense* of quantity and value; the second a recognition of mutuality; the third is sociological and legal.

Cognitive theories of the mind comprise both computation and also the social mutuality of recognition and seek to account how these processes function. As explained by Eck and Turner, these capabilities are not learnt, but as with language and the realization of intentionality in children they arrive, fully formed, around the age of four. Adam Smith can hardly be criticized for holding truck and barter to an "original principle of human nature," but what is questionable is that the innumerable generations of Smithean economists proclaim that same principle. In language philosophy this is an appeal to dubious mental entities. It assumes that there is a desire to truck and barter, and Menger in his criticism observes that for Smith exchange is a "pleasure" (*eine Lust*) for both parties. That may or may not be the case, who can know? The philosophical problem is linking up desire and intention on one side to actions and behaviors on the other. Intentionality is a crucial bit in the vocabulary of motives that dominates economic analysis and intention is supposed to drive the economic act or transaction. So "the profit motive" leads someone to make an economic transaction and the deeper impulse behind this is the propensity or pleasure of conducting exchanges. There are actions and behaviors and "things like beliefs, reasons and desires … are there to be inferred from them [the actions]" (Turner 2018a: 293). Actions are observable, intentions and other mental states are not. The falsities of misattribution and circular arguments are rife. The "explanatory task is to say how we act, and not only to give some story on how action might be brought about by whatever fictional entities one cares to invent" (Rüdiger Bittner quoted in Turner 2018: 295). As Stephen Turner comments: "The explanatory relation is fundamentally circular, since the only evidence for these 'fictional entities' is their effect, which is also what they are supposed to explain" (Turner 2018a, 295).

The world manages to tick over despite the solecisms committed against language philosophy; the ascription of intentionality to another person or party enables sociality.[1] But the issue is far more serious for economics as a science, because whatever the intention that is assigned to driving economic actions it is frequently used to justify not only economic theory but economic doctrine and ideology. Adam-Smithean economics is pervasive through dint of ascribing "the profit motive" to the natural propensity to barter. Menger indicates one way out of these difficulties. His three prerequisites define in an externally observable manner the conditions under which one party might choose to barter and exchange with another. The situation in itself explains the action without relying solely on ascribed motives. To put it more strongly, Menger's essential prerequisites become an imperative to act and not to act would indicate willful irrationality.

The belief-desire model of action has slightly detoured the discussion of cognitive capacities involved in marginalist calculations. Menger is compatible

---

1 See tacit theory and what Turner calls a "good bad theory" (Turner 2018a, 294–5).

with the standard model of theories of the mind: people have the capacities to work out their advantage, to enter into mutual arrangements, and to assess, however accurately or inaccurately, other people's intentions. "But people also have a ToM [Theory of Mind] and can make inferences about the beliefs and desires of others, and this is at the core of the mutual calculations that make up social action and determine institutional arrangements" (Eck and Turner 2018, 158–9). There are further extensions of cognitive theories of mind and these eat into the territory that is occupied by sociology, anthropology and culture. Bottom-up cognitive theory (of the mind) seeks to explain areas claimed at the macro level. Cognitive theory also seeks to argue that the mind is embedded, embodied, extended and enactive - the so-called "4Es" (Eck and Turner 2019, 159). The mind is not a brain in a jar but the corporeal surrounds within which it sits and interacts become constituents of an environment of an expanded theory of the mind.

In my view this expansion of the scope of the theory of the mind is illegitimate, for it is importing properties that have determinate force apart from cognitive properties.[2] Menger again is interesting on the issue, since he places explanatory emphasis outside the individual, in culture and the development of civilization. In this sense most subsequent members of the Austrian school in putting the stress on individual motivation and rationality betray the master.

It is *possible* to advance features of the "4E "argument to Menger's analysis. A cereal farmer has no horses and a livestock farmer has no cereal. At the margin the cereal farmer will pay highly for one horse and reciprocally the other farmer for grain. In a second transaction of horse against bushels of grain the prices will be lower—the extra purchase does not quite have the same impact on each farm economy and is worth less (Menger 1981, 203ff). Menger's farmers are homely people not quantitative analysts. They are not computing an exact number, but working from a knowledge of their farm and its prospects. Their knowledge is embedded in their literal environment and accumulated farming acumen—soil, weather, seasons, risks to crops and livestock. The same point can be made for industrialists the viable success of whose firms is founded upon decades of experience.

Subsequent to Menger, a host of economists have taken the path of exact calculation as mediated through the overall price of each good and its equilibrium price arrived at in a market. Menger argued that the conditions of cost and market price, by the complex nature of economic interrelations and time

---

[2] Stephen Turner discusses the merits of cognitivists' appropriation of culture (Turner 2018b, 26–39).

horizons, simply did not allow prices for goods to be arrived at so exactly. (Nor can they be arrived at today, if we accept the arguments for market disequilibria.) His figures, simple arithmetic tables (and just to note he was mathematically gifted), were illustrative.[3]

If the argument is that the reckoning of a farmer's advantage owes more to the environment in which he was brought up and lives than it does to computational capability, then we might want to say that habitus *à la* Bourdieu is primary.[4] Habitus has been incorporated into the standard model as an add-on box. The mind absorbs, interacts and selects from its environment giving it extra functional capacities. For Menger, however, the local environment is a reflection of the wider state of knowledge and culture, which is not out there as some ideal but belongs to the nature of things. It is the relation between goods which provides the culture of an economy.

Rather than individualize the mind we can equally conceive of the subject's "economic mind" as deriving from the composition of economic goods. Menger graduates goods into first, second, third and fourth orders and so on. Consumption goods are the first order, but are composed of goods (second order) used to produce those goods, and these allow further orders until we come to those goods (the final order) come out of the soil or beneath the ground. The value of goods is determined by subjective perception of how they fulfill human needs and for economic actors their value in production processes, and not any inherent value in the things themselves. Economic analysis, for Menger, lays bare the causal connection between the orders of goods.

We can extend this line of argument into Durkheimian territory—that the "economic mind" is the collective consciousness and perception of the order of goods, standing behind which is the level of civilization and its division of labor. The causal relation between the orders of goods represents the stage a civilizational has reached. Primitive societies are hand to mouth, so to speak, and the division of labor is gendered and simple. Advanced societies have more complex and extended relations between things, and a more advanced division of labor. But for Menger this division of labor is more than that described by Adam Smith; instead, it is determined by the range of commodities and the extent of their orders. Culture/civilization is the driver. Smith's "technical division of labor" is a *consequence* of this and not a prime mover. With respect

---

3   "Marginalism is introduced in the middle of Menger's *Grundsätze*, but it is for this very reason not central to, not the keystone of, this very logical construction" (Streissler 1973, 160–1).
4   Notions of habitus have a long history going back to Le Play's monographs on households. See Hacking 1990, 138–41.

to the subjective value imagined or perceived of goods, Menger wrote: "the quantities of consumption of goods at human disposal are limited only by the extent of human knowledge" (1871, 29). As knowledge extends, so does the *conscience collective*.

We could add, by way of *Wirtschaftskritik*, that Menger's Austria and Vienna are about culture and civilization not computational arithmetic. In the same way, for Max Weber, the economizing subject was determined in the final instance by culture and religion and its residues. Economics as a secularizing discipline treats only with a disenchanted world. Carl Menger dedicated his *Principles of Economics* to Wilhelm Roscher, who was then Germany's leading political economist and, as a neo-Aristotelian, defined economic utility in terms human needs (Menger 1871, 2, starred note). The intellectual debt (to Roscher) was how to think about societies, their arrangements (*Verhältnisse*), and knowledge (*Erkenntnis*).

This appeal to evolving human needs and requirements according to the development of knowledge, which is instantiated in the orders of goods and their relationality, does not disable the claims of theory of mind arguments. "It can be expanded to account for any functional capacity" write Eck and Turner (2018, 158). The short term can be modelled alongside habitus and environment in their long term aspect. The model can be still further expanded by bringing in "affordances," an idea borrowed from psychology theories of evolution. In the process of the satisfaction of human needs, economizing individuals will avail themselves of anything in the wider societal environment that they perceive as useful (technology, professional services, the sciences). This suggests a way around difficulties in the standard model whose program has to come up with an explanation of the mind's ability to reason. Embedding in a long term environment and the use of affordances look a better bet as part of an extended theory of mind.

But, against these cognitive theories, Menger makes the environment determinative, it has causal power. His theory does not make the macro economy the outcome of (tacit) beliefs and preferences structured by the rational mind and made harmonious through the market. The wider economy of the changing orders of goods determines the possibilities of choice. "The producers of each individual article usually carry on their business in a mechanical way, while the producers of the complementary goods realize just as little that the goods-character of the things they produce or manufacture depends on the existence of other goods that are not in their possession" (Menger 1981, 63). "Only in their entirety do these goods bring about the effect that we call the satisfaction of our requirements, and in consequence, the assurance of our lives and welfare" (Menger 1981, 75).

Two features follow, or are determined, by this analysis. One is property: "The entire sum of goods at an economizing individual's (*Individuum*) command for the satisfaction of his needs, we call his *property*." The second is the mutuality of property. The property (*Besitz*) of the individual (where individual equates to the individuation of subjects within an economy of orders) is not some "arbitrarily combined quantity of goods, but a direct reflection of his needs, an integrated whole, no essential part of which can be diminished or increased without affecting realization of the end it serves" (Menger 1981, 76; 1871, 31).

4 Economics as Decision-Making under Conditions of Uncertainty

In the above part theories of mind force a genuine re-evaluation of Menger's own analysis. In this part a different "cognitivist" turn is considered.

Erwin Streissler, as the longtime professor of economics at the University of Vienna, is very much the dean and curator of the Austrian school. In his chapter "To What Extent Was the Austrian School Marginalist?" he mounts a rescue operation to save Menger from his successors (Streissler 1973, 160–75). Marginalism, as noted above, was not central to his *Grundsätze*, even though his pupils (Böhm-Bawerk and von Wieser) gave it primacy. It was a set of calculations that could be made to illustrate a point. Streissler argues that Menger was achieving "a change in our understanding" and, quoting Menger, it is the "increasing understanding of the causal connections between things and human welfare" and is only limited by human knowledge. Streissler goes on to paraphrase Menger: this "alone constitutes the correct 'subjective value' view of progress" (1973, 165).

Streissler, in his analysis of Menger, despite placing the emphasis on knowledge and a wider understanding of progress, turns this in an informational direction: "marginalism in its essence is a decision theory; in the language of mathematical programming it focuses on the objective function first, on the choice variables second, and on the restraints not at all" (Streissler 1973, 160). Knowledge, let alone *Erkenntnis*—a concept more open to learning from experience—becomes information and uncertainty. This is a trend in economics that predates Streissler (going back to Frank Knight at Chicago) and it tops out with Ackerlof and colleagues' Nobel Prize for economics in 2001, which was awarded for decision-making: asymmetric knowledge giving firms advantage over ignorant consumers. Information and decision-making become the new cognitive science (though not as a theory of the mind). Streissler re-reads Menger according to the informational turn in economics (which was underway by the 1970s). Entrepreneurial activity is above all about the dissemination of information about the economy. The entrepreneur needs to know about not just the quantity, quality, and variety of goods at his disposal but "we also have to add *informational* content, variable over time, and, at any given moment, over individuals" (Streissler 1973, 166).

The cognitive turn in economics marked a turning away from quantitative aggregates and the assumption that economic actors have exact information on prices at their finger-tips, and were capable of rational decisions. Menger's "conditions under which men (*Menschen*) engage in provident activity" becomes the imperfection of knowledge, the limits of rationality with its heuristic biases, and the probabilistic estimation of future states.

5   The Case of Friedrich Hayek

As an economist working in the 1920s and 1930s Hayek contributed to a general theory of prices, market equilibrium, interest rates, investment, and cycles of trade and capital formation. All of this was predicated on the idea that economic decisions are made on the calculation of marginal advantage by individuals. The generality of this model (not exclusive to Hayek) was held to by policy makers with a doctrinal rigidity, so that the return to the gold standard was acceptable for Austria in the 1920s (whose deflationary consequences had peasants dying of starvation); government intervention was condemned after 1931 (market equilibrium had to restore and reset itself whatever the costs in human welfare); and in the post 1945 world the introduction of a welfare state was caricatured as the road to serfdom (in the book of that name). The mirror image of these doctrines, we might have supposed, would be that economic actors were effortless calculators of marginal advantage. The motivation driving action was self-interest, held to be axiomatic. The cognitive part of the brain could remain shut, as a "black box."

Hayek while rigid on market theory adopted an approach to the validity of science, one influenced by his fellow Austrian émigré Karl Popper. Republic followed the end of the Hapsburg Empire in 1917, and communist rule followed for a period in 1919. In the neighboring "free state" of Bavaria there was a serious endeavor by economists (Otto Neurath) to create a socialist planned economy which aimed at replacing an exchange economy with one responsive to communal needs. Austrian intellectuals of non-Marxist hue attacked the underpinnings of Marxist determinism (so-called historicism), empiricism (represented by Ernst Mach), objectivism, and behaviorism. At a later date

Hayek characterized these erroneous epistemologies as "scientism"—and in this he was not out of line with Max Weber's methodology.

illustrative here was Max Weber's 1908 critique of Lujo Brentano's attempt to buttress marginal utility with Fechner's psychological study of marginal responses to stimuli (Weber 2012, 242–51). For Weber, marginalism was an economic form permitted, and only to an extent, by the configuration of economic power (see Whimster 2019, 28). The mistake with regard to behaviorism, or Machian imprinting on the brain, or of Fechner's diminishing response was to look for a *physical* basis in the brain for human decisions; rather than today, following Dennett's approach, to let the brain, and the little brain compartments within it, to function.

Hayek's epistemology argued that there was no direct correspondence between an external stimulus and a sensation and that "when something becomes a part of our consciousness, it assumes a position in relation to our other past impressions" (quoted in Caldwell 2007, 19). This is his position in *The Sensory Order* (from ideas drafted much earlier in 1920) and it is repeated in his critique of behaviorism. "Behaviorism insists on making recourse only to observable phenomena in order to remain 'objective' and to avoid acts of interpretation." We *might* say that Hayek was an early adopter of current enactive theories of mind (Eck and Turner 2018, 161–2); "all sensory data are themselves products of the mind—they are themselves acts of interpretation," as Bruce Caldwell puts it (Caldwell 2007, 30).

But for Hayek minds do not speak to each other on the basis of inherent mutuality or recognition capacities. As an avowed methodological individualist—where in a market n always reduces to one—knowledge never coheres into an ordered and socially constructed world but is dispersed. Institutions are formed not through the assumption of order (as in Max Weber where the consolidation lies in the common orientation of groups of individuals to an order) but as a spontaneous process resultant from "the unintended consequences of purposeful human action" (Caldwell 2007, 29). Changes in prices in a market act as signals which are quickly diffused through an economy. Consumers and producers react to these changes.

Hayek's arguments here are interesting. He does not have to specify tacit beliefs-desires on the part of economizing individuals. They can do whatever they want in the face of market price signals—they can remain ignorant, they can interpret them incorrectly, they can alter their choices in a way that proves advantageous, and so on. The validity of the theory lies in the empirical evidence. If there is a hike in the price of tin, that part of the production and consumption related to tin changes pattern, quickly and spontaneously, even though economic actors have no idea why there has been a change in price.

Unfortunately his status as an economist was more or less destroyed, notably by Keynes and Kaldor, who pointed out that the magic of the market did not cure Depressions. People reacted to price signals in a manner that destroyed the market. His later book on capital theory was regarded as impenetrable (by Milton Friedman among others). It was only through the unexpected award of a Nobel Prize for economics in 1974 that his reputation was restored—with devastating effect as it was taken up in the new conservatism of Reagan and Thatcher. The Nobel Prize committee had decided to give the Mount Pèlerin Society a massive, and undeserved, public stance. What was being celebrated was the Popperian fallibility of scientific knowledge that segued into a romanticist notion of free will over all forms of determination. In raising up an epistemology, a rigid and unforgiving free market ideology was set loose upon the world.

Hayek's hour in the sun was short-lived, for it had little affinity with the new economics of the 1980s, other than a hatred of social democracy and the welfare state. The post-war settlement, a continuation of Roosevelt's New Deal, had irretrievably blocked off the return to the neoclassical Austrian model. Neoclassical, like classical economics, contained not only a theory of the market but also the distributional consequence. For both, the market achieved harmony (equilibrium) and wherever that fell, it determined *and justified*, who got what—not just the returns to labor and capital, but each sector within the various markets. The welfare state had altered the sovereignty of property, it welcomed state industries into national economies, and it used taxation to achieve harmony and security between generations. Equilibrium theory was about markets moving from one market state at t_1 to a new state t_2. But government took control of t on a generational and planned timescale. This destroyed the game for the supposed market harmony and economists wanted their t back. The new conservative economics demanded that the state be rolled back, socialized industries—mostly public utilities—should be privatized, and all markets liberated from government control.

6 Ludwig Lachmann's Theory of Expectations

Lachmann's intellectual formation started with reading economics at the University of Berlin in 1924, where he absorbed the writings of Carl Menger. Then he studied with Friedrich Hayek in England, and as he developed into a mature economist he discovered Max Weber's theory of social action, whom he had previously read as an economic historian. Max Weber was formative for the Austrian school through Ludwig von Mises who admired his critique, in 1920, of Otto Neurath's socialists' plan to abolish the exchange market economy in favor of community-oriented mechanisms of resource allocation.[5]

Lachmann was true to the master, Carl Menger, and it is doubtful that he would have approved of late twentieth century economic theory, outlined in the next part below. Like Menger he was highly skeptical that capital could be aggregated and priced, and this also made him a critic of Keynesian theory whose aggregation of economic categories (debates in the 1960s and 70s) he regarded as fictitious.

"Lachmann's work during the 1950s may be described as a fusion of (1) his concept of the role of expectations in capital theory, (2) the Misesian view of human action as purposive, and (3) the *verstehende* sociology of Max Weber. [...] To understand action is to comprehend the thought that sets that action in motion" (Grinder 1977, 16). In Lachmann's own words "observable events as such have no significance except with reference to framework of interpretation which is logically prior to them. From this there follow two conclusions, a narrower one concerning expectations, and a broader one pertaining to the formulation of the economic problem in a dynamic World" (Lachmann 1977, 72). In the 1950s Keynesian theorists, such as John Hicks, were inquiring why after a financial crash investors in the real economy are not tempted by low interest rates (engineered by state treasuries and central banks). This led these economists to talk about the elasticity of expectations, which would be impacted variously by higher or lower interest rates. Lachmann's point is that expectations remain inelastic (1977, 78–9), as investors hold off mulishly until they are entirely satisfied that demand for their products is picking up. Hence there is a need to understand, in Weber's terms, the orientation of investors to an economic situation. Contra Mises there was "no logic of choice." Lachmann interposes in the assumed causation of price signals and action an all-important chamber of forethought which itself is, less us say, ambient in a climate of opinion. "To investigate in what conditions what type of expectations is likely to have a stabilizing or destabilizing influence is no doubt one of the next tasks

---

[5] Weber took the proposals seriously and devoted some pages of *Economy and Society* to rebutting them (Weber 2013 [1921], 277 ff; see also editors' "Einleitung" 2013, 73). The socialist calculation debate is far from over. In 1919 the vulnerability of a free market exchange economy was plain to see after the viability of a planned war economy (though this threw up some obscene inequalities). Later commentators have also noted that market equilibrium was achieved, for Leon Walras, by a central auctioneer who set market prices. Neurath was proposing to replace the imaginary auctioneer with a planning department. Big tech today is half way to reaching a similar mechanism, but with outcomes extremely favorable to shareholders.

of dynamic theory. We submit that it cannot be successfully tackled unless expectations are made the subject of causal explanation" (1977, 79).

Lachmann is attacking the positivist trait of economics that there is always a scientific solution or answer to an economic problem. Indeterminacy prevails, and in this he is like Hayek in deriding the scientific pretensions of economics. This still leaves the status of the subjective within the social un-inquired. Lachmann goes on to state—this was in 1943: "In a properly dynamic formulation of the economic problem all elements have to be subjective, but there are two layers of subjectivism, rooted in different spheres of the mind, which must not be confused, viz. the subjectivism of want and the subjectivism of interpretation" (1977, 73). It is how we interpret the world leading to our actions that causes and governs change. "We now realize that ultimately it is the *subjective* nature of these beliefs which imparts indeterminateness to expectations as it is their *mental* nature which renders them capable of explanation" (1977, 72–3). (This approach is manifest in George Soros's ideas on reflexivity, and his speculative wealth made possible by the "affordances" of financial markets—as any UK tax-payer of a certain age can attest.)

This certainly cuts down the scientific-positivistic claims of economists and allows the interpreting human being some breathing space. But we are left with a number of difficulties. Appeals to Weber's theory of social action can only come good if it refers to the mutuality of *social* interaction, or its near cousin intersubjectivism. Individual subjectivism, seemingly mandatory in all economic models, blocks the way to how *verstehende Soziologie* works. Lachmann remains wedded to the naturalism of the subject's utility. This postpones the discussion of just how the intersubjectivism or the meaning laden *Zusammenhang* of "scaredy" investors operates as a cause in plain sight. Lachmann is content to let his approach rest with interpretive causes and indeterminateness of outcomes. However, in a Weberian direction, it needs to translate interpretation into a method of attribution of cause and the decidability of outcomes (Turner 2003, 33; 2019).

Lachmann also falls foul of the belief-desire issue. On expectations Lachmann, to repeat, writes, "it is their *mental* nature which renders them capable of explanation." But this leads us into the dark woods of the mind. We require a Dennett-like homunculus or some other social-psychological theory to come to the rescue. It's probably safe to surmise that Lachmann in 1943 (outside Princeton) was not directing us to cognitive homunculi in his use of "the mental." Nevertheless it forces social theory to make up *its* mind. Are interpretations events in an external world, and how do they link to theories of mind as currently researched?

7 Rational Expectations Theory

Rational expectations theory is currently in vogue in economics and common to both Chicago school monetary theorists and New Keynesians. Whether Ludwig Lachmann would recognize it in its present form is doubtful. Offer and Söderberg provide this health warning: "rational expectations macroeconomics was the most insulated from falsification, the most empirically empty, and in terms of adoption by economists, by far the most successful" (Offer and Söderberg 2016, 25). Economic decisions, by individuals, are made on the basis of all the available information, and each individual is a utility calculator of a sophisticated kind. At this point, in the model, a market participant is able to anticipate (on average) future prices correctly. These choices in total become determinate for the macro economy. This applies not just to experts but the public as well, which is "assumed to be applying the economist's own statistical model, regardless of technically difficult that might be" (Offer and Söderberg 2016, 25).

Determinateness here is based on assumptions alone: everyone has access to information, they use it rationally and calculate optimally. The result is the best of all possible worlds. "Rational expectations is an 'invisible hand' theory that implies that markets cannot be improved upon" (Offer and Söderberg 2016, 29). The policy implications of this is that any government intervention detracts from the perfection of the model. So, intervening institutions like central banks should either be abolished or reduced to minimal importance.

It is hard to see how this theory gained wide academic legitimacy, and it certainly bears out Thomas Kuhn's ideas on paradigm shifts. But its practitioners may well believe that it has ecological validity (to use a research methods term). Rational expectations theory assumes that "all market participants behave as if they are a single individual endowed with uniform assets and preferences." Any differences in assets and preferences are treated as random and cancel each other out. The individual person is termed a "representative agent" (Offer and Söderberg 2016, 27). Whatever the collective might be, it is reduced to the agent who, nevertheless, is someone who acts in real time absorbing all incoming information to make the best guess on future decisions. Just ignoring for the moment what kind of extended explication of cognitive theories of the mind this would require (see below), we are nevertheless dealing with a real person and this gives a naturalistic gloss to the theory. Indeed the assumption is that all individuals advance their utility through recourse to innate cognitive abilities. Rationality of action is grounded in an individual embedded in the noise of information. Rational expectations theory is not necessarily incompatible with theories of the mind.

Offer and Söderberg pose a rhetorical question at this point in their critique of rational expectations theory: "why reduction only to persons, and not their psychology, biology, chemistry, physics?" (2016, 27). To which it could be answered, why not? Not in a physicalist solution, but rather that these elements are in play in theories of the mind. The person in the rational expectations model does not have to be cast as imaginary or heuristic. They also pose a second critical question asking why start with the individual and not operate the other way round; "markets are governed by social rules and conventions, and depend on social media like language and calculations" (2016, 27). Economic sociologists will concur with the statement, but this does rather enforce the antinomy between bottom-up and top-down explanations. Social media today flow through the mind in ways yet to be investigated (and Google is a major employer of neuroscientists).

However, we are rather giving a helping hand to rational expectation theorists, who themselves display remarkable incomprehension of the issues. Their account of determinateness is quite striking. One advocate of rational expectations theory boasted: "All agents inside the model, the econometrician, and God share the same model." And a critical economist wrote: "The 'hypothesis' of rational expectations is like the 'hypothesis of the knowability of God'. There is hardly any point in looking for evidence" (Offer and Söderberg 2016, 26, 28). The advocate is closer to the essence of the model than the critic, however sarcastic the latter may be. The economic actor, who in this branch of economic theory is designated "representative agent," could just as well be a Leibnizian monad. The soul of the economizing subject is not windowless—as in Leibniz's strange theory of non-interacting substances—"but every monad mirrors the universe not because the universe affects it, but because God has given it a nature which spontaneously produces this result" (Russell 1946, 606). For rational expectations theory outcomes of individual choices become determinate of (objective?) reality. Such an approach restricts explanatory causation exclusively to the individual agent's situational choice; no other explanatory candidate need apply.

This does not *seem* to be a promising line of inquiry. But—for the sake of imaginative argument—if all human beings are monads, they all possess the same (God-given) cognitive capacities. If we substitute the Bayesian model of perception for theology, the argument becomes more promising.[6] Evolutionary biologists and psychologists hold that species survival has depended on a

---

[6] The determinateness of the world was an issue for the Rev. Bayes for whom the irregularities of chance could be explained. See Karl Pearson 1978, 363.

form of inferential decision-making, and recently this has been modelled on Bayesian theory. Psychologists have pursued this with experiments on people's perception of objects, like estimating the shape of a light shade, under conditions of reflectants and illuminants. Those two are conditional on each other and the mind has to calibrate this conditionality. The philosopher, Michael Rescorla, notes: "There is no evidence that the perceptual system explicitly represents Bayes's Rule or expected utility maximization. The perceptual system simply proceeds in rough accord with Bayesian norms" (Rescorla 2013, 697). He endorses the experimental psychology:

> Bayesian perceptual psychology offers illuminating, rigorous explanations for numerous constancies and illusions. It is our best current science of perception.
>
> I assume a broadly scientific realist perspective: explanatory success is a prima facie guide to truth. From a scientific realist perspective, the explanatory success of Bayesian perceptual psychology provides prima facie reason to attribute representational content to perceptual states. The science is empirically successful and mathematically rigorous.
>
> RESCORLA 2013, 701, 704

This is a confident statement by Rescorla. It is even more jarring when we work out that he has turned the economists' *explanans* (utility and/or profit maximization) into some kind of perceptual sub-routine. Goal attainment, however characterized, is achieved through a semi-automatic mental process. "The model seeks to describe, perhaps in an idealized way, how the perceptual system actually transits from sensory input to perceptual estimates" (Rescorla 2013, 698). The invitation to economists here is to theorize economizing decisions as an inferential capacity of the mind when reading the "market" environment and to do this on the basis of "prior" expectations of prices relative to each other, and updating those "prior" likelihoods into "posterior" likelihoods on the receipt of new market price information. The economic agent is treated as capable of absorbing information and making probabilistic calibrations in real time.

Parsimony tends to lead Rescorla's approach not to take on board the social environment in the construction and operation of perception and its computational capacities. Social psychologists do this and place the "4Es" as determinative of how the mind functions. For Sloman and Fernbach the mind is embodied in its surroundings. Here the economic agent is interdependent on other agents and the shared nature of social interaction. Economic decisions and calculations come preformed with their answers embedded in the situation. This replaces the heroic individual who chooses between ends and desires of different utility *and* at the same time works out the probability of each end being achievable: the theory of subjective expected utility established by Morgenstern and Neumann (in 1944). "Rather than doing calculation on a mental blackboard, thinking takes place through actions that engage the objects of thought" (Sloman and Fernbach 2017, 102). Individuals are not sovereign in their reasoning. "We live under the knowledge illusion because we fail to draw an accurate line between what is inside and what is outside our heads" (Sloman and Fernbach 2017, 15).[7] They argue for a "cognitive division of labor" - in the same way that Durkheim argued for the interdependence of society based on a social division of labor.

Social psychologists and theorists of mind are not at one on the matter of perception, but both approaches downgrade the sovereign omniscience of economic agents. Instead of speaking of "representative agents" a very average agent suffices to explain the routines of economic life, though *not* its overall structuring.

8 Rational Expectations and the Inharmonious Market

In rational expectations theory markets are *in*harmonious, which is an interesting version of the best of all possible worlds. This places further emphasis on the Hobbesian (natural) individual. The Austrian "tradition," exemplified by Hayek and Mises and taken up by Chicago monetarist theories, pushed the state out and gave markets freedom. The hostile reaction to social democracy was accompanied by "a shift from extolling the harmony of interests to an assumption of bad faith." There was "no longer a single best outcome, which economists could recommend with confidence; instead a range of possible equilibria, none of them certain and many of them bad" (Offer and Söderberg 2016, 164). This overturned the axioms of neoclassical economics where the "core vision is simple: self-interest is harmonized by the invisible hand. The economy is driven by individuals, each seeking to maximize their private preference" (Offer and Söderberg 2016: 261). In the neoclassical world individuals were maximizing their marginal advantage in good faith believing that the

---

7   For another take on this, see Nick Chater, *The Mind is Flat* (2019). Or, more radically: "Eliminativists take the view that ordinary mental concepts are just bad concepts that need to be replaced with scientific ones, or not replaced at all" (Turner 2019, 25). By this account of a theory of the mind marginalist calculations are better explained by neuroscience.

market outcomes, while not equal, were legitimate; or if not just were justifiable in terms of the overriding mechanism of the market.

The assumption now becomes that in any market transaction (still between individuals) the other party is acting in bad faith. She will be gaming you, will have an "asymmetric" knowledge advantage, be exploiting moral hazard and the incompleteness over time of contracts etc. Opportunism, in the words of Oliver Williamson is "self-interest seeking with guile." As Offer and Söderberg conclude: "In sum, markets were no longer guided by an invisible hand, but could equally inflict an 'invisible backhand'" (Offer and Söderberg 2016, 164).

It is an unfriendly world since in any transaction, the other party's behavior has to be gamed and assumed to be not worthy of trust, i.e., bad faith is the existential condition. These theoretical insights are used to justify freedom of contracts in pension decisions, an argument when advanced justifies the superiority of individual choices in funded pension schemes, and health provision insurance over joint occupational schemes, and state provided medical care from taxation. Individual provision buttressed by contract take the place of collective provision. Such is the ideological momentum and human misery derived from "self-evident" naturalistic assumptions about human rationality.[8]

---

[8] This last sentence circumvents, for reason of space, the more fundamental argument on "natural" drivers of human actions. Piers Rawling makes some very perceptive comments. "On the Humean account rationality determines only the means, and has nothing to say concerning the relative preference ranking of any two ends" (a position taken up extensively by Max Weber). Total utility theories can only decide on the probabilities of achieving a given end, but they cannot rank the ends themselves. Hobbes assumed that man existing in a state of nature is a predator in the pursuit of self-interest, and the taming of these instincts requires all men to be subjugated to a sovereign who guarantees order and contracts (Rawling 2003, 115–16). Adam Smith assumes that is natural for men to truck and barter, and that the pursuit of profit leads to increased welfare and the wealth of the nation. If we turn to Thorstein Veblen on Adam Smith, the natural inclination to barter is socially constructed. Smith took it for granted that the country [Great Britain] has moved from feudal authoritarianism to a mercantile legal order. John Locke established "the doctrine of the 'natural' right to property based on productive labor." "The whole sequence of growth of this natural right is, of course, to be taken in connection with the general growth of individual rights that culminated in the eighteenth-century system of Natural Liberty" (Veblen 1904, 43). It was on this presumption that Smith could speak with confidence of the propensity to truck and barter as an original principle of human nature. For Veblen the assumption of what is taken as "natural" is a feature of the times these theorists lived in; they strike us now as naive—just as now the naivety of thinking that the business enterprise is concerned with production and welfare and not pecuniary speculation. The lesson is that appeals to inherent motives quickly turn out to be naive and false.

9   The Turing Solution

In all of the above parts it is apparent that there is an elective affinity between economic theories and cognitive theories of the mind. The potential is marked in the micro foundations of economics where marginalism, probability and utility calculations as well as games theory are key elements. All of these are susceptible to cognitive theories of the mind. This places a responsibility on economists *not* to exploit and theoretically misuse the general goal-directedness features of mind in the human species.

One way of characterizing the project of Stephen Turner and his colleagues is the critique of delusional social science. At the individual person level beliefs, desires, preferences, and tastes cannot be invoked as cause and explanation without demonstrating how this operates. Preferences and self-interest are not validated by empirical behavior; they are merely inferred back as motivations. Economists confidently bolt together beliefs and motives and acts assuming certain beliefs. They show little interest in the philosophy of social science and the philosophy of mind. Friedrich Hayek did try (unsuccessfully) to re-orient economics through epistemology. But across the board economists animate a natural person fully loaded up with tastes, preferences, and attitudes. This assumed person is used to justify the coherence of economic theories *and* to justify the ideological correctness of free markets. Insofar as economists are always invoking the cognitive in various ways, theories of mind can offer greater precision, thereby allowing a clearer boundary between what is scientifically argued and the prescriptive.

Carl Menger is exceptional among the tribe of economists in his reluctance to rest everything on a computing rational person; also his demand that the wider culture and civilization was the prime mover in defining needs and meeting them. Menger, I argued, negotiated successfully the boundary between culture and action—by stipulating the conditions under which people act. Menger in his day tutored the crown prince, a constitutionally legitimate legislator (in his time). Economists today have become self-appointed legislators, ignoring their Austrian founder.

The stand-out delusion is that a theory at the level of micro foundations projecting unvalidated assumptions can build an all-embracing theory of the macro. This relates to the ambition that economics is capable of coming up with a complete economic theory that will explain everything and leave no problem unsolved. The scientific ambitions are akin to mathematics at the start of the twentieth century. The way Alan Turing and colleagues handled the ambitions of theoretical mathematics could be illuminating for economics. My argument here is to suggest that the routine computational aspects of economics be taken away from economists and that this rationalistic core is not used to justify theories that are highly ideological and injurious to survival and security of citizens.

The analogue of mathematics to modern economics offers a different journey into theories of the mind. It was thought early in the twentieth century that in principle there would always be a method that would ascertain whether any mathematical assertion was provable or not. (This was Hilbert's third problem, the "decidability problem," that awaited a solution or proof, which Hilbert thought would be forthcoming.) In 1935 Alan Turing, then a mathematical fellow at Cambridge University, turned his attention to this. He did not approach it as if it was some sort of examination question that through dint of hard thinking and creativity would be solved. Instead he removed the problem from the mathematician's brain, so to speak, and argued that mathematical reasoning could be reduced and converted to mechanical processes that would test out the provability of mathematical assertions.

This, perhaps, is akin to solving a half-completed crossword puzzle. You run every letter of the alphabet through your mind for every empty space in a clue until the correct answer is found. A machine can do that, trying every combination of letters from its memory bank of words. Whether artificial intelligence can now complete crossword puzzles, I do not know. The point here is the initial approach, which says that numbers and symbols can be represented by machines, and be read by them. Instruction notes are fed into the machine telling them what to look for. A calculator is a mathematical brain on the desk. Advanced mathematical research on prime numbers is a field wholly dependent on computers that generate numbers so large that while they are identified by the computer as primes they are foremost computer numbers, mechanically generated. Instead of thinking of how to get a machine to do arithmetic, think of arithmetic as a machine process.

> ... the goal of this development was the development of what Hardy [a Cambridge mathematician] had called a "miraculous machine" - a mechanical process which could work on Hilbert's decision problem, reading a mathematical assertion presented to it, and eventually writing a verdict as to whether it was provable or not. The whole point was that it should do so without the interference of human judgement, imagination or intelligence.
>
> HODGES 2012, 125

The hint to economists here is to clear the brain of the economic individual of unnecessary attributes. In 1947 the British mathematician Sir Charles Darwin (grandson of the Charles Darwin) wrote in *The Times*:

In popular language the word "brain" is associated with the higher realms of the intellect, but in fact a very great part of the brain is an unconscious automatic machine producing precise and sometimes very complicated reactions to stimuli. This is the only part of the brain we may aspire to imitate. The new machines [Automatic Computing Engine] will in no way replace thought, but rather they will increase the need for it. ...

quoted in HODGES 2012, 449

Overheard at lunch, in 1937, in the Bell Corporation canteen, Dr. Alan Turing opined:

"No, I'm not interested in developing a *powerful* brain, I am just interested in a *mediocre* brain something like the President of the American Telephone and Telegraph Company." A machine would be fed data on the prices of commodities and stocks and be asked for example "Do I buy or sell?"

HODGES 2012, 316

In 2019 this is exactly how CEOs act. A machine is fed instructions and comes out with the answer: buy or sell. The same applies to capital markets, where hedge fund operations are controlled by "quants". Or take consumer behavior. On line shopping is machine controlled: search engines offer us a choice, determined by the instructions programmed into the search engine, and that same program learns from our previous choices, further determining or narrowing our choices. Taste and preference are secondary, though need—basic or imagined—remain primary. A given order of goods, to use Menger's conceptualization of the economy, can be and is handled by machine intelligence. Macro economies are controlled by central bank technicians. An instruction, which has only a tenuous connection to economic theory - here Wicksell's (imaginary) natural rate of interest—is fed into a machine that controls a digital money economy (Black et al 2018: 57–59).

Macroeconomics is not a field of problems awaiting further theoretical solutions; it is the sum of what happens at the level of machine intelligence plus its cognates as are identified by cognitive theories of the mind. Seen from the viewpoint of the latter, all routine behavior and their possible variants are algorithmic. Computers mirror this, placing the routine functions of the mind on the bench, so to speak, and successfully incorporating it. "The key principle, in short, is the substitutability of some other means for a mental or at least partly mental process" (Eck and Turner 2018, 162). The computer stands in for the same function in the mind. We no longer have farmers steeped in the habitus of their surroundings. The North American harvesting of cereals is controlled though satellite information relayed to decision making computers. The farmer turns the steering wheel. I pass over the related subject of speculative machines manipulating grain futures.

Cognitive processes and machines cannot, however, control the weather.[9] Menger's grasp of the meeting of needs on a survivable and sustainable basis becomes the issue for social theory, and economists as social theorists, faced with a mechanized civilization. What lies outside the dual functionality of minds and machines becomes the proper subject of human goal-directedness.

References

Black, A., V. Bojkova, M. Lloyd, and S. Whimster. 2018. *Federal Central Banks. A Comparison of the US Federal Reserve and the European Central Bank*. London: Forum Press.

Caldwell, B. 2007. "Hayek and the Austrian Tradition." In the *Cambridge Companion to Hayek*. Edited by E. Feser. Cambridge: Cambridge University Press.

Chater, N. 2019. *The Mind is Flat. The Illusion of Mental Depth and the Improvised Mind*. London: Penguin.

Dyson, George. 2012. *Turing's Cathedral. The Origins of the Digital Universe* London: Penguin.

Eck, D., and Turner, S. 2019. "Cognitive Science and Social Theory." *The Oxford Handbook of Cognitive Sociology*. Edited by W. Brekhus and G. Ignatow. Oxford: Oxford University Press. DOI: 10.1093/oxfordhb/9780190273385.013.9.

Grinder, W.E. 1977. "In Pursuit of the Subjective Paradigm." In *Capital Expectations and the Market Process: Essays on the Theory of the Market Economy*. Edited by L. Lachman. Kansas: Sheed Andrews and McMeel, 3–14.

Fregert, K. and Jonung, L. 1996. "Inflation and Switches between Specie and Paper Standards in Sweden 1668–1931: A Public Finance Interpretation." *Scottish Journal of Political Economy* 43 (4): 444–467.

Hacking, I. 1990. *The Taming of Chance*. Cambridge: Cambridge University Press.

Hodges, A. 2012. *Alan Turing: The Enigma*. London: Vintage.

Lachmann, L. (Ed.) 1977. *Capital Expectations and the Market Process: Essays on the Theory of the Market Economy*. Kansas: Sheed Andrews and McMeel.

Malmqvist, Peter. 2019. "Negative Rates and the Swedish Experience." *Financial Times*, Letters, 29 October 2019. https://www.ft.com/content/c7c0a782-f96d-11e9-98fd-4d6c20050229.

---

9 Though weather forecasting with computers grew out of John von Neumann's ambition to *control* the weather (Dyson 2012, 160–1).

Menger, C. 1871. *Grundsätze der Volkswirtschaftslehre*. Vienna: Wilhelm Braumüller.

Menger, C. 1981. *Principles of Economics*. Trans. J. Dingwall and B. F. Hoselitz. New York: New York University Press.

Offer, A. and G. Söderberg. 2016. *The Nobel Factor. The Prize in Economics, Social Democracy, and the Market Turn*. Princeton and Oxford: Princeton University Press.

Pearson, K. 1978. *The History of Statistics in the 17th and 18th Centuries*. Edited by E. S. Pearson. London and High Wycombe: Charles Griffin.

Rawlings, P. 2003. "Decision Theory and Degree of Belief." In *The Blackwell Guide to the Philosophy of the Social Sciences*. Edited by S. Turner and P. Roth. Oxford: Blackwell.

Rescorla, M. 2013. "Bayesian Perceptual Psychology." In *The Oxford Handbook of Philosophy of Perception*. New York: Oxford University Press. DOI: 10.1093/oxfordhb/9780199600472.013.010.

Russell, B. 1947. *The History of Western Philosophy*. London: George Allen and Unwin.

Streissler, E. 1973. "To What Extent was the Austrian School Marginalist?" In *The Marginal Revolution in Economics. Interpretation and Evaluation*. Edited by R. D. Collinson Black and A.W. Coats, et al. Durham NC: Duke University Press.

Turner, S. 2018a. "The Belief-Desire Model of Action Explanation Reconsidered: Thoughts on Bittner." *Philosophy of the Social Sciences*, 48 (3): 290–308. DOI: 10.1177/0048393117750076.

Turner, S. 2018b. *Cognitive Science and the Social. A Primer*. London: Routledge.

Turner, S. 2019. "Causation, Value Judgments, *Verstehen*." In *The Oxford Handbook of Max Weber*. Edited by E. Hanke, L. Scaff, and S. Whimster. New York: Oxford University Press. DOI:10.1093/oxfordhb/9780190679545.013.38.

Veblen, T. 1904. *The Theory of Business Enterprise*. New York: Charles Scribner's Sons.

Weber, M. 2012 [1908]. "The Theory of Marginal Utility and the 'Fundamental Laws of Psychophysics'." In *Max Weber. Collected Methodological Writings*, trans. H.H. Bruun; edited by H.H. Bruun, and S. Whimster. London and New York: Routledge.

Weber, M. 2013. *Wirtschaft und Gesellschaft. Soziologie*, MWG I/23, edited by K. Borchardt, E. Hanke, and W. Schluchter. Tübingen: Mohr (Siebeck).

Whimster, S. 2018. "Pure Relationality as a Sociological Theory of Communication." *Frontiers in Sociology*, Jan. https://doi.org/10.3389/fsoc.2018.00001.

Whimster, S. 2019. "Economics and Society and the Fate of Liberal Capitalism." In *The Oxford Handbook of Max Weber*. Edited by E. Hanke, L. Scaff, and S. Whimster. New York: Oxford University Press. DOI: 10.1093/oxfordhb/9780190679545.013.3.

Interpretivism and Qualitative Research

Julie Zahle

Abstract

Interpretivism is commonly associated with the employment of qualitative methods. In philosophical discussions of interpretivism, however, the way in which qualitative research is conducted and may serve as basis for the advancement of interpretations is almost never considered. In this paper, I explore how the philosophical discussions may benefit from taking into account the way qualitative researchers go about their business. From this perspective, I examine Taylor's influential defense of interpretivism and two objections to it, the argument from lack of brute data and the argument from underdetermination. I argue that, by bringing into view how qualitative research proceeds, it may be shown that Taylor's position should be amended, that the argument from brute data should be dismissed, and that the argument from underdetermination has a much smaller scope than assumed by its proponents.

Keywords

interpretivism – qualitative research – Taylor – underdetermination – brute data – Jones – Turner

1   Introduction

Interpretivism is the view that the social sciences should only, or at least mainly, offer accounts in the form of interpretations of meaning. It is commonly taken that, in the process of arriving at these interpretations, researchers make use of qualitative methods. For instance, Mark Risjord observes that "[t]he research methods associated with interpretation are often called 'qualitative research'" (Risjord 2014, 57). Likewise, Malcolm Williams writes that "[a]part from the analysis of pre-given texts (books, film, archive material etc.) interpretivists use two principal methods […] of Participant Observation and Unstructured Interviewing" (Williams 2000, 90–91). Or, to mention one last example, Mark Bevir and Jason Blakely comment that "[s]ocial science today has largely reduced the interpretive turn to a commitment to 'qualitative' methods" (Bevir and Blakely 2018, 88).

In philosophical discussions of interpretivism, the way in which qualitative research is conducted and may serve as basis for the advancement of interpretations is almost never considered. In this paper, I explore how these discussions may benefit from taking into account how qualitative researchers go about their business.[1] From this perspective, I examine both an influential defense of interpretivism and two objections to it. I argue that, by bringing into view how qualitative research proceeds, it may be shown that the interpretivist position should be amended, and that one of the objections should be dismissed and the other regarded as less significant than assumed by its proponents.

I concentrate on Charles Taylor's highly influential defense of interpretivism in his "Interpretation and the Sciences of Man" (1985). In the paper, Taylor does not directly state that interpretations should be based on qualitative research. Yet, at one point, he notes that advancing interpretations requires the researcher to examine individuals' self-interpretations and the streams of actions in which they are set (Taylor 1985, 26). And qualitative methods are well suited to this task. Moreover, Taylor forcefully criticizes the use of quantitative methods in political science and implies that they are not usable for the purposes of offering interpretations. This makes it tempting to ascribe to him the view that the standard alternative to quantitative methods, viz. qualitative methods, should be employed instead. Perhaps for these reasons, Taylor's interpretivism is sometimes explicitly associated with the use of qualitative research. For instance, Bohman comments that one of Taylor's examples of an interpretation "requires slow ethnographic [i.e., qualitative] and historic description" (Bohman 1993, 106). In any case, the sheer fact that Taylor is a key proponent of Interpretivism makes his account fitting to serve as the focal point of the subsequent discussion.

In the following, I begin by presenting Taylor's position. Next, I provide an introduction to qualitative research while showing how this account brings into view that Taylor's interpretivism is in need of amendment. I then turn to two objections to Taylor's account and show how they apply to his amended position. In the philosophical debate on interpretivism, the approach has first and foremost been opposed on the ground that interpretations lack justification.[2] The two objections exemplify this line of criticism. One is the

---

1 It should be noted that, by adopting this focus, I do not mean to suggest that only qualitative methods may be used for the purposes of offering of interpretations.
2 For alternative discussions of these and other objections to both Taylor's interpretivism and other formulations of the approach, see, e.g., Bohman 1993, 102ff; Fay 1998, 112ff; Kincaid 1996, 191ff; Little 1991, 68ff; Martin 2000, 159ff; Roth 1987.

argument from lack of brute data that Taylor brings up himself. The other is the well-known argument from underdetermination. I argue that, by taking into account how qualitative research is conducted, it may be shown that the argument from lack of brute data must be found wanting and that the argument from underdetermination has a much smaller scope than assumed by its proponents. I end by briefly summarizing the findings of the paper.

Before embarking on this task, however, a few words about Stephen Turner's work is in order. One of Turner's main contributions is his dissection and criticism of theories of practice in "The Social Theory of Practices" (1994) and succeeding publications (see, e.g., Turner 2002, 2014). Turner's work on this topic is highly influential and, personally, I keep returning to it for insight and inspiration. I have elsewhere discussed various aspects of Turner's objections to theories of practice (Zahle 2017, but also 2014, 2013). In this paper, I continue my "conversation" with Turner's work by taking up his argument from underdetermination as it applies to Taylor's interpretivist position.

2   Taylor's Interpretivism

According to Taylor, the social sciences should exclusively, or at least mainly, offer interpretations of actions and practices. These are accounts, which purport to make clearer the meaning of actions and practices.

An interpretation of an action identifies the action (the kind of action performed). Moreover, it states why the individual performed the action through a specification of the acting individual's emotions/feelings and desires in response to the situation. Also, it may detail the individual's beliefs as prompted by the situation or acquired on an earlier occasion (Taylor 1985, 23). Taylor refers to the emotions, desires, etc. as an individual's subjective meanings. An example of an interpretation of an action might be that the minister broke off the negotiation because she felt angry about her negotiation partner making unreasonable demands and didn't want to waste any more time futilely trying to reach an agreement.

An action may be part of a practice. The latter refers to a social activity that is constituted by (could not exist without) distinctions in the language that accompanies the activity. For instance, the activity of negotiation is a practice in this sense. It is constituted by descriptions like "entering into negotiation," "breaking off negotiations," "offering to negotiate," "negotiating in god (bad) faith," "concluding negotiations," and "making a new offer" (Taylor 1985, 32).

An interpretation of a practice identifies its practice-actions, as I shall call them, that is, the types of action that are part of it. Further, it specifies the ideas about the individual and her relations to others and society, and the norms that together "are constitutive of the social matrix in which individuals find themselves and act" when they take part in a practice (Taylor 1985, 36). Both the ideas and norms are implicit in a practice in the sense of being not merely in people's minds but also "out there in the practices themselves" (Tayor 1985, 35). This being the case, Taylor refers to the ideas and norms as intersubjective rather than subjective meanings. By way of illustration, consider an interpretation of the practice of negotiation. It would lay out the different types of actions that are part of it and make clear that the practice presupposes the idea of distinct parties entering into a willed relationship, and norms like that of good faith (one should negotiate with the genuine intention of reaching an agreement) and of rationality (agreement should correspond as much as possible to one's goals) (Taylor 1985, 35).

Interpretations of practices may also point to common meanings. These are values—notions of what is significant—that individuals share and which are part of their common reference world. Because of this latter feature, Taylor maintains, they are not subjective meanings either. Common meanings may give rise to and sustain practices and consequently an interpretation of a practice may also draw attention to the common meanings that accompanies it. An example of an interpretation along these lines might be that the ideal of a free society, that assigns an important role to bargaining, has served to sustain the practice of negotiation (Taylor 1985, 40).

It may now be specified in what sense interpretations of actions and practices make clearer their meaning. Taylor observes that individuals interpret—and as such articulate or put into words—the meanings of their actions, practices, and the accompanying subjective, intersubjective, and common meanings. However, individuals' self-interpretations are often confused, incomplete and partly erroneous (Taylor 1985, 26). The researcher's interpretations purport to be clearer compared to these self-interpretations.

Lastly, it may be noted that Taylor holds that interpretations of actions and practices may only be justified by appeal to their coherence with other interpretations (Taylor 1985, 17). Accordingly, the interpretation of an action may only be supported by pointing to its coherence with other identifications of actions, interpretations of subjective meanings and interpretations of actions (actions plus subjective meanings). Similarly, interpretations of practices may only be justified by reference to their coherence with other identifications of practices, interpretations of intersubjective and common meanings, and interpretations of practices (practices plus intersubjective and/or common meanings) (Taylor 1985, 52). In this fashion, there is no way out of the circle of interpretation. Consequently, if the correctness of an interpretation is still disputed, that is, after its coherence with other interpretations has been demonstrated, there is no other option but to tell the critic that she needs to develop her intuitions or change more radically (Taylor 1985, 54).

3 Qualitative Research

The advancement of interpretations is commonly associated with the use of qualitative methods. In order to spell out this linkage as it applies to Taylor's interpretivist position, it is helpful first to say a few words about qualitative research. In this section, I offer a brief introduction to participant observation and qualitative interviewing that are likely the two most frequently used qualitative methods of data generation (Bryman 2012, 493).

In participant observation, the researcher participates in the research participants' ways of life. The researcher may participate to different degrees. For instance, she may participate in the weaker sense of simply hanging around or in the stronger sense of engaging actively in the research participants' activities. In any case, she should try to effect the ways of life she studies as little as possible. While participating, the researcher observes, i.e., notes, what goes on. Typically, the researcher carries out participant observation over an extended period of time. Earlier on, in anthropology, this meant that the researcher should stay in the field for at least a year. Today, studies of a much shorter duration are also regarded as perfectly acceptable.

The researcher's descriptions of her observations make up her field notes, i.e., field data. As DeWalt and DeWalt explain it, field notes provide a detailed account of the situations observed by the researcher and as such they "should include description[s] of the physical context, the people involved, as much of their behavior and nonverbal communication as possible, and in words that are as close as possible to the words used by the participants. Indeed, verbatim quotes should be included to the extent to which the researcher has jotted them down or can accurately remember them. Specific words, special language, terms, and vocabulary should be recorded" (DeWalt and DeWalt 2011, 165–6).

In qualitative interviewing, the researcher poses questions to an interviewee who, in her replies, is permitted or encouraged to digress, to expand on her views, to exemplify her points, to introduce her own concerns, and the like. Qualitative interviewing is semi-structured or unstructured, or somewhere in between. In semi-structured interviewing, the researcher has a list of questions that she goes through. She may pose them in whatever order seems natural during the interview just as she may add questions. In unstructured interviewing, the researcher has at most a list of topics that she wants to cover. She does not introduce these in any pre-fixed order and formulates her questions as she goes along. As a result, the interaction comes close to an ordinary conversation. In both cases, the researcher should make an effort not to influence what people say on the issues that come up during the interview. Lastly, a qualitative interview is typically conducted in a setting familiar to the research participant who may be interviewed on one or several occasions.

The interview notes, i.e., interview data, consist in transcriptions of audio-recordings, or in descriptions of what was said during interviews as based on the researcher's observations and scratch notes. In addition, interview notes detail other aspects of the interview situation such as the setting in which it took place, the research participants' facial expressions, and their nonverbal behavior during the interview.

The analysis of field and interview data usually begins while data generation is still ongoing and then continues more intensively after the researcher has left the field. While there are various qualitative methods of data analysis, these have received comparatively less attention than qualitative methods of data generation. For the present purposes, there is no need to go into different ways of analyzing qualitative data. It suffices to note that the researcher uses her data as evidence base for her research findings. In the following, I focus exclusively on the employment of participant observation and qualitative interviewing and, in line with common practice, I assume that they are used in tandem.

4 Taylor's Interpretivism and Qualitative Research

Taylor's interpretivist position is that social researchers should offer interpretations of actions and practices. I now explicate how qualitative research may serve as basis for these interpretations. Also, I show that paying attention to this issue makes it apparent that Taylor's interpretivism is in need of amendment.

Following the outline offered in the last section, the qualitative researcher starts by generating field and interview data that describe the research participants' doings and sayings, their contexts of action, etc. Note that field and interview data describe the research participants' doings, sayings, etc. in words that come as close as possible to those they use. Since the research participants are likely mainly to describe their doings, sayings, etc. in meaningful terms, the researcher should strive to do the same. Accordingly, her field and interview notes will mostly be interpretations. To underline this point, I shall often refer to the notes as data-interpretations though this is a simplification as all the data may not, to repeat, be interpretations. In any case, the researcher uses her data as the evidence base for her research findings in the form of interpretations of actions and practices.

This rough depiction of the research process shows that it is quite straightforward how qualitative research may be used with the aim of providing interpretations of actions and practices. Yet, it also points to aspects of Taylor's position in need of clarification. In the account of the research process, a distinction is made between qualitative data and the research findings (the interpretations of actions and practices) based on these data. I shall formulate this distinction as one between data-interpretations and data-based interpretations in order to highlight that qualitative data are interpretations too (at least for the most part). Taylor does not draw a distinction of this sort. How does it apply to his position?

In response, consider the types of interpretations Taylor mentions. These are: identifications of actions and practices, interpretations of subjective, intersubjective and common meanings, and finally interpretations of actions (actions plus subjective meanings) and interpretations of practices (practices plus intersubjective and/or common meanings). All of these, except identifications of actions, may plausibly be classified as data-based interpretations. With respect to action-identifications, Taylor at one point comments that, in order to offer interpretations of actions and practices, the researcher should examine the research participants' streams of actions (Taylor 1985, 26). Since this likely means that the researcher should also identify their actions, the remark suggests that Taylor thinks of action-identifications as data-interpretations. In the passage just mentioned, Taylor also states that the researcher should look to the research participants' self-interpretations. This indicates that he would agree that data-interpretations comprise descriptions of individuals' sayings that express their self-interpretations.

The application of the distinction between data-interpretations and data-based interpretations to Taylor's position brings into view that he works with too thin a conception of data-interpretations. A qualitative researcher does not limit herself to describing individuals' doings and their stated self-interpretations. Research participants say many things unrelated to their self-interpretations and a qualitative researcher typically notes them down too. Moreover, she details the research participants' contexts of actions, that is, their settings (a church, a private home), their furniture and equipment (a desk, a computer, a hammer), their outfits (a nurse uniform, a swimsuit), and the like. These material data are important. They are taken into account when the researcher identifies actions as when she sees that the person, who wears a police uniform and stands in the middle of an intersection where the stoplight doesn't work, is directing the traffic. Also, many actions and practices involve, or are directed towards, the material circumstances of social life. For these reasons, Taylor's position should be modified so that it recognizes a broader range of data-interpretations.

Another issue raised by the application of the distinction between data-interpretations and data-based interpretations to Taylor's interpretivism is how it affects his view of the justification of interpretations. He holds, remember, that interpretations may only be justified by their coherence with other interpretations. In light of the distinction, there are different ways in which to understand this claim.

Consider first the suggestion that both data-interpretations and data-based interpretations may only be justified by other interpretations. Intuitively, this view seems difficult to defend in relation to data-interpretations: a data-interpretation may also be justified by pointing to the researcher's competence to identify the sayings, doings, or material circumstances that it describes. For instance, the researcher's description of what a research participant said may be justified by noting that the researcher is a competent speaker of the research participant's language and that there was no background noise that prevented her from hearing what was said. Accordingly, Taylor's claim about justification should be limited to data-based interpretations only: these (and not data-interpretations too) may solely be justified by other interpretations. This still leaves it open what interpretations justify data-based interpretations. Once the category of data-interpretations has been recognized, it is reasonable to hold that data-based interpretations must always cohere with the researcher's data-interpretations. At the same time, and in line with Taylor's thinking, it may also be taken to count in favor of a data-based interpretation that it coheres with other such interpretations. In sum, Taylor's view should be specified as the claim that data-based interpretations may only be justified by their coherence with the researcher's data-interpretations and other data-based interpretations.

The upshot of the foregoing considerations is that, taking into consideration how qualitative research is conducted, Taylor's interpretivist position should be slightly amended. To bring it into line with qualitative research practices, it should: incorporate the distinction between data-interpretations and data-based interpretations, acknowledge that the qualitative researcher generates other data-interpretations than identifications of the research participants' actions and their stated self-interpretations, and specify that data-based interpretations may be justified by their coherence with data-interpretations and other data-based interpretations. There may well be other ways in which Taylor's account is in need of revision (I think there are). Here, though, I shall not go into these. My sole concern has been to point to revisions that may be prompted by taking into account how qualitative researchers go about their business.

5 The Argument from Lack of Brute Data

As part of his defense of Interpretivism, Taylor discusses, and rejects, the argument from lack of brute data, as it may be called.[3] Evidently, he considers the argument as it applies to his un-amended position. However, it is easily adapted so that it targets the amended version of his account presented at the end of the last section. Thus adjusted, the argument goes as follows: In order for interpretations of actions and practices to be justified, it is necessary that they cohere with brute data, i.e., data that do not involve any interpretation and cannot be challenged by offering a different interpretation (see Taylor 1985, 19). Yet, interpretations of actions and practices may only be justified by their coherence with data-interpretations that may always be questioned by offering an alternative interpretation. Therefore, interpretations of actions and practices lack justification.

Taylor's response to the argument is to deny the premise that a necessary condition of interpretations of actions and practices being justified is that they cohere with brute data. In support of this move, he contends that this is to set the standard of justification way too high; it "is to adopt an absurdly severe criterion of 'certainty', which deprives the concept of any sensible use" (Taylor 1985, 18). By the lights of a lower and reasonable standard of justification, interpretations of actions and practices are justified by their coherence with data-interpretations.[4]

Though I sympathize with the gist of Taylor's reply, I think it is unsatisfactory as it stands: it fails to show why and when it is reasonable to maintain that interpretations of actions and practices are indeed justified by their coherence with data-interpretations that may always be challenged by offering a different interpretation. I now show how such an account may be developed by taking into consideration how qualitative research proceeds.

---

3 It should be noted that Taylor does not explicitly state and rebut the argument. Rather, I take the argument and its rebuttal to be the gist of his discussion on pp. 17–21 just as it also surfaces pp. 28–31 (Taylor 1985).
4 In the last section, it was specified that interpretations of actions and practices are also justified by their coherence with other data-based interpretations. To keep the focus on data, I simply leave out this addition in the subsequent discussion.

Consider a qualitative researcher who carries out participant observation and conducts qualitative interviews. Imagine that she is a native Dane who does her research in Denmark in a familiar context. Sometimes she works under standard conditions, i.e., she can properly hear what people say, she is not drunk, etc. Other times the conditions are difficult: the music is too loud for her properly to hear what people say, there is too little light properly to see what goes on, her recording of an interview is of poor quality, or the like. In the latter case, she makes sure to confirm the correctness of the data by appeal to other data-interpretations.

It is worth briefly to go over different ways in which some data-interpretations (that the researcher is confident are correct) may lend support to other more uncertain data-interpretations. First, field or interview data about what a research participant says about some situation may confirm the researcher's description of that situation in her field or interview notes. This is the case, insofar as the research participant describes the situation in a similar manner to the notes. Second, data-interpretations of a research participant's actions may provide a reason for holding that other field or interview data correctly describe some situation if the action may be taken to suggest that the research participant would agree to the researcher's description of the situation. Finally, the researcher may show her field or interview notes to a research participant. If the latter approves of the notes, this constitutes evidence in support of their being correct unless there is reason to think that the research participant is not frank, is overly polite, and the like.[5]

Insofar as the Danish researcher proceeds in this manner—she carefully notes down what transpires in the situations she observes and she makes sure to confirm data that describe observations made in difficult conditions—her research is relevantly well conducted. In this case, it is highly likely that her data-interpretations correctly describe the research participants' sayings, doings, contexts of action, etc.

The scenario in which the researcher is familiar with the ways of life she studies while being also fluent in the research participants' language is ideal from the perspective of obtaining qualitative data that correctly describe the research participants' doings, sayings, etc. Less ideal scenarios may also be contemplated. Envisage that the Danish researcher still conducts research in

---

5 This last strategy exemplifies a form of respondent validation. In respondent validation, the researcher asks research participants to confirm the correctness of her data, preliminary analyses, or research findings. Among these, the presentation of the research findings to research participants seems to be the most discussed and commonly recommended form of respondent validation (see, e.g., Bryman 2012, 391; Seale 1999, 61ff; Stake 1995, 115ff).

Denmark but now in an unfamiliar context. As a result, she is not acquainted with all the research participants' actions, practices, ways of describing them, and so on. Next, picture that the researcher studies more and more unfamiliar ways of life and/or research participants whose language she speaks less and less well. The further the researcher moves away from the ideal scenario, the longer it likely takes, and the more effort it requires, to become familiar with the research participants' ways of life and to be in a position correctly to describe their actions, sayings, etc. The researcher will increasingly need to generate data-interpretations that confirm that she is able correctly to describe their actions, sayings, etc. even in standard conditions. Still, insofar as the researcher takes these steps, her research is well conducted: she is highly likely to end up with data-interpretations that correctly describe what transpired when she carried out participant observation and conducted her qualitative interviews.

In light of these reflections, it may now be explicated why and when it is reasonable to maintain that interpretations of actions and practices are indeed justified by their coherence with data-interpretations that may always be questioned by offering a different interpretation. This is the case when the generation of the data-interpretations exemplify relevantly well conducted research since this means that the data are likely correctly to describe the research participants' doings, sayings, etc. It may be granted that even so a data-interpretation may always be challenged by coming up with an alternative, i.e., conflicting, data-interpretation. In well-conducted qualitative research, this challenge is not in any way a serious one: when there are good reasons to hold that a data-interpretation is correct, any conflicting interpretation is unlikely to be correct; it is implausible.

The addition of this account to Taylor's reply amounts to a more convincing rebuttal of the argument from lack of brute data since it shows, to repeat, why and when it is reasonable to maintain that interpretations of actions and practices are justified by their coherence with data-interpretations that may always be questioned by offering a different interpretation. It should be stressed that I do not claim that this is the sole way in which to dismiss the argument from brute data. My line of approach reflects my concern with exploring how taking into account the way qualitative researchers go about their business may contribute to the philosophical debate about interpretivism.

6 The Argument from Underdetermination

The other objection to Taylor's amended interpretivism is the argument from underdetermination. It states that interpretations of actions and practices are underdetermined by their data: the data-interpretations are equally compatible with different data-based interpretations. In consequence, the claim that a particular data-based interpretation is correct lacks justification. In this section, I discuss two different ways in which to push this line of argument put forward by Todd Jones (1998, 2000) and Stephen Turner (1994) respectively. As Taylor does not defend his position against the argument, I respond on his behalf by appealing, once more, to the way in which qualitative research is conducted. While my responses do not amount to dismissals of Jones' and Turner's versions of the argument, they show that the problem of underdetermination likely occurs less frequently than they acknowledge.

In his paper "Ethnography, Belief Description, and Epistemological Barriers," Jones argues that the evidence qualitative researchers offer in support of their ascriptions of particular beliefs is usually inadequate: it underdetermines their belief ascriptions (Jones 2000, 145).[6] Moreover, he contends, qualitative researchers run into this predicament because they typically use a combination of two basic strategies of belief ascription.

One is the behavioral strategy. Here, the researcher observes a research participant perform a particular action. Then the researcher makes the assumption that a certain belief tends to bring about an action of that sort. On that ground, she infers that the individual has the belief in question (Jones 2000, 120). The problem with this strategy, Jones states, is that a given action is compatible with the ascription of multiple different beliefs in combination with diverse desires and auxiliary beliefs.[7]

The other main strategy is the environmental one. Here, the researcher observes that a research participant is exposed to a certain social or natural environment. Next, she adds the assumption that an environment of that kind typically results in the adoption of a given belief and then she concludes that the individual has the belief in question (Jones 2000, 124). Jones asserts that this way of proceeding runs into the obstacle that the belief an individual forms in response to an environment depends on her auxiliary beliefs. As a result, an environment is consistent with ascribing to an individual multiple

---

6 Jones mainly talks about ethnographers rather than qualitative researchers though he does use the latter term on a few occasions. Still, he may plausibly be taken to hold that ethnographers use qualitative methods. Thus, in order to streamline the terminology, I phrase his view in qualitative research terms.

7 Jones further expands on his criticism of this strategy and the same applies to the strategy that I consider next. For the present purposes, however, his more elaborate considerations need not be taken into account: doing so will not make a difference to the objections that I raise in a moment.

different beliefs in combination with diverse auxiliary beliefs. In this manner, qualitative researchers who employ the two basic strategies invariably run into the problem of underdetermination.

Jones continues by explicating that qualitative researchers sometimes try to patch up the two basic strategies by adding the approach of asking the research participants about their beliefs (Jones 2000, 126). Equipped with these data, researchers may be reasonably confident about their ascriptions of "ordinary consciously accessible beliefs [...to] people much like [themselves]" (Jones 2000, 138). Unfortunately, however, the approach is not really effective in relation to exotic beliefs and unconscious symbolic beliefs. Exotic beliefs are ones harbored by people who are very different from the researcher. These people may not tell the researcher what they truly believe as they often fail to trust outsiders. Further, the researcher may not speak their language sufficiently well to gather exactly what they are saying. In connection with unconscious symbolic beliefs, asking the research participants about these beliefs is not of much help either as the beliefs are not consciously accessible. For these reasons, the problem of underdetermination persists with respect to the ascription of exotic and unconscious symbolic beliefs.

Jones' argument poses a challenge to Taylor's interpretivism as there are two obvious ways in which interpretations posit beliefs. Interpretations of actions typically involve the ascription of beliefs to the acting individual. Moreover, interpretations of practices include specifications of the ideas that are constitutive of a practice. Because the ideas are in individuals' minds too, the interpretations should be seen as ascribing these ideas—beliefs—to the participants in a practice. This means that, by the lights of Jones' argument, interpretations of both actions and practices, or the beliefs they posit, are underdetermined by the researcher's data.

In order to assess this contention, consider first a qualitative researcher, who competently employs the method of participant observation. Her field data describe the situations she observes in detail: they list the people present in the observed situations, what they did, what they said, what the contexts of the action were (i.e., their settings, equipment, furniture, outfit), and so on. These points sit badly with the first part of Jones' argument: they show that a qualitative researcher, who competently employs the method of participant observation, does not confine herself to observe either particular actions (the behavioral strategy) or the environment in which an individual finds herself (the environmental strategy). Rather, she makes, to repeat, observations and detailed notes about the people under study, what they did, what they said, their contexts of action, etc. Moreover and crucially, it is reasonable to think that the researcher uses *all* these data—and not merely data about either particular actions or environments—as the basis for her belief ascriptions. Why wouldn't she? In other words, competent participant observers do not employ the behavioral and environmental strategy as their two main strategies and, by implication, they do not run into the problem of underdetermination that accompany their employment.

Further, unless the researcher participates in the limited sense of merely staying silently in the background, she typically has conversations with the research participants. As part of these exchanges, she is likely sometimes to ask them about their beliefs. In addition, recall that participant observation is commonly used in combination with qualitative interviewing where the researcher evidently has ample opportunity to prompt the research participants to state their beliefs. These considerations indicate that it is also a mischaracterization of the way qualitative research is usually conducted to maintain that qualitative researchers only *sometimes* ask the research participants about the beliefs. Rather, doing so is typically part and parcel of carrying out participant observation just as the method is commonly used in tandem with qualitative interviewing.

These misgivings about Jones' argument do not undermine its second part. It may be granted that the qualitative researcher generates a wide variety of data-interpretations, while still insisting that these data underdetermine ascriptions of exotic and symbolic unconscious beliefs because the approach of asking people to report these beliefs is of no avail. I shall not dispute this point in relation to unconscious symbolic beliefs. Instead, I challenge it with respect to exotic beliefs.

Jones thinks that people with exotic, i.e., very different, beliefs may not tell the researcher what they truly believe because they often fail to trust outsiders. However, as noted in the presentation of the method, participant observation should be carried out over an extended period of time and this means that the researcher has time to build up relations of trust with the research participants (a point Jones acknowledges but makes nothing of [Jones 2000, 132]). Moreover, the researcher being an outsider may sometimes be an advantage. The fact that she is not, and will not, become a permanent member of the community she studies may at times make the research participants more inclined to talk truthfully to her than if she had been an insider: being an outsider, she is not a threat to those in power, she has no stake in ongoing struggles, and so on.

Jones' second reason for maintaining that asking people about their exotic beliefs is an ineffective approach is that the researcher may not speak the research participants' language sufficiently well to gather exactly what they are saying. Yet, as Jones also recognizes, people with exotic beliefs include individuals who are marginalized within the researcher's own language community.

Needless to say, the researcher will not have any difficulties comprehending what they say. With respect to research participants who do indeed speak a different language, the researcher may improve her knowledge of their language during the extended period of time in which she carries out participant observation. In addition, she may sometimes resort to help from an interpreter. In view of these reflections, Jones' claim about exotic beliefs should be qualified: asking people about their exotic beliefs is only sometimes—rather than mostly or always—an ineffective approach. Thus, exotic beliefs are not for their most part underdetermined by the researcher's data. On a more general note, therefore, Taylor's interpretations of actions and practices—the ascriptions of beliefs that they contain—are likely to be much less frequently underdetermined by the researcher's data-interpretations than Jones' argument asserts.

In his influential book "The Social Theory of Practices," Turner pursues a different version of the argument from underdetermination that targets the ascription of tacit presuppositions (Turner 1994, 28ff). These are an individual's beliefs, norms, values, and the like, that she has not explicitly formulated and to which she has no conscious access. Researchers ascribe tacit presuppositions to research participants whose self-reported beliefs, norms, etc. do not suffice to account for their doings and sayings: only by positing the tacit presuppositions is it possible fully to make sense of what the research participants were up to.

In line with this latter point, Turner emphasizes that tacit presuppositions are ascribed on the basis of data about the doings and sayings in need of explanation: it is data about the (supposed) behavioral manifestations of tacit presuppositions that first and foremost serve as evidence for their ascription. In passing, Turner notes that additional data are available when it comes to positing tacit norms. Here, observations of situations in which the norms are breached also constitute evidence for their ascription (Turner 1994, 28). Lastly, Turner makes it clear that ascriptions of tacit beliefs are also constrained by considerations of consistency. More precisely, at one point, Turner maintains that ascriptions of explicit beliefs to research participants (their stated beliefs) may *perhaps* be used to rule out ascriptions of tacit beliefs that are inconsistent with them (Turner 1994, 30). The "perhaps" is due to the fact that it is perfectly possible, psychologically speaking, for individuals to harbor inconsistent beliefs. A little later, Turner seems to make the slightly stronger claim that a posited belief, a tacit one included, should be consistent with the other beliefs attributed to an individual (Turner 1994, 33). Putting these points together, I shall take it that, in Turner's view, a posited tacit belief should, prima facie, be consistent with the other beliefs ascribed to an individual.

Turner contends that ascriptions of tacit presuppositions are underdetermined by a researcher's data. The observation of a research participant's action or claim is typically compatible with the ascription of different tacit presuppositions to her. Thus, the assertion that one of the ascriptions is the correct one lacks justification. Further, the point that different tacit presuppositions may account for the same action or claim carries over to situations in which the research participants perform the same type of action or make the same type of claim: in these cases, the tacit presuppositions may well vary among the individuals (Turner 1994, 31). The data underdetermine the contention that the same type of tacit presupposition brings about the similar actions or claims. Moreover, Turner's discussion implies, adding data about situations of norm breach and allowing consistency considerations to constrain ascriptions of tacit beliefs makes little or no difference to this situation.

On this basis, consider how Turner's argument applies to Taylor's interpretivism. Taylor maintains that individuals routinely engage in self-interpretation, that is, try to articulate their subjective meanings (beliefs, desires, emotions), their intersubjective meanings (the practice-constitutive ideas and norms that are also in their minds), and their common meanings (shared values). Individuals' self-interpretations, however, are often confused, incomplete, and partly erroneous. When this is the case, it is reasonable, I think, to regard their beliefs, desires, norms, values, etc. as tacit: they remain unarticulated and individuals have no conscious access to them. It follows from these points that interpretations of actions which ascribe tacit presuppositions (beliefs, desires, emotions, etc.) to single individuals, are underdetermined by the researcher's data-interpretations. Further, Taylor thinks that the participants in a practice subscribe to the same ideas, norms, and values. Insofar as these are tacit, Turner's second point of underdetermination has a bite too: interpretations of practices which maintain that the participants endorse the same tacit presuppositions (norms, ideas, and values) are also underdetermined by the data-interpretations: it may well be that the research participants' tacit presuppositions differ.

In response to Turner's argument, contemplate once again the data generated by a competent qualitative researcher. These include descriptions of multiple situations in terms of the people present, their doings and sayings, their context of action, etc. Further, the data about individuals' sayings may comprise not only their stated beliefs, but also their reported values, feelings, desires, long-term aspirations, and the like. A qualitative researcher is likely to draw on all these data when she ascribes tacit presuppositions to research participants. Why wouldn't she? Accordingly, there is no reason to think, as Turner seems to, that the data qualitative researchers use as the basis for their ascriptions of tacit presuppositions are almost exclusively ones that describe their (alleged) behavioral manifestations.

The foregoing discussion fails to take into account Turner's point that the evidence for ascriptions of tacit norms include observations of situations in which the norms are breached. It may now be elaborated that breaches are informative to the extent that they prompt expressions of disapproval: the research participants reacting to an action or claim in this manner indicates that they regard it as inappropriate. But that is not all. Observations of research participants who express their approval of an action or claim may suggest that they deem it appropriate—in accordance with a tacit norm (see Zahle 2016). Hence, unrecognized by Turner, data about situations of this latter sort are likewise informative when positing tacit norms.

Finally, return to Turner's claim that the ascription of a tacit belief should, prima facie, be consistent with the other beliefs ascribed to the individual. There is no reason not to broaden out this claim: the positing of a tacit belief, norm, value, etc. should, prima facie, be consistent with all the other ascriptions of mental states (beliefs, norms, values, desires, etc.) that the researcher makes on the basis of her rich data. These additional considerations of prima facie consistency should likewise constrain a researcher's positing of tacit presuppositions.

The upshot of these reflections is that a wider range of data-interpretations and posits of mental states inform and constrain the ascription of tacit presuppositions than recognized by Turner. Intuitively, as the researcher takes more types of data and posits of mental states into account, the number of possible ascriptions of tacit presuppositions likely decreases. The researcher is put in a better position to show that some ascriptions of tacit beliefs, ideas, norms, etc. are more plausible than others, and to rule out alternative ascriptions of tacit presuppositions. As a result, there are likely more occasions where the wider range of data and posits of mental states are consistent with the ascription of only a *single* presupposition, or set of presuppositions, whether to an individual considered on her own, or to all the participants in a practice. In this way, Taylor's interpretations of actions and practices—the tacit beliefs, norms, values etc. they posit—are likely to run into the problem of underdetermination less frequently than Turner's discussion suggests.

It goes without saying that this finding is compatible with holding that there are also other difficulties that the ascription of tacit beliefs, norms, values, etc. run into (for their discussion, see, e.g., Turner 1994, 2002, 2014). Further, I do not mean to claim that there are not other ways in which to question the argument from underdetermination. I have simply explored how attentiveness to the way qualitative research is carried out may serve as the basis for a criticism of Jones and Turner's versions of the argument.

7 Conclusion

Interpretivism is commonly associated with the use of qualitative research. In this paper, I have shown that considerations as to how qualitative research is conducted may be brought to bear on the philosophical discussion of interpretivism. From this perspective, I first demonstrated how Taylor's interpretivist position was in need of clarification and elaboration. Then I moved on to examine two objections to Taylor's amended position. By bringing into view, once more, how qualitative researchers go about their business, I established that the argument from lack of brute data should be rejected and that the scope of the argument from underdetermination is significantly smaller than assumed by Jones and Turner. While there are many ways in which to approach the critical scrutiny of interpretivism, I hope, in this paper, to have shown the fruitfulness of taking into account how qualitative research actually proceeds.[8]

References

Bevir, M. and Blakely, J. 2018. *Interpretive Social Science. An Anti-Naturalist Approach.* Oxford: Oxford University Press.

Bohman, J. 1993. *New Philosophy of Social Science.* Cambridge, Massachusetts: The MIT Press.

Bryman, Alan. 2012. *Social Research Methods*, 4th edn. Oxford: Oxford University Press.

DeWalt, K.M., and B. R. DeWalt. 2011. *Participant Observation. A Guide for Fieldworkers*, 2nd edn. Lanham: AltaMira Press.

Fay, B. 1998. *Contemporary Philosophy of Social Science.* Oxford: Blackwell Publishers.

Jones, T. (1998). "Interpretive Social Science and the 'Native's Point of View': A Closer Look." *Philosophy of the Social Sciences* 28(1): 32–68.

Jones, T. E. 2000. "Ethnography, Belief Ascription, and Epistemological Barriers," *Human Relations* 53(1):117–152.

Kincaid, H. 1996. *Philosophical Foundations of the Social Sciences.* Cambridge: Cambridge University Press.

---

[8] I would like to thank Christopher Adair-Toteff, Kevin Cahill, Harold Kincaid, and Stephen Turner for their helpful comments on the draft of this paper.

Little, Daniel. 1991. *Varieties of Social Explanation*. Boulder: Westview Press.

Martin, Michael. 2000. *Verstehen. The Uses of Understanding in Social Science*. London: Routledge.

Risjord, Mark. 2014. *Philosophy of Social Science*. New York: Routledge.

Seale, Clive. 1999. *Introducing Qualitative Methods: The Quality of Qualitative Research*. London: Sage Publications Ltd.

Stake, R.E. 1995. *The Art of Case Study Research*. Thousand Oaks: SAGE Publications, Inc.

Roth, Paul A. 1987. *Meaning and Method in the Social Sciences*. Ithaca: Cornell University Press.

Taylor, Charles. 1985. *Philosophy and The Human Sciences. Philosophical Papers 2*. Cambridge: Cambridge University Press.

Turner, Stephen P. (2014). *Understanding the Tacit*. New York: Routledge.

Turner, Stephen P. 2002. *Brains/ Practices/Relativism*. Chicago: The University of Chicago Press.

Turner, Stephen P. 1994. *The Social Theory of Practices. Tradition, Tacit Knowledge, and Presuppositions*. Chicago: The University of Chicago Press.

Williams, Malcolm. 2000. *Science and Social Science: An Introduction*. London: Routledge.

Zahle, J. 2017. "Ability Theories of Practice and Turner's Criticism of Bourdieu." *Journal for General Philosophy of Science*, 48 (4): 553–567.

Zahle, J. 2016. "Methodological Anti-Naturalism, Norms and Participant Observation." In *Normativity and Naturalism in the Philosophy of the Social Sciences*, Mark Risjord (ed.). London: Routledge, pp. 78–95.

Zahle, J. 2014. "Practices and the Direct Perception of Normative States: Part II." *Philosophy of the Social Sciences*, 44 (1): 74–85.

Zahle, J. (2013). "Practices and the Direct Perception of Normative States: Part I." *Philosophy of the Social Sciences*, 43(4): 493–518.

Sociology, Expertise and Civility

John Holmwood

Abstract

This chapter discusses Stephen Turner's contribution to the role of expertise in liberal democracy. It addresses the shift from expertise understood as certain knowledge that can be applied to policy problems to the role of expertise as staging arguments for public consideration. Drawing on Talcott Parsons' arguments about the relation between the professions and the modern citizenship complex, the chapter argues that the current problem of expertise lies in the dismantling of citizenship associated with neo-liberal policies, which have created the conditions for populist partisanship. The marketisation of higher education has also facilitated the presentation of knowledge as the expression of interests. The chapter concludes by suggesting that the problem of expertise is better understood as a problem of democracy where the issue is less the contested nature of knowledge claims and more a new incivility – that undermines the staging of arguments in public domains.

Keywords

democracy – knowledge – professions – public opinion – universities

Turner's work extends across a wide range of theoretical and philosophical topics, always challenging dominant understandings and upsetting apple carts. Unusually, he brings a deep engagement with the philosophy of social inquiry, and of social action more generally, together with a concern for the practical (sociological) conditions of possibility of warranted knowledge. His approach is reflexive in the best sense; engaged with sociological understandings as social constructions, but also with their material (institutional) conditions.

I have known Stephen Turner for several decades, mainly through participation in conferences organised by social theory and history of sociology sections of the American, European and International Sociological Associations. We collaborate as editors of a Palgrave Pivot series on the History of Sociology in different national contexts. We do not share sociological assumptions, or political opinions, but his sharp and distinctive observations about the nature of the academic craft and the misapprehensions of standard positions have been the goad I have needed. Indeed, I can think of few other sociologists and social philosophers who regularly force a re-think of how we understand our practices. It is an honor to contribute to this *Festschrift* and to acknowledge his significance and his influence.

1

In this chapter, I want to address the issues raised by his discussion of "expertise" and "professional knowledge." This brings together his contributions across a number of areas. First is his concern with democratic knowledge, as set out in *Liberal Democracy 3.0* (2003). With characteristic economy of expression he defines democracy as "government by discussion" (2003, 5) and he goes on to set out that civility is one of its necessary conditions.

An overall thesis of the book is that the increasing role of expertise in government has undermined the role of the public. This is an argument that goes back to Walter Lipmann and his argument of the "phantom public" (1925). What makes Turner's argument different is that he sets out different epochs of the role of science in government, alongside an account of the problem "after the sociology of science" and its deconstruction of the politics of expertise. The latter has culminated in claims that we are in post-truth times and that this is something prefigured in developments in the sociology of science across the last few decades (Fuller 2018). Turner is setting out something more sophisticated than Fuller's knowledge as a "power game." He is seeking the institutional conditions for the public discussion that he argues to be integral to any meaningful liberal democracy.

The book was written before the Obama and Trump presidencies in the US. The former's extensive use of "administrative orders" and their background justifications through commissions, regulatory agencies and the like (Rudalevige 2016), rather confirms the prescience of Turner's arguments about the usurping of democracy by administration. However, the excessive use of administrative orders was not occasioned by any specific logic of government, but rather by the rise of bi-partisan incivility and the refusal of Republican cooperation. This incivility has been ratcheted further by the populist presidency of Trump, including attacks on expertise which have taken place alongside a disdain for discussion.

Liberal Democracy 3.0 begins on a pessimistic note and, throughout, he invokes the figure of a future historian and the judgement she might make on what we are living through. When we look back at the situation in 1944, liberal democracy would have seemed fragile to those living through the time, with only anglophone countries showing any evidence of a deep cultural commitment to its principles and institutions that strongly embodied them. By 2003, after the collapse of communism, the situation looked very different, with liberal democracy triumphant and affirmed across the globe with few hold outs. Barely two decades later, and our future historian would see that populist governments are resurgent, whether in Poland, Hungary, the Philippines, Brazil, Russia, or India. More poignant, the erstwhile strong anglophone liberal democracies have fallen victim to the virus, with Trump in the US and Brexit in the UK each governing with an uncompromising "mandate from the people" based on support from a minority of voters. Incivility is perhaps too decorous a word for the pathologizing of opposition, but, nonetheless, incivility reigns.

What are we to make of this situation and what are its implications for sociology, Turner's "home" discipline (notwithstanding that he is a restless traveller to other disciplines, too)? What can we say derived from his own earlier analysis?

2

In essence, Turner offers philosophical reflection on a sociological account of the rise of professional knowledge and its changing contexts in the organisation of political life. His focus is the changing nature and organisation of public life in the post second world war period (although, of course, his interests in sociological knowledge have a broader historical range), including the changing role of the university in public life, and the role of sociology within the university. Paradoxically, this was one of the gaps in *Liberal Democracy 3.0*; there is no discussion of the university—a primary space in which knowledge is made, even if it has no monopoly on its production, and in the arguments of some, declining significance (Barber et al 2013).

Any critical account of expertise necessarily raises the question of the authority of its own claims and its broader disciplinary warrants. The nature and possibility of sociology was something he addressed together with Jonathan Turner in *The Impossible Science* (1990). Many commentators found the conclusions dispiriting. The possibility of sociology as a coherent and cumulative science was argued by them to be *institutionally* impossible (or, at the very least, unlikely). Changes since they wrote have, in my view, made that conclusion more, rather than less, plausible. These changes are associated with neo-liberal public policies that have asserted private goods over public goods, including the subordination of universities to market processes of revenue generation—including, for example, leveraged revenue from student fees justified as investment in human capital (Newfield 2016; Holmwood 2019).

The changes, I will suggest, are part of a broader shift in the privatisation not only of public assets, but also of the functions of government and their replacement by the market. The university is late to this development, and it is one that has gone further in the UK (more properly England) than in the US because of the system of public higher education that preceded it. However, it is a situation that must compromise any straightforward claim for public sociology (Burawoy 2005), in terms both of its internal (student) and external audiences.

In the reviews of the book (for example, *Social Epistemology* 1994), there was little reflection of the nature of the disagreement between the authors—with Jonathan Turner arguing that such a science was intrinsically possible and Turner that it was not—despite the fact that their fundamental disagreement facilitated cooperation rather than an inability to work together. Given that arguments for the impossibility of sociology frequently point to fragmentation and the lack of consensus over foundational concepts as obstacles to scientific sociology (see Balon and Holmwood 2019), this did not seem to trouble the authors' cooperation. In this way, the book itself models an important insight of Turner's work, namely that we are witnessing a shift in sociological sensibility from expertise as the *statement of certain knowledge* as a possible instrument of policy to its role in *the staging of arguments for wider public engagement and deliberation*. For its sociological audience, *The Impossible Science* modelled discussion, rather than (failed) foundationalism as the necessary way forward, even if its reviewers did not get it. The institutional setting of the university, however, does not favour that self-understanding, nor the loosening of the boundaries between academic social science and wider publics (Turner 2014).

But I am getting ahead of myself. I want first to discuss what I will term the "standard view" of the professions, democracy and sociological knowledge as set out by Talcott Parsons. Of course, I am conscious that, as befits a member of the "disobedient generation" (Sica and Turner 2008), albeit a maverick voice within that generation, Turner had no great respect (in truth, no respect at all!) for Parsons' work believing it to be both over-rated in its own terms and not at all the dominant voice within US sociology that it was frequently perceived to be (especially, perhaps from those outside US sociology). However, in the spirit of Turner's own contributions, I will present a non-standard view of the standard view, one that I believe will bring into relief the significance of his own contribution.

3

Parsons was one of the few major sociologists to write extensively on the nature of the university and the academic role and what he had to say is surprisingly pertinent to our own times and quite different to what is usually attributed to him even by those sympathetic to his position. Alexander, for example, describes Parsons' justification of the specialized functions of the university as deriving from, "the impersonal morality of cognitive rationality" (1988, 177). His critics, most famously Alvin Gouldner (1962), also took aim at what they saw as his technocratic conception of value freedom and social scientific objectivity, supposedly derived from Weber, but which erased all the agonism of Weber's own account. On this view, Parsons was perceived as being concerned with the articulation of a "liberal consensus" (Jewett 2012) and committed to sociology as an expert discourse separated from wider publics (see, for example, Haney 2008). The radical criticism developed by Gouldner also argued that this technocratic approach was tied to quiescence in the face of the corporate power structures of modern capitalism.

Absent the radical critique of corporate power, this is not far removed from Turner's own criticisms of Parsons' project for general theory, its patrician nature and (failed) attempts at disciplinary hegemony. His co-author, Jonathan Turner, took a different tack. The problem was less Parsons' positivism, but his failure to take it to its logical, behaviorist conclusion, which was implicit in the collaborative project associated with the short-lived Department of Social Relations at Harvard (Isaac 2012). This interpretation was reinforced by his wider professional activities, with him having been asked in 1946 to provide a report justifying the inclusion of the social sciences for funding by the National Science Foundation which was under discussion at the same time as the new Department at Harvard (see Haney 2008). The latter body and the politicians that oversaw it needed to be persuaded of the credibility of the claims of social science to be included among the natural sciences and Parsons provided a justification in terms of the rigour of concepts and methods and the mutual relations among the disciplines (Parsons 1986 [1947]). The bid was unsuccessful, but it seemed to confirm Parsons' positivism.

The wider political context also provided ammunition for Parsons' later critics to see him as raising professional expertise over democratic engagement. Somewhat earlier, Walter Lippman (1925) had argued that the "eclipse of the public" was a consequence of the complexity of modern society. This view was reinforced by the recent political experiences of authoritarianism evident in Stalin's Soviet Union and fascism in Europe. According to Haney, the dominant sociological response —in which he includes Parsons—was a suspicion towards democracy, the advocacy of the importance of experts and a denigration of public opinion as easily swayed and subject to non-rational impulses. In part, this was associated with arguments about the emergence of a mass society and the dissolution of intermediate groups between elites and non-elites (Kornhauser 1959). I will suggest, however, that the concerns about mass society apply rather better to our own times.

These are however, at best, partial understandings of Parsons' approach. It would be too simple to suggest that he was part of a wider conservative and elitist turn as Haney (2008) suggests. Parsons' argument involved a claim about the wider significance of professions in society, within which he would locate the emergence of sociology itself (and other social sciences) as a profession. The *apparent detachment* of the academy from public life, that he proposed, itself depended upon *its mediated attachment to democratic values*. His political commitments were those of a broadly social democratic amelioration of inequalities and realisation of social rights (see Nielsen 1991; Gerhardt 2002). These were integral to his sociological arguments rather than additional to them.

As I shall argue, Parsons ultimately justified the university by reference to its role in what he called the "citizenship complex." While he disagreed with his radical critics, he shared with them a commitment to sociology as a form of democratic knowledge even where they differ in how it is constituted. However, he also regarded the development of corporate capitalism as indicative of a new kind of individualism, what he called "institutional individualism" and suggested that the fears of corporate capitalism were misplaced. The corporation, he argued, was undergoing a process of transformation which meant that it could not simply be understood in terms of an unfettered exercise of property rights and the pursuit of profit. Indeed, as Howard Brick (2006) has argued, a dominant theme of US sociologists in the period was that capitalism had been transcended—certainly as understood by Marx. This was indicated by Parsons' use of the term, "modern society," rather than that of "capitalist society." The latter would have indicated one in which capitalist economy determined social formation, whereas modern society indicated one where capitalist economy was embedded and regulated by values that included and modified property rights.

Parsons' argument rested on a form of the 'end of ideology' thesis, which, in other writers, was associated with the idea of a mass society (Bell 1960; Kornhauser 1959), but, again, Parsons was proposing something different. The institutional developments associated with the rise of professions are central, he argued, to the resolution of an "individualism-socialism" dilemma that had characterized an earlier phase of capitalist development. For Parsons, this brought into being the era of sociology which, while it overlaps with the psychological and economic era, involves the recognition that the complexities of large-scale society require an analysis that goes beyond individual behaviour and, therefore, beyond the individualistic assumptions of economics and psychology. Parsons' claims represent a powerful mix. Sociology, itself, had come of age into a new professional role. The "end of ideology," as understood by Parsons, presaged the "age of sociology" (Parsons 1959).

In this context, Turner's representation of Parsons' conceptualisation of the professions as being, "squarely within the nineteenth century paradigm of 'interests' " (2003, 136), rather misses the latter's critique of that paradigm. Indeed, while Parsons is clearly influenced by Durkheim's arguments about professional ethics and civic morals, it is misplaced to suggest that the issue for Parsons was one of "professional *morality*" (Turner 2003, 136). It is clear that Parsons understands professionalism in terms of socially structured motivations, rather than morality per se (Holmwood 2006). As I shall argue, the social structures that are involved, according to Parsons, are those of the modern citizenship complex, linking professional development directly with the issues of democracy that are of concern to Turner.

4

My "revisionary" account of Parsons' arguments is made easier by a recent convergence upon them from within the critical theory tradition of the Frankfurt school. This is unexpected in the light of that tradition being associated with a radical account of mass society taken from Horkheimer and Adorno's critique of mass consumption capitalism and the entertainment industry.[1] It is a convergence which is largely unacknowledged in the case of Habermas (see, Holmwood 2009), but explicit in the case of Honneth (2014) who has presented Parsons' sociological account of modernity as the successor to that of Marx and the one which is required by a reinvigorated (critical) Hegelian normative theory of modernity.

Turner is (rightly, in my view) rather dismissive of Habermas's idealized conceptualization of discussion under conditions of undistorted communication (Turner 2003, 98ff) precisely because of its utopian view of social structures and failure to grasp the sociological conditions of modernity. This is not a criticism that can be levelled at Honneth. For the latter, the issue is how to

---

[1] For an early discussion of US and Frankfurt school approaches to mass society, see Bramson (1961).

understand the different spheres of modern society as expressing normative values. Essentially, for him, these spheres are those of personal relationships, market, and political will-formation (or family-household, market and public sphere). In this way, values are not assigned to the sphere of a distinct and separate lifeworld, but also embed spheres otherwise usually understood as instrumental, or only "externally" regulated. Instrumentalization—what Habermas (1987) would refer to as the colonization of the life-world—is a possible "deformation," within each sphere, but it is not intrinsic to any sphere as its internal "logic."[2] This, then, begs the question of what the normative basis of each sphere might be and how they are interrelated.

It is here that Parsons' treatment of modernity has interest for Honneth (albeit, in common with others, he does not address the role of the university, and education more generally, in the former's account). In effect, Parsons' theory of modernity has the form of a projection forward of tendencies he believed to be evident in the 1960s and 1970s as representing intrinsic features of modern society. Rather than the reduction of modern society to capitalist economy, what was occurring, he argued, was the embedding of capitalist economy within modern values of achievement and egalitarianism, providing, thereby, not simply a normative grounding of the public sphere, but also of the market economy itself.

Parsons broadly accepted T.H. Marshall's (1950a) account of this process in terms of the development and extension of civil and political rights to include social rights. These refer to membership in what Parsons calls the "societal community," a domain broadly equivalent to civil society in Habermas (see, Mayhew 1997). Civil rights provide the framework of the boundary relations between the societal community and the state in terms of issues of free expression and assembly. Political rights determine participation in the selection of government and are expressed through the extension of the franchise. Finally, social rights address the welfare of citizens, "treated as a public responsibility" to secure the "provision of realistic opportunities to make good use of such rights" (Parsons 1971, 21); that is such rights represented as political and civil rights. Social rights seek, "to ensure that adequate minimum standards of 'living', health care, and education are available" (1971, 22). Parsons goes on to argue that "it is particularly notable that the spread of education to ever wider circles of the population, as well as an upgrading of the levels of education

---

2 "Instrumentalization" in Habermas's terms also entails the rise of "administered" capitalism and thus of expertise which now necessarily functions as "ideology" behind a veneer of "objectivity." See especially, Habermas 1976.

has been closely connected with the development of the citizenship complex" (Parsons 1971, 22).

Notwithstanding that Parsons was much less sympathetic than was Marshall to framing these issues in terms of *class*, he does provide a similar discussion, which is, perhaps, more telling for our purposes. For Parsons, the "citizenship complex" is understood as transforming the corporation, *not from below, but from above*. In effect, Parsons traces the "civil," "political," and "social" development of organizational forms. This occurs first in terms of the orientation to the market, where increased scale introduces distinct occupational roles associated with management and its separation from labor. This is found in the rise of bureaucratic forms of organization. Finally, "associational" forms of organization emerge. These extend throughout the societal community and become increasingly important in the fiduciary boards' of large corporations. With significantly much less emphasis on struggle than Marshall, Parsons nonetheless identifies employment as a form of membership of a collectivity (beyond a simple contract). Different forms of associative membership both define a modern societal community and interpenetrate with organizational forms.[3]

What is significant about this account is that Parsons explicitly understands the core structure of the university to be "associational" (that is, "collegial") and uses its mode of organization to understand wider developments. In other words, if the modern university becomes more like a corporation, as Habermas (1971) suggests, this is also because, at the same time, the *corporation becomes more like a university*. In part, Parsons attributes this to the rise of the large corporation and the separation of ownership from the functions of management. This latter development assigns managers a "political" role in the corporation, reconciling different claims upon it. In this way, management is able to take on the status of a profession similar to the rise of other professions.

The development and transformation of the professions was, for Parsons, one of the key features of associative membership in the modern societal community. Professions enjoy a monopoly of practice in the light of claims for special expertise requiring considerable trust on the part of clients who are not able to judge services provided in terms of a principle of *caveat emptor* that might operate in other contractual relations. This poses a moral hazard, or information asymmetry, where clients may be vulnerable to a self-interested

---

[3] Significantly one of Parsons' severest critics, David Lockwood, also came to a similar view, drawing on Marshall to argue for an "institutional unity consisting of citizenship, market and bureaucratic relationships" (1996, 532). What I am arguing is that it is this "institutional unity" that has been broken, with citizenship and bureaucracy increasingly reduced to the market.

professional's pursuit of profit. However, according to Parsons, professional associations serve to regulate the relations between practitioners and clients and do so both by certifying knowledge and by codes of practice that establish a "professional ethics" (something he develops from Durkheim). The point is not that the professional person is less driven by self-interested motivations, but that these are constrained by new social structures toward a reconciliation of private and public interest in terms of self-conscious duties and responsibilities.

Once again, this is an argument also set out by Marshall (1950b). In an article first written in 1939, but specifically selected by him for publication alongside his more well-known "Citizenship and Social Class" (1950a), he makes the point that the development of rights also requires special occupational groups to deliver them, namely professions. Under the dominance of civil and political rights, the professions are associated with an "individualist" form of transcendence of self-interest related to pecuniary advantage. This involves, "the belief that the individual is the true unit of service, because service depends on individual qualities and individual judgement, supported by an individual responsibility which cannot be shifted on to the shoulders of others … it is not concerned with self-interest, but with the welfare of the client" (1950b, 140). With the development of social rights and services provided directly through public authorities, however, this involves that, "the professions are being socialized and the social and public services are being professionalized" (1950b, 147). With regard to the first aspect, professions are brought to connect the welfare of the individual client with obligations to the wider public. With regard to the second, the professionalization of services means that they are provided in a manner befitting social rights of citizenship. They are provided as a service to individuals regarded as equal members of the political community, rather than as recipients of charity.

To some extent, then, the development of the professions follows the track of the university itself. Just as the professions once recruited from those with high status backgrounds because they served people of a similar status (an argument that goes back to Adam Smith), so the university was initially associated with the reproduction of elite culture. However, with the development of the "citizenship complex," as the professions are democratized, so, too, is the university. This is not the democracy that might be claimed by a student movement concerned to disrupt all hierarchies (a situation that confronted Parsons and led to him being accused of conservatism), but the latter orientation, for Parsons, was a symptom of changes to the university and not in itself the direct expression of the new meaning of the university for democracy.

This is so not least because the university is responsible for what Parsons calls the "cognitive complex" and its normative significance within modern societies. While the professions are the outward face of the knowledge society and its demand for specialized expertise, the university is increasingly the guarantor of the knowledge base of that expertise and its development through research. Professional associations continue to regulate practice, but increasingly the knowledge they certify is credentialized through universities and their professional schools (including business schools). At the same time, for Parsons, this means that the "profession of higher education, and of scholarly research, has also been acquiring greater relative importance" (1971, 26), along with the notable fact that the educational revolution has begun to "transform the whole structure of modern society. Above all, it reduces the relative importance of the two major ideological concerns, the market and bureaucratic organization. The emerging emphasis is on associational organization, especially its collegial form" (1971, 98).

It should be stressed at this point that Parsons' functional analysis of systems (cultural, social and behavioral) and sub-systems within systems creates a complex set of locations (nodes) and exchanges (see Holmwood 1996 for discussion). While associational forms arise in different organizations, they also have an expression specific to their functional location. A university is not the same as a business organization, although it does have its business side (for example, it has to generate revenues and make material provision for its activities and this requires a distinctive —functionally specific—type of employee different from the academic). In a similar way, the business organization has its aspects similar to the university, but with a different ordering under the pursuit of profitability over the long term, while the university is defined by its pursuit of cognitive rationality.

By emphasizing the rise of associational organization, Parsons is, of course, mobilizing a theme of American democracy that goes back to Tocqueville. Nowhere does Parsons use the language of the "public sphere" to account for the changing roles of the university. However, as I have suggested, he does locate the university centrally within the societal community as an expression of a citizenship complex that secures social rights and defines overall legitimacy within the societal community by reconciling private and public interests. The "autonomy" of the university, then, takes on a new meaning within this citizenship complex. Its knowledge is at service to a societal community in which, "the principle of equality has broken through to a new level of pervasiveness and generality. A societal community as *basically* composed of equals seems to be the 'end of the line' in the long process of undermining the legitimacy of … older, more particularistic ascriptive bases of membership" (1971, 119).

5

It is not my purpose to argue that Parsons was right in his characterisation of the professions and democracy, only to point to the connections he was making with the development of a citizenship complex grounded in social rights. Turner is similarly oriented to the relationship between expertise and democracy. Admittedly, he has a simpler definition of democracy as government by discussion, whereas Parsons' definition extends to the idea of government of and by equals. Once again, we can allow that Turner's definition is intended to encompass the equal status of the parties to discussion. Indeed, it is the very substantive inequality in comprehension of topics brought forward for discussion that expertise creates that exercises him. Parsons suggests that this problem can be overcome through social structure and the direction toward inclusive membership in the societal community.

This construction is not subject to the same criticism that Turner makes of Habermas. Parsons may be wrong about the development of social rights of citizenship, but it is a substantive argument not a utopian construction against which all extant social structures will fail. However, Turner is correct to argue that Parsons' sociology of science is Mertonian in character and that subsequent developments in the field have proceeded with knowledge itself, not simply its institutional frameworks, as the object of analysis. This has coincided both with the expansion of knowledge claims and more extensive coalitions of practitioners. The diversity of knowledge claims involves competing expertises and the idea that consensus is a (conditional) achievement *within* coalitions and not *across* them.

Just as sociology must be conducted in fragments (see, for example, Abbott 2001), with no overarching consensus, so is this the case with other disciplines. Even where they exhibit greater internal consensus—for example, economics—that consensus evaporates once expert claims travel outside the bounds of the academy. Experts are frequently in name only and self-identified. As Turner nicely puts it, there is a difference between a scientific consensus and a consensus among scientists (2003, 121). The former is less secure than the older sociology of science proposed and it is both contingent and time limited. The second is merely a gambit within a political game (frequently carried out via signatures and petitions), which can simply reveal the distance between experts and wider publics.

Turner ends his book on *Liberal Democracy 3.0* with a discussion of the "withering away of civil society" and a hope for a new facilitation of democratic discussion with a holding to account of expert opinion. In fact, he does not say very much about the nature of recent developments except in terms

SOCIOLOGY, EXPERTISE AND CIVILITY 233

of the rise of administrative decision-making. Significantly, he describes social democratic Sweden as its apotheosis with decision making delegated to Royal Commissions. The treatment here is somewhat anecdotal deriving from a book by the British translator, Paul Austin, written in 1968. Turner regards the Swedish situation to be an expression of "expert bureaucratic power" as the ideal type of one solution to the conflict between expertise and opinion in liberal democracy 3.0. As he says, it describes a process where "expert opinion establishing fact-surrogates alone suffices" (Turner 2003, 133).

It is significant that this is described as having legitimacy, but there is no discussion of the wider implication of social democracy for establishing that legitimacy. At the time, Sweden was also the apotheosis of a welfare state embodying social democratic social rights. I am not concerned for present purposes with the issue of whether or not it retains this character. However, it is precisely the future anticipated by Talcott Parsons, in his outline of the modern citizenship complex. What I suggest is that the inclusive membership that is integral to that complex is also integral to the legitimacy of the ideal type discussed by Turner. Parsons was wrong about the future development of the welfare state in the US, which turned out not to be found in the development of social rights of citizenship, but their demise. A similar outcome is found in other anglophone countries, most especially the UK.

Elsewhere, I have suggested that the underlying reason is found in racial divisions intrinsic to the liberal state (Bhambra and Holmwood 2019). Indeed, Parsons, himself, regarded one of the obstacles to the institutionalising of social rights in the US to be the failure to resolve the problem of race. "Inclusion" was something that would require the agency of African Americans. As Parsons put it, "he can become the spokesman for the much broader category of the disadvantaged, those excluded on this egregious ground. The Negro movement, then, can become the American style 'socialist' movement. This is to say that the basic demand is for full inclusion, not for domination or for equality on a basis of separateness" (1965, 1040). Notwithstanding the general character of his theory, his realism about the likelihood of full citizenship—and it is significant that he punctuated the title of his article discussing the topic with a question mark—placed a significant query over the future of social rights in the US at the moment of their apparent embrace. At the same time, he identified the obstacle to lie in the re-emergence of the radical right under Barry Goldwater. Thus, Parsons suggested that, while social rights complete the citizenship complex, they do so in circumstances where they are likely to be contested on racial grounds. He writes that, "the alignment of the resistance to Negro inclusion, directly or through resistance to various measures essential to its success (such as federal support of education and the war against poverty), with a generalized political conservatism is a highly important development" (1965, 1043).

Parsons thought that this resistance was not likely to succeed. In retrospect, we can see that it did, with profound implications. Inclusion in social rights could be avoided if social rights were themselves to be withdrawn (a withdrawal, which if the Marshall-Parsons argument about the relation between civil, political, and social rights oc citizenship is correct, would entail consequences for other rights within the citizenship complex). What, at the time, was referred to as the rise of the "new right" (King 1987) and is retrospectively understood as the rise of neo-liberalism, would seem to be coterminous with liberal democracy 3.0, but, at the same time, undermines liberal democracy itself.

6

What is at issue involves the widening social inequality and stagnant real incomes that have characterised the decades of neo-liberal public policy in the US and UK (Piketty 2014). The dismantling of the citizenship complex can be considered as a shift from "thick" to "thin" citizenship, not a denial of citizenship as such. Nonetheless, "thin" citizenship will involve the return of problems that thick citizenship sought to resolve. Notwithstanding a continued emphasis on equal opportunities, inheritance of social position has become more evident, not least in low and stable, or declining, rates of social mobility, against the expectation that modern societies were becoming increasingly open. Social rights of citizenship are under challenge, but this is not simply an issue of distributive justice and the withdrawal of a public commitment to "adequate minimum standards of 'living', health care, and education" (Parsons 1971, 22). Given the way in which Parsons also argues that associationalism is a characteristic of the societal community, it also involves a transformation of the latter, involving the greater dominance of market and bureaucratic orientations. Another corollary is the "de-professionalization" of public and social services, as their recipients are transformed from clients to undeserving recipients and/or customers of services who would be better served by private providers.

Ironically, at the same time as sociological theory was developing the idea of the citizenship complex as the embedding of markets and bureaucracy, economic theory was addressing the problem of restrictions to the market that such embedding represented. It is not possible to do justice to this literature here, but my main concern is how some of it was taken up in a new economics of private property rights (Bartzell 1989; Eggertsson 1990) that became especially influential in neoliberal policy circles and as an ideology of shareholder value. The core idea involved market exchanges as both the paradigm of efficiency securing maximum aggregate welfare and grounded in an idea of economic liberty. In this context, social rights are perceived as both inefficient, when they are delivered in the form of public services, and unjust because they entail a restriction on private property rights and the liberties they embody. In effect, what is proposed is a reorganization of the citizenship complex around an austere concept of simple freedom expressed through ownership, including that of self-ownership (Tomasi 2012).

"Self-ownership" in the context of declining returns to "self-investment" in human capital (Newfield 2016) is fraught. It does not override ascriptive bases of membership, but re-instates them and, at the same time constitutes politics as a competition for advantages. In so far as neo-liberalism represents the hollowing out of intermediate organisations in civil society it ushers in a new form of mass society, one which is the fertile ground for the excesses of social media. It is the sociological condition for opinion formation as occurring within 'echo chambers', because of the decline of both overlapping groups and common interests transcending private or group interests (as described in the citizenship complex).

In this context, the problem of democracy identified by Turner is less that of expertise and much more that of a structurally-produced incivility, something he discusses at much less length. The neo-liberal preference for markets also involves the representation of professional organisation as a monopolistic producer interest. Equally, acceding to a neo-liberal project for universities—"putting the student-consumer at the heart of the system," as a UK white paper has it (Department for Education 2015)—opens the university to a wider neo-liberal project, one in which matters previously subject to public discussion are made matters of private decision. At the same time, professional motivations are separated from citizenship and represented as self-interested.

Ironically, this can seem to be no more than an extension of the radical critique of the professions that emerged in the 1970s. This is also part of the heritage of the sociology of science, perhaps most vividly encapsulated by Fuller (2018) in his recent book, *Post-Truth: Knowledge as a Power Game*. The idea of post-truth (or perhaps, more correctly, of multiple—competing and irresolvable—truths) has been widely seen as a consequence of the post-modern turn associated with late capitalism. Put very simply, Fuller endorses the idea of post-truth as the logical conclusion of the arguments of the sociology of science and its deconstruction of philosophical attempts at demarcation—reason from emotion, knowledge from belief, and so on. For him, there is little to be gained from lamenting the situation and everything to be gained from joining the game. Post-truth, for Fuller, is nothing less than a consequence of the democratization of knowledge, especially in the context of social media and the internet where information and counter-information is readily available.

Turner provides a more sober account. Incivility, itself, is an enemy of democratisation, once we understand democracy as discussion. Fuller conflates self-determination within the market and democracy.[4] We can understand the conflation by going back to an older sociological (pragmatist) understanding of democracy in terms of "publics" and discursive processes of decision-making. The wider project of neo-liberalism is to displace publics with markets, and thus the displacement of democracy itself by the market. Little wonder that a 'hollowed out' public sphere is vulnerable to populism. In the history of reflection on the nature of the university, the figure of Kant reigns large—the Faculty of Philosophy, for him, was emblematic of the university's relation to truth. Without irony, Fuller suggests that the emblem of the University in the age of post-truth is the Business School, writing, "if any part of the university deserves to carry the torch for anti-expertism, it is business schools" (2018, 22).

7

Part of the hollowing out of the public sphere is the very privatization of the public university itself. Collegiality has given way to the corporate brand with academics expected to act in ways to support it. At my own university, with branch campuses in Malaysia and China, this involves alignment with a mission statement that can embrace the University's contribution to well-being, but eschews democratic values and the criticism of a regime that has built concentration camps for its Uighur minority. Turner's invocation of the historical perspective on liberal democracy in 1944, with fascism yet to fully reveal its horrors, is mocked by our individual institutions which might once have understood themselves in the pursuit of truth, but, in giving up truth, have also sacrificed democracy in the pursuit of revenue and, in the

---

4 Interestingly, an early radical critic of the professions and specialist in the field of the sociology of science, Randall Collins, wrote of the problem of credentialism created by the struggle for advantage under a meritocratic ideology (Collins 1979). He offered two solutions—markets or social democracy. Significantly, radical sociology, including the sociology of science, was always close to the embrace of neo-liberalism.

process, have contributed to the sociological process that diminishes expertise itself.

References

Abbott, Andrew. 2001. *Chaos of Disciplines*. Chicago: University of Chicago Press.

Alexander, Jeffrey C. 1988. *Action and Its Environments: Towards a New Synthesis*. New York: Columbia University Press.

Balon, Jan, and John Holmwood. 2019. "The Impossibility of Sociology as a Science; Arguments from within the Discipline." *Journal for the Theory of Social Behaviour* 49 (3): 334–347.

Barber, Michael, Katelyn Donnelly, and Saad Rizvi. 2013. *An Avalanche Is Coming: Higher Education and the Revolution Ahead*. London: IPPR. https://www.ippr.org/publications/an-avalanche-is-coming-higher-education-and-the-revolution-ahead.

Bell, Daniel. 1960. *The End of Ideology: On the Exhaustion of Political Ideas in the Fifties*. New York: Free Press.

Bartzell, Yoram. 1989. *The Economics of Property Rights*. New York: Cambridge University Press.

Bhambra, Gurminder K., and Holmwood John. 2018. "Race, empire and the European Welfare State." *New Political Economy* 23 (5): 574–587.

Bramson, Leon. 1961. *The Political Context of Sociology*. Princeton: Princeton University Press.

Brick, Howard. 2006. *Transcending Capitalism: Visions of a New Society in Modern American Thought*. Ithaca, NY: Cornell University Press.

Burawoy, Michael. 2005. "For Public Sociology." *American Sociological Review* 70 (1): 2–28.

Collins, Randall. 1979. *The Credential Society: An Historical Sociology of Education and Stratification*. New York: Academic Press.

Department for Education. 2011. *Higher education White Paper - Students at the Heart of the System*. UK Government. https://www.gov.uk/government/consultations/higher-education-white-paper-students-at-the-heart-of-the-system.

Eggertsson, Thrainn. 1990. *Economic Behavior and Institutions*. Cambridge: Cambridge University Press.

Fuller, Steve. 2018. *Post-Truth: Knowledge as a Power Game*. New York: Anthem Press.

Gerhardt, Uta. 2002. *Talcott Parsons: An Intellectual Biography*. Cambridge: Cambridge University Press.

Gouldner, Alvin W. 1962. 'Anti-minotaur: the myth of a value free sociology', *Social Problems* 9(3): 199–213.

Gouldner, Alvin W. 1970. *The Coming Crisis of Western Sociology*, London: Heinemann.

Habermas, Jürgen. 1971. *Toward A Rational Society: Student Protest, Science and Politics.* Translated by Jeremy J. Shapiro. London: Heinemann.

Habermas, Jürgen. 1976. *Legitimation Crisis.* Translated by Jeremy J. Shapiro. London: Heinemann.

Habermas, Jürgen. 1984. *The Theory of Communicative Action, Volume I: Reason and the Rationalisation of Society.* Translated by Thomas McCarthy. London: Heinemann.

Habermas, Jürgen. 1987. *The Theory of Communicative Action, Volume II: Lifeworld and System.* Translated by Thomas McCarthy. Cambridge: Polity.

Haney, David Paul. 2008. *The Americanization of Social Science: Intellectuals and Public Responsibility in the Postwar United States.* Philadelphia: Temple University Press.

Holmwood, John. 1996. *Founding Sociology? Talcott Parsons and the Idea of General Theory*, London: Longman.

Holmwood, John. 2006. "Economics, Sociology, and the 'Professional Complex': Talcott Parsons and the Critique of Orthodox Economics." *American Journal of Economics and Sociology* 65 (1): 127–160.

Holmwood, John 'From 1968 to 1951: How Habermas transformed Marx into Parsons' in G.K. Bhambra and I. Demir (eds) *1968 in Retrospect: History, Theory, Alterity*, London: Palgrave.

Honneth, Axel. 2014. *Freedom's Right: The Social Foundations of Democratic Life.* Cambridge: Polity.

Isaac, Joel. 2010. "Theorist at Work: Talcott Parsons and the Carnegie Project on Theory, 1949-1951." *Journal of the History of Ideas* 71 (2): 287–311.

Isaac, Joel. 2012. *Working Knowledge: Making the Human Sciences from Parsons to Kuhn.* Cambridge, Ma: Harvard University Press.

Jewett, Andrew. 2012. "The Politics of Knowledge in 1960s America." *Social Science History* 36 (4): 551–581.

King, Desmond S. 1987. *The New Right: Politics, Markets and Citizenship.* London: Macmillan Education.

Kornhauser, William. 1959. *The Politics of Mass Society.* Glencoe, IL: Free Press.

Lippman, Walter. 1925. *The Phantom Public.* New York: Macmillan.

Lockwood, David. 1996. "Civic integration and Class Formation." *British Journal of Sociology* 47 (3): 531–550.

Marshall, T. H. 1950a. "Citizenship and Social Class." In *Citizenship and Social Class: and Other Essays.* Cambridge: Cambridge University Press, 1–85.

Marshall, T. H. 1950b. "The Recent History of Professionalism in Relation to Social Structure and Social Policy." In *Citizenship and Social Class: and Other Essays.* Cambridge: Cambridge University Press, 128–155.

Mayhew, Leon H. 1997. *The New Public: Professional Communication and the Means of Social Influence*, Cambridge: Cambridge University Press.

Newfield, Christopher. 2016. *The Great Mistake: How We Wrecked Public Universities and How We Can Fix Them.* Baltimore: Johns Hopkins University Press.

Nielsen, Jens Kaalhauge. 1991. "The Political Orientation of Talcott Parsons: The Second World War and Its Aftermath." In *Talcott Parsons: Theorist of Modernity*. Edited by R. Robertson and B. S. Turner. London: Sage.

Parsons, Talcott and Platt, Gerald M. 1973. *The American University.* Cambridge: Harvard University Press.

Parsons, Talcott. 1959. "Some Problems Confronting Sociology as a Profession." *American Sociological Review* 24: 547–558.

Parsons, Talcott. 1965. 'Full citizenship for the American Negro? A sociological Problem,' *Daedalus* 94(4): 1009–1054.

Parsons, Talcott. 1971. *The System of Modern Societies*, Englewood Cliffs: Prentice Hall.

Parsons, Talcott. 1986 [1947] 'Social Science: A Basic National Resource' in *The Nationalization of the Social Sciences,* ed Samuel Z. Klausner and Victor M. Lidz, 41–112, Philadelphia: University of Pennsylvania Press.

Piketty, Thomas. 2014. *Capital in the Twenty-First Century*. Cambridge. MA: Harvard University Press.

Rudalevige, Andrew. 2016. "The Contemporary Presidency: The Obama Administrative Presidency: Some Late-Term Patterns." *Presidential Studies Quarterly* 46 (4):868–890.

Sica, Alan, Stephen and Turner, eds. *The Disobedient Generation: Social Theorists in the Sixties.* Chicago: University of Chicago Press.

Social Epistemology. 1994. "Symposium on the History of American Sociology Portrayed in *The Impossible Science* by Stephen Turner and Jonathan Turner." *Social Epistemology* 8 (1).

Tomasi, John. 2012. *Free Market Fairness*. Princeton: Princeton University Press.

Turner, Stephen P., and Jonathan H. Turner. 1990. *The Impossible Science. An Institutional Analysis of American Sociology*. Stephen Park Turner and Jonathan H. Turner. Newbury Park: Sage.

Turner, Stephen P. 2003. *Liberal Democracy 3.0: Civil Society in an Age of Experts*. London: Sage.

Turner, Stephen P. 2014. "From Edification to Expertise: Sociology as a 'Profession'." In *The Politics of Expertise*. London: Routledge.

Response

Normativity, Practices, and the Substrate

Stephen Turner

Abstract

In this reply to the commentary in the volume, some intellectual, historical, and biographical context is provided for the writings discussed. This includes a brief account of the trajectory from Sociological Explanation as Translation, and a discussion of the general problem of the substrate of social explanation and the status of social theories as ideal-typical constructions with a problematic relation to this substrate. On this basis, the themes of practices, normativity, and the problem of the meaning of reasons explanations are reconsidered. An outline of a view of norms based on the notion of Jellinek of the normative power of the real is given and related to Russian developmental psychology. This extends and gives a psychological base to the pragmatic account of norms and practical normativity that runs through these texts. The chapter concludes with a discussion of social science, including the problems of the status of economic theory, the objectivity of field work and the problem of underdetermination, and the political significance of Parsons.

Keywords

Jellinek – normativity – ideal-types – practices – Parsons – Verstehen – folk psychology

Let me first thank the contributors for their gratifying response, which confirms for me that these were issues worth dealing with, and worth continuing to deal with. I will discuss all of the papers in this short response, however briefly. All I can do in this space is to provide what amounts to meta-philosophical observations, and perhaps no more than prejudices, about the issues discussed here, but I hope that by doing so I can provide the context for the arguments that people have objections to. So this response will be more an attempt at explication than an assemblage of arguments.

1 Overviews

There is considerable continuity and intertwining in the texts discussed in this volume, but there is also a trajectory, which Paul Roth, Mark Risjord, and Rafał Wierzchosławski take up, in different ways. Roth points out my continuing concern with the question of what the object of social explanation is; Wierzchosławski answers this question in terms of practical normativity; Risjord gives a rich history of the rationality and other cultures problem of the 1960s and its fate. The three are of course closely related. My dissertation, published as *Sociological Explanation as Translation* (1980), focused on the problem of the occasion for sociological and anthropological explanation, which I took, like Peter Winch (1958), to be a matter of getting into trouble, but for me it was with the application of our practices, rather than, as Winch had it, with our concepts. Our default social position was to operate with what I called the "same practices" hypothesis: a sociological puzzle or problem arose when it failed—when we encountered people in different social settings who did things differently. The solution, as I described it, was a kind of translation, or showing one game, the one we didn't understand, to be a variation of another, which we did.

There was no intent to ontologize "games": indeed, the stress was on the fact that these problems arose from a particular starting point, one in which we already had a tacit understanding of the world that was failing us in a new setting. It didn't depend on the unitary notion of culture, and was strictly instrumental, in the sense that translations were, and was subject to the same indeterminacies. Nor was it holistic in its approach to the web of beliefs; context, it was claimed, was whatever was relevant to the specific translation problem or the failure of the same practices hypothesis. As Roth notes, this was a way of answering the question of what the explanatory object of sociology was: it was about how one identified something to explain sociologically. Risjord's history points to the more publicly discussed and contested side of the problem, which began or was at least concretized in the rationality debate. He divides the sides between localizers and universalizers, and suggests that the localizers, on whose side he places me, won—mostly as result of the game changing paper by Donald Davidson on conceptual schemes ([1974] 2001). Moreover, as Wierzchosławski points out, the games were exercises in practical normativity, though this was not the language used at the time. It is worth noting that the two main examples in *Sociological Explanation as Translation* (1980) were a case in which the prevailing moral code led to collective failure and another in which a group professed a blatantly untrue belief. They were anomalous from the point of view of functionalism, and also from the point of view of the doctrines that replaced functionalism, such as rational choice, game-theoretic accounts of norms, or evolutionary accounts.

The term practices pointed to something more than language and concepts, as did my examples, namely the substrate on which practices were based. This was also pointed to in a backhanded way by Winch, who acknowledged that concepts rested on habits ([1964] 1974, 93). The issue of the substrate has been with me from the start—with my interest in Claude Levi-Strauss and the idea that there might be general structuring forms of thought rooted in something sub-social that explained the common structure of myths, the categories that went into social organization, and so on—in the fashion of the Chomskyian account of syntax. But I would now agree with the idea, nicely formulated in a recent Times Literary Supplement review, that

> As much as we all might admire what is fresh and innovative, we all learn by imitating patterns. Babies learning to speak do not immediately acquire the full grammar of their mother tongue and a vocabulary to slot into it but inch slowly into the language by repeating basic phrases and varying them.
>
> DUMITRESCU 2020

Levi-Strauss's myth structures, the spatial division of villages, and so forth now seem to me to be the product of good patterns to think with.

Why "patterns"? I think both Jerry Fodor, with his notion of an innate semantics, and the long tradition of thinking of reasons as mental causes had the right instinct in one respect: it is necessary to have some concepts that, so to speak, face both ways: into the causal world and the *Verstehen*, "meaning," one. Neither Fodor's account nor "reasons as mental causes" work out, the latter for reasons well-attested to in the series of little red books published in the 1950s and 60s, which included Winch's. Pattern recognition faces both ways. It has the advantage of being a well-attested psychological phenomenon, basic to thought, and also largely involuntary, with some prospect of being grounded in brain processes. Yet patterns themselves can be the subject of joint attention and discourse, and are therefore "social." There may be other candidates for concepts that face both ways, such as dispositional notions like altruism, notions like pain, and what Wittgenstein called natural symbols and Russian psychology called the first signal system. Without them we are paralyzed in relating mind to brain, or the causal world generally.

A picture of the substrate problem as I now understand it would go like this. The bounds of what we "understand" as like ourselves, or meaningful, can be thought of as a circle, what I called the *Verstehen* bubble (2018, 205–18), within two larger circles of causal relations. In the first circle are differences which causally produce differences in human behavior. Outside this circle are differences that don't cause differences in human behavior. The limits of these circles, as I take it, are empirical. Weber tried to define the substrate he wanted to consider as socially meaningful action. Others, like Dorothy Smith, liked the term experience. But these approaches define the limits from within, or based on criteria taken from within the category—a category whose contents are problematic simply because of the limits of "understanding." To the extent that we can devise a neuroscientific account of "understanding," and an empirical marker, such as mirror neuron activation, we can get an independent "objective" criterion, and an empirical one. By the same token we can discover what is and what is not causally related to behavior. If there are quantum level differences that produce differences in behavior, they are in the circle; if not, we can ignore them. It would be an empirical question in each case.

Let me say briefly that, like Sam Whimster, I consider most if not all basic level social science theory to be, in epistemic terms, ideal-types, but that in practice, in their explanatory uses, they are basically analogies. I discuss this informally in "Mundane Theorizing, *Bricolage* and *Bildung*" (2014). I take it that applications of game theory, the abstract idea of the market, and even the concept of norms itself are analogical—social norms are analogous to legal or explicit norms, but are neither legal nor explicit. These analogies float far above the causal processes that determine outcomes, and often far from actual interpretations of behavior, which helps sustain the illusion that they are causal forces—such as "market forces"—on their own, or that there is such a thing as "symbolic capital" outside of the vague analogy between this "capital" and reputation. At best, these are shortcuts that represent casual processes for a particular purpose; at worst, they substitute for and obscure and misrepresent them.

2   Practices and Beliefs

Several of the papers deal with the concept of practices, my critique of it, and the question of whether there is something more that is different from, beyond the reach of, or better conceived that answers to the name of practices, and which is collective or supra-individual in a sense I deny. Some of the comments are irenic, and I appreciate the attempt to reconcile my criticisms of what I constructed as a "collective object" account of practices with alternative accounts that escape, or try to escape, the argument. As Theodore Schatzski points out, the differences may turn out to be quite narrow, and the criticisms may not apply to such a central figure as Pierre Bourdieu, something argued elsewhere by Julie Zahle as well (2017).

What these issues come down to, however, is something simple, and it applies not only to practices but to collective beliefs, shared schemata, scripts, and so forth. The issue is whether these things get transferred intact from a collective source, or even intact from one person to another, or whether people acquire something resembling these things in their own way, with their own learning history, and with their own individual nuances, ultimately associated with the individually diverse set of connections in their own brains.

I will start with the issue of the substrate, which provides a motive for my response. At the brain level, a highly plausible basic story about how the individual mind develops goes like this. There are some basic dispositions and capacities, some of which develop over time, some of which are genetic. Then there is a process of learning. This involves making associations, and doing this is something the brain actively and proactively does, at an unconscious level, all the time, and in such a way that additional associations between associations, patterns of patterns (call them meta-associations), are also being proactively produced. Pattern recognition, predictive processing, and other very basic brain processes go into this learning. Things that are done, things that are seen and especially those that produce some sort of feedback, get built into memory and become the preferred route for new memories and actions. Patterns are built on patterns, and meta-cognition about patterns makes for meta-cognitive patterns—patterns of thinking about patterns, which are or become tacit.

This is how what is called cognitive architecture gets constructed, and it seems to get constructed in early developmental stages by pruning connections. Though there is still plasticity, a lot gets fixed in place early, and provides, so to speak, the rapid route to perception and action with the inputs that fit with the patterns that get established early. In this respect the Freudians, but also Ferdinand Tönnies, were right: basic habits of mind, especially those that give rise to "moral" responses, get established early in the developmental process. The inputs are heavily "social": the developing child is part of and responding actively to an environment of other people, and interacting, from birth and even in utero. Mirror neurons may be a big facilitator of interaction and crucial for imitation. The moral or normative aspect raises some other issues, which I will return to shortly.

The learning process includes lots of universal things—finding one's body, for example. But it proceeds in an idiosyncratic way, simply because the events that become inputs are different for different people. And because the basic process of neurons firing together wiring together is a process of building on what is there, what gets built is idiosyncratic on the deepest level. But there are lots of constraints on the process that produce uniformity of a kind on the observed not-so-deep level: social interaction, language or what the Russians called the second signal system, training, and a shared world of objects to which a great deal of joint attention is given all serve to shape cognition in the direction of something like common tacit knowledge. But this process never gets to the point of complete uniformity. A recent AI learning experiment giving a common task to identical learning set-ups with the same inputs produced slightly different results in each case. In the case of human learning, we can expect much more variation because the inputs vary.

This has a lot of implications, but also a lot of caveats. One implication is that the distance between basic inherited dispositions and the dispositions that ultimately drive behavior, which is filled with idiosyncratic events, is so great that any reductive account of social life to these impulses is a non-starter. Evolutionary psychology, and for that matter the "modules" beloved of cognitive scientists, can only go so far. The settings in which we have the experiences or exposure that go into learning—at this point in the story meaning tacit learning rather than training or learning from explicit inputs—are "social," or local and specific, often associated with a specific group of people. But this comes with its own caveat. There is nothing special about groupness or "the social" at this stage of the exposition, other than as a shorthand way of describing the settings themselves. Whether this ever changes, for example into "collective intentions" or "shared scripts," and how, is a key question.

Social interaction, however, disciplines and creates (at least surface or behavioral) uniformity. But it also individualizes—into people of different types and different personalities, with different aims, out of different social settings. The development of basic social skills, including a theory of mind—or at least its equivalent in processes of simulation, recognition of the directionality of the actions of others, and mirroring—is a huge part of early childhood development, and very demanding. Studies of the false belief problem have put a wedge between the verbal skills needed to articulate correct answers and the apparent tacit understanding of the phenomenon: the two are not the same. That wedge is important, because the gap between the discursive and the gut or automatized responses to inputs is a persistent fact of social experience. Language, or the Russians' second symbol system, changes things tremendously: the Russians spoke of it as reorganizing the brain. Language use changes the cognitive architecture, the neuronal connections, and enforces a kind of uniformity. But it also re-individualizes, in that as the linguistic habits become tacitized and automatic, they change as well, and in accordance with the prior experiences they link together in memory which differ from person to person.

3 Normativity

I have not written about this elsewhere in precisely these terms, but a brief discussion of the sources of "normativity" will help explain some of what follows. Ways of doing things, practices and all that goes with them, are cases of practical normativity which are learned pragmatically, often by imitation of conduct that is normal in the factual or descriptive sense, and in which the normative and pragmatic are not differentiated. There is good psychological evidence of this (Bear and Knobe 2017; Phillips and Knobe 2018), and it fits with Georg Jellinek's idea of the normative power of the factual or real (Jellinek 1905; Bezemek 2019). The developmental question is this: when does the factual normal, the pragmatically successful one, or simply what people do, become distinguished from the normative one? A simple answer to this is that the normative one is conveyed by and distinguished by the approval and disapproval communicated by others. A simple example is the story of being taught how to respond to a yellow light while driving: the novice driver imitates the experienced driver by speeding up to make the light; the experienced driver and teacher says "why did you do that?" to which the novice replies "but that is what you do!" to which the teacher says "well, you are not supposed to do that." We get two kinds of messages from the world that conflict, and the normative and the pragmatic (and descriptively normal) come apart. The approval part is associated with various social payoffs and associations, and becomes emotionally and cognitively entrenched as a sense of correctness. It gets further entrenched and stabilized in a social group by something explicitly shared, namely theories that justify the approvals and disapprovals. But it is not necessarily the actual normal, the thing people find pragmatically normal—to cross the street against the light when there is no traffic, for example.

The "right way" in the "normative" sense usually means "our way," and gets bound up with group identity, signaling, belonging, conformity, and so forth, and produces a moral sensibility, or a normative attitude." One needn't go far to find this process at work: Nancy Friday, in her best seller *My Mother My Self* (1977), gave many examples like these: women becoming upset when their spouse filled the kitchen cabinet with dishes differently than the way she was used to from her mother—and of course her response was that it was the "wrong" way. It felt wrong, so it was wrong. All that is needed to produce this reaction is to violate expectations. This violation is a kind of condition of "normativity": she would not have even known that there was a right or wrong to have a normative attitude about if she had never encountered a different way of arranging the dishes. It is at least the beginning of "normativity." Perhaps it is also the whole of it.

David Henderson and Terence Horgan say that "What one is looking for is, in effect, a kind of minimal characterization of the normative sensibilities posited in terms of what these do in the production of coordinated behavior." I take it that this is also the sociological "problem of order." Nietzsche would have thought that herd-like conformity was enough to answer this question, and perhaps expectations are all that is needed for coordinated behavior. There is evidence that normal practices become normativized automatically in the developmental process (Schmidt et al. 2011). Only at some later point does the normal way, which is "right" in the pragmatic sense that it works, get differentiated into "things that work" and "the right way." I suspect that this differentiation depends on some sort of "theory," such as the theory that only superior people do things a particular way. The theorization and justification of a preference for "the right way" can be elevated far beyond the pragmatic: the imitation of Christ, for example, is a long standing Christian ideal, but it is also impossible to achieve. It is when normal practice conflicts with theory that it becomes possible to say "the community practice is wrong."

"Normative language," an issue also raised by Peter Olen, is ubiquitous. What this language, with terms like beautiful, correct, evil—or the language I experienced in being taught to ride a horse with an English saddle, which was wordless but consisted of a whip cracked on the rump of the horse—have in common is some sort of commendation or disapproval, or express wishes and desires. That this kind of use of normative language is ubiquitous should be no mystery—it is one of the major ways we manipulate other people and co-ordinate with them. Nor should the fact that it also gets used to signify social status, identity, and so on, and that it can be refined into elaborate justifying theories: they become the good bad theories that stabilize the practice. Theories justify the approvals and disapprovals.

Vilfredo Pareto made a point of the arbitrariness of these theories—based on the observation that the practices in societies went on unchanged for a long time, but the justifications changed often. For him that meant that they were largely ornamental. There is a grain of truth in this—a big enough grain to lead to questioning any account of normativity that concentrates on the justifications and ignores the pragmatics. But the fact that these theories can be shared explicitly means that this idea of correctness can be stabilized for a group and become part of our expectations about what other people approve of—not a personal normative attitude but a group one. The theories are as heterogenous as the motives for commending and disapproving. People who believe in tabu believe in a natural fact that a mechanical force acts when a tabu is violated. This provides coordination. It is false, from the scientific point of view. From the point of view of the tabu-thinker, the fact that everyone around him honors the tabu and fears the mechanical result is reason enough to do the same: it is convenient to believe, and creates problems if one doesn't (Turner 2015). This produces impressive coordination: enough for a rudimentary political order in which the "Big Man" is himself tabu. But co-ordination also happens through using a concept like quarks. What is universal is co-ordination. But there is nothing in the way of a special force here, beyond the pragmatic, and the stabilizing. And I think this is also going to be true of any universalizing notion of normativity, which will be only an abstraction from the practical normativity discussed earlier, and particular coordinating relations, and not a separate "universal" phenomenon.

Our thinking—at the substrate level—is transformed by our actions, by our practices of commendation, and by our public justificatory reason-giving. And in this way justifications become not only justifications, but reasons for action: they become part of our predictive processing of situations. We begin to think in advance in justificatory terms. And this is how social constructions enter the brain itself. The connections that get made by the act of justification, in its "culturally specific" sense, transform our brain organization and therefore our thinking. And the associations are there, activated by our actions, when we are called upon to justify or explain. This is why the hypnotized subject is so facile in producing explanations for his actions. Moreover, the associations hook into such universal "moral" dispositions as altruism, equality, the recognition of hierarchy, and such feelings as pain, disgust, and fear, and give them targets.

This is what I take the substrate of social life to be. All these "social realities" are transmitted, created, and become neuronal through joint attention, ostentation, discipline, habit, and so on—through social interaction. They never escape their basis in the physical brain, in the sense that there is always something neuronal happening when they happen. But they do escape, or are never at the level of, consciousness, introspection, or mutual understanding: the level I call the *Verstehen* bubble (2018). This is my answer to the question raised by Henderson and Horgan of why I think there is a principled difference between what goes on in the bubble and the casual processes of mind that go on outside it. Reflection and introspection are a small and cloudy window on mental processes. This is something we know both from common knowledge, for example from the fact that we cannot introspect the processes that convert irradiations

4 Shared Cognitive Objects

Schatzki's critique of my account of practices focuses on the claim that Bourdieu does not deny that individuals have different learning histories. But the issue with taking practices as a unit goes beyond this—one can imagine people with different learning histories converging more or less on a common practice (though one would like a cause for this convergence, such as the ones I suggested, namely common rituals and discipline, imitation, convenience, and so forth). The problem is with the Bourdieuvian idea that this convergence creates something novel in kind and agent-like, with aims or teleology obscured to the actual agents, who misrecognize it, which also adjusts itself to new circumstances (in a changing "field") while keeping its aims in mind. That is a lot to claim, and a lot more than "practice as convergent behavior that has the unintended effect of making other kinds of behavior easier or more effective, or alternatively more difficult and less effective," which I obviously accept. One can debate the meaning of Bourdieu. But to give up these agentive elements of "practice" would make the social world consist of individual agents whose acts have unintended consequences. This would be to revert to Boudonism, the position of his main rival.

I agree with Schatzki on a crucial issue: the physical environment, planned or unplanned, and the world of objects, do have a profound effect on people's habits, reactions, on the convergence of behavior, and the organization of the brain. I have argued in a chapter that was not in print when this paper was written ("'Habit Is Thus the Enormous Flywheel of Society': Pragmatism. Social Theory, and Cognitive Science," 2020), that there are many actual "things," public and physical rather than mental objects, that are in fact shared, and I suggested that their ubiquitous role even in religion was revealing about their relation to abstract thought. This was also a point I made in the last chapter of the *Social Theory of Practices* (1994). The question is whether actual objects, along with the means of convergence mentioned above, are enough to explain the "social life" in question, without appealing to something else.

Schatzki appeals to an ontology of "pools" which he uses to define practice:

> A practice is a certain clumping of doings and sayings that hang together through a pool of items ... [i.e. what is in "*in* the open arrays of doings and

sayings"] Whether, furthermore, a given activity belongs to the clump (the practice) is established by reference to this pool.

I struggle a bit to see the issue here, as Schatzki himself does. We can talk about fields, or pools, in a descriptive sense, and of a pool of items that hang together and are there to be used in idiosyncratic ways by individuals. For me the issue is not whether this is a fruitful way of thinking: clearly it is, in the sense of identifying something *to* explain. The question is whether one slips into circularity by turning pools into something with its own agency or with a coherence other than the coherence that can be lent to it by practices in the sense he rejects: namely patterns of behavior and thought that reside in the individual.

There is, however, a middle ground here that preserves the sense—that recurs throughout the history of this topic— of some special coherence in social formations. I think the idea of niches is a useful way to talk about this, The niche idea is this: the social world provides various affordances, in the form of people's predictable responses, which become one's own habits, and which make possible other predictable responses, which allow for stabilization in good bad theories which are accepted because they are convenient to believe and out of pluralistic ignorance, workarounds that become kludges, uses of the physical world and inventions in the physical world—the usual mix of social stuff—in which one element builds on another to form a complexly intertwined social world that resists change because of the mutual dependence of the elements. Cases I discuss, such as Patterson's analysis of the traps of the ghetto (2001, 2015) and Banfield's account of southern Italy (1958), can be usefully understood in these terms. What I would reject is a teleological account of "niche construction," for which there are adequate non-teleological alternatives (Gatti et al. 2020).

Henderson and Horgan provide an interesting, and different, account of what must be shared for there to be norms, which raises much the same issues, but in relation to normativity. Changing the terminology here doesn't change the problem. Cristina Bicchieri herself relies very heavily on the notion of shared scripts (Bicchieri and McNally 2018), since she needs shared expectations and more to apply game theory. Henderson and Horgan propose "conceptions." Can we get by without any mental "thing"—prototypes, concepts, conceptions—being shared? I have instead referred to the work of L. W. Barsalou, who has advanced a more Gestalt-like picture of what people actually do when they size up situations for action (Barsalou 2013). I called the things they recognize "Barsalou bits" (which are essentially matters of pattern recognition) which I take to be personal rather than shared (Turner 2019, 259–61), in line with Barsalou's own critique of the concept of concept as a psychological fact (Yeh and Barsalou 2006). The question is whether these kinds of person-specific means of engaging with the normative social world, together with personal attitudes, dispositions (including natural "normative" ones, such as altruism) are sufficient to explain what needs to be explained.

5 Folk Psychology, Collective Beliefs, and the Ubiquity of Normative Language

There is a long-running dispute between people who think that reasons explanations have a close relation to thinking and that attributing beliefs and desires corresponds to the major explanatory factors of action (e.g., Fodor 2008), and those who think that these have more to do with social institutions of blaming and justifying action and less to do with explanation (Mercier and Sperber 2017, but also Strawson [1962] 1993). Steuber wants to defend "the framework of folk psychology as providing us with a genuine and, at its core, autonomous explanatory domain," that is primary and basic, concerns features of persons embedded in a social context rather than mental contents, and also claims that despite the fact that vocabularies for the different versions of folk psychology vary, we can still claim objectivity for claims about things in this domain using our own terms. Moreover, for Steuber this is just an extension of what we ordinarily do in the course of understanding people in social interaction, as rational agents, using our re-enactive empathetic capacities.

This does highlight a key issue: the extent to which this interpretation can be scientific, objective, and reveal actual causes of action. Stueber thinks it can be, and thinks that I regard cultural relativity as an obstacle to objectivity, whereas he thinks cultural difference is only an obstacle to access. To take his example, we may have different cultural resources for understanding Caesar, but we can come to share them and thus share an objective understanding. I would first separate the two questions: we can, plausibly enough, come to an "objective" evaluation of Caesar's guilt, justifications for actions, and thus his rationality as an agent. We can understand why others may have judged him differently, historically or across cultures, and put the judgments aside in doing this. Doing this is already an external exercise, like that of a legal procedure, which merely happens to be formulated in terms of our folk psychological conventions.

But if justifications are not more or less equivalent to causes, we still don't have an *explanation*. There is good reason for thinking they are not. We are quite facile, after coming out of hypnosis, at giving justifications for our actions—to rationalize them and make ourselves out as rational agents. It is certainly also true that we associate our actions with justifications, and subconsciously as well as consciously are affected by these associations. But there is plenty that goes on in the course of action that we are not aware of, can't articulate, but nevertheless plays a role in the cognitive processes related to action, including pattern recognition, which Stueber complains about. These all go into the stew that makes up the causes of action, and can't be reduced to the model of rational justification. This is something Weber asserts specifically. The meaningful part of action, the rational part, is merely an imposition on a more complex reality. This is his point in calling rational action an ideal type. That we can anchor and test these impositions at least to some extent by relying on our empathic capacities is important, and this may yield the "reasons" for their actions, but these reasons are not the same as causes, though they may be part of the stew. Do we understand this stew? No: neither for ourselves nor for others, because we don't "understand" most of its elements, which include much that is outside the *Verstehen* bubble, nor how they work together. Nor is this claim all that radical: Davidson himself regarded reasons explanations as at best low probability causal explanations.

The larger question here is about concepts like belief and desire, and the objectivity of our claims about them. We know that there are pitfalls, even within the limits of folk psychology, such as fundamental attribution error and cultural differences in the way actions are explained. A claim made in the growing anthropological literature on "belief" is this: that the fact that the meaning of the term "belief" has changed over time does not have any bearing on the validity of our ascriptions of beliefs to historical agents (or indeed to agents in any cultural context, assuming they can make assertions [see Streeter 2020]). I take it that this is Steuber's claim as well—that *their* folk psychology doesn't matter to *our* ascriptions. I agree with this, up to a point: the "our" in this formulation is correct, because our ascriptions need to be translated back into our locution if it is going to make sense to us. But the situation at the substrate level is different. The second signal system, which includes their folk psychology, is not just an alternative interpretation of the same facts about belief and motivation. The language they use gets fed back into the brain and reorganizes it in a different way from ours. So there is an objective difference that makes for a mismatch between our ascriptions and their cognitive processes—in addition to the mismatch between our ascriptions and our own cognitive processes.

Does this mean that we cannot arrive at objective results in making claims, for example, about Caesar, at least if we remain in the *Verstehen* bubble, i.e., the space of interpretation? The issue here, which I will take up again below in relation to Zahle, is how much of indeterminacy there is in interpretation and how it gets resolved. Obviously historians of different eras and cultures interpret (and judge) Caesar differently—what is problematic for us is what is normal and human for them, for example. Can this be overcome by sharing of perspectives and information to construct a whole, objective picture? Or is it always limited by the limitations of the perspectives being integrated? I think the latter, for reasons that fall under what I called the Mauss problem: what is unusual and needs explanation, within the bubble, is a matter of what we take to be normal or merely human and not noticeable. We "interpret" the noticeable. We do not interpret the fact that someone breathes. That can change in the future—we may become differently attuned to matters that were formerly unproblematic and unproblematizable. But the idea that the second signal system reorganizes the brain is also relevant: it suggests that there may be physical limits to our capacity to empathize, to follow the thinking of others in other cultures, and therefore to integrate their perspective. Weber explicitly acknowledged this possibility.

Alban Bouvier takes up the problem of collective beliefs, and particularly the role of false beliefs, and their rhetorical construction. I am highly sympathetic to this approach, especially as it relates to "normativity," in part for reasons he mentions in relation to Alexis de Tocqueville and Jon Elster, namely the role of hypocrisy and pluralistic ignorance in explaining the gap between norms in the empirical sense of what people actually do and in the ideal sense of what they are supposed to do. I have touched on some of these issues here and there (2011), but never at any great length. My emphasis in relation to "collective belief" has been on the interweaving of tacit and explicit—the existence and profusion of creedal statements, folk sayings, and their use in reminding people of what is "right," is a particularly clear example of this. What is "collective" here is the explicit. This inverts Durkheim, who thought that the explicit things he listed in the chapter on social facts in *The Rules* ([1895] 1982) were manifestations of the shared collective consciousness. My suggestion is that the supposed manifestations, which are public, such as laws, rituals, and proverbs, do the collective work. For me what is tacit is not collective, but personal, though in a pragmatic sense there may be a high degree of convergence in behavior.

I would agree with Bouvier's structural-individualist model, in large part, and add the following. There is a very interesting question, one which originally motivated my turn to the problem of tradition, of what we might call deep tradition, the tradition that persists even when explicit belief not longer holds. Bouvier gives several examples of this. The obvious ones are the Christian roots of "Europe," and the Confucian ethic in China, honor societies all over the place, notably in the Arab world, and so on. These have characteristics that seem not only to persist but to reproduce themselves, adapt, and are independent of religious belief, though religious belief is used to justify them. My guess is that their persistence is not an illusion, but rests on multiple bases. Kinship relations, business practice, authority relations, friendship, and much more depend on expectations that persist, each for its own panoply of reasons, and get rearticulated in novel ways, sustaining the interweaving of explicit and tacit. They are niches, or niche-like.

What is intriguing is rapid change. The sexual revolution followed the pill and appeared to be rapid; in contrast, the removal of the threat of hell in most people's minds, which the Victorians thought would unleash moral chaos, had little effect. In these cases, the mistake was probably this: we mistook the justificatory (and condemnatory) language people used, and the theories that justified it, for the real determinants of behavior. The role of argument, and rhetoric, in these cases may have been less direct than one might think: just admitting doing something that is normally kept private or secret can eliminate the pluralistic ignorance that sustained a practice. This is a point made by Bichierri (2017) which I think is especially important, but it also serves to reduce the apparent need for a collective object solution to the problem of the stability of beliefs and practices.

Bouvier's useful reconstruction of various approaches to the idea of collective beliefs speaks to some of these issues, especially by considering the role of explicit argumentation in changing beliefs. I would say that the success of explicit argumentation depends on the relation between the tacit bed, so to speak, of the individual, which receives the arguments, and the explicit argument itself. What makes an argument persuasive depends, in short, on how the brain has been reorganized by the second signal system and the connections that are produced by its use, including the tacit "beliefs" that determine how people respond. That these can be similar is just to say that responses can be similar, not that there are literal collective tacit beliefs. But the interesting thing here is the way in which niches differentiate the people who function within them.

To take Bouvier's examples, operating within the niche of religious people who speak and respond non-verbally in a particular way, and do so consistently, reorganizes their brains in a particular way, just as living within the niche of a university and academic discipline does. How powerful these effects are, meaning how much they differentiate people from people in other niches, seems to me to be an empirical question, and thus the question of "how social" are these determinants of cognition is also empirical. Pluralistic ignorance is an important feature of niches: the fact that we are ignorant of what people know, do, or think, forces us to rely on public utterances that mislead us about this, possibly because they are consciously or unconsciously attempts to manipulate us, for example to improve the reputation of the speaker. All of this is consistent with a sense both that justifications do not represent cognitive processes very well and that they nevertheless play a role in preparing the tacit bed for persuasion.

Olen works through possible objections from the Sellarsian tradition to my criticisms of the use of normativity as a mysterious explanatory mechanism. One defense he suggests is that something like score-keeping, rather than any particular content, is universal, and normative, and unproblematic. I take it that all this means is that coordination is universal. The other defense is that local notions of normativity might be universally necessary from the human point of view, which I think amounts to the same thing. Beyond this, but related to them, is the idea that normativity is not really an explanatory notion at all, but a way of explicating the kinds of practical lives of people in communities. I agree with this, but would radicalize the point, with a caveat, by extending it from "normative" justifications to reasons explanations.

There is a tradition of claiming that reasons explanations are not explanatory, but are characterizations or descriptions. The basis for this is the fact that claims about reasons, understood as internal facts, are not based on any information added to what one knows externally about the person and their situation. They are mere placeholders in a narrative. I have discussed a particular version of this argument by Bittner, and made some emendations to it (2017b). Steuber's comments are in part a response to that paper. But the picture of explanation I have outlined above adds reasons and justifications back in, though in a somewhat different role. I suggested that part of the predictive processing that precedes action includes the anticipation of the possible need to justify or explain the act. Thus anticipated justifications are part of the set of connections that go into the explanation of action, and therefore explanatory, but not in the sense of the reasons as mental causes tradition.

The underlying puzzling issue, as Olen notes, is the ubiquity of normative language in the conduct of practical affairs. The presence of normative language is universal among human communities, and therefore in some sense the mark of the human point of view. Or so this argument goes. But is it true? Probably not. The commonalities to the "normative" are illusory. What is universal is the distinction between what people do and what other people want or expect them to do, and the role of this distinction in coordination. The category of expressions of this difference is massively heterogenous: telling people how to do something, telling people what one likes, telling people how it is normally done in a specific setting or community, ranking things so the ranking is taken as objective, saying what makes one "belong," saying what God wants ... the list goes on endlessly. And these expressions all can be turned into justifications. To call all this "normative" is unproblematic: thinking that this means that there is a special ingredient or attitude that makes them normative, which amounts to importing an explanatory notion, is not.

6 Social Science

I am grateful for Whimster's discussion of economic thought, because it goes to the heart of many of the problems that social science faces generally, given that its "theories" are ideal-types some of them seem especially powerful and seductive and because the concepts that make up "folk" understandings of social life also have this character. A University of Chicago theoretical economist was quoted to me by a scientist on the faculty as having said that his models were more real than reality. This is in a sense an idea that came from science itself: that the world of mere apparent factuality is not real, but the world of scientific abstractions is. Whimster traces accounts of the problem from Carl Menger through Ludwig Lachmann, who was a student of Werner Sombart and perhaps the most consistent Weberian in economics.

Lachmann grasps the radical significance of the problem of making economic thinking consistent with what people actually do, how they actually think, and how they act. The key implication, for me, is this: Models, or idealtypes, have an "apply when they apply" character. Although the model or ideal type works for a given set of circumstances, we don't know what the circumstances are, so generalizing from them is always hazardous. This was Clark Glymour's argument about statistical causal models (1983) and implicitly my own argument against Simon's claim that the assumptions of these models were "empirical" (Turner and Wilcox 1974: 587). The form of the models often deludes us into thinking that they should generalize. Getting back to ordinary motives and reasons, in the fashion of Lachmann, is a kind of protection against this error; it is not just another way of constructing things. Rather it is an appeal to a more basic level. Models and ideal-types are shortcuts that work as long as the basic level does not change.

Zahle raises the question of underdetermination, which I have taken up in a variety of contexts and indeed can be seen as a red thread through my writings, from my dissertation to the present. She discusses these issues in relation to Charles Taylor, whose "Interpretation and the Sciences of Man" ([1985] 2012) was an important source of legitimation for interpretivism. Her focus is on the relation between the kind of data qualitative researchers actually collect and interpretation. Taylor is inclined to reduce all data to interpretation; she notes that qualitative researchers separate the data they collect in field notes, which she calls data-interpretations, from interpretations of a more theoretical or speculative kind, and that data-interpretation is not only less subject to underdetermination but that data-interpretations can support one another in ways that make them even less subject to underdetermination.

Edward Banfield's *Moral Basis of a Backward Society* (1958) provides a nice example of this problem. Banfield collected all sorts of qualitative data, from the Pinocchio legend and its status, local religious traditions, justifications of behavior, observed behavior, to thematic apperception tests, and constructed his key theoretical notion or interpretation, a culture of "amoral familism," out of all of this material—all of which I would regard as "behavioral manifestations." The thesis was controversial. Moreover, it was generalizable: one could see similar cultural traits in other "culture of poverty" situations. No one really denied the primary observations in these cases, consistent with what Zahle argues. But they nevertheless rejected the thesis. My concern in *Sociological Explanation as Translation* (1980) was to show that there was a coherent process of criticism in the discourse about the subject. I defended a position not that different from hers, in the sense that I sought to explain how underdetermination could be overcome, though my approach was to show that this was done mostly by citing new aspects of the context, aspects that were made relevant by providing a coherent alternative interpretation.

The issue between us, if there is one, comes down to this: can enough mutual support be given on the level of data-interpretations to preclude alternative theoretical interpretations, i.e., to reduce the level of underdetermination at the theoretical level? In the highly politicized culture of poverty literature that followed Banfield, the answer seemed to be "no." For decades a debate has raged over whether ghetto conditions are the product of a pathological ghetto culture or ghetto culture is the rational response to ghetto conditions. The data settled nothing. I would like to think that one can get beyond this level of underdetermination to a better account, and I have discussed Orlando Patterson's attempts to do so (2001, 2015), which included doing what I described in *Sociological Explanation as Translation*: providing an interpretation that expanded the context, and thus changed the explanatory problem. But this kind of analysis is governed, as Zahle notes that I implied, by a certain constraint. The hypothesis, in my case a translation-like hypothesis, the translation itself needs to make sense in the new language. One cannot translate into gibberish. Constructing such an account depends on "data-interpretation," because the newly relevant contextual facts are data, but this is not enough. Making their relevance clear requires a higher-level interpretation, which is what Patterson and Banfield supplied. Coherence and relevance go together.

I was overoptimistic about the ability of a process of criticism of the sort I discussed to reduce underdetermination. I don't think the kind of convergence at the level of data-interpretation she discusses fares any better. The problem of relevance gets tangled up with a related problem: salience. In the study of race relations in the US, for example, there have been a few outstanding moments where the facts were able to settle important issues. I would rank Charles Johnson's report on the 1919 Chicago race riots as perhaps the best (1922). The people studying the topic, agreed, and had an audience that agreed, on what was relevant, and on what mattered or was salient. A century later there is no such agreement. What is relevant now is contested, or disagreed about, and in ways that the data can't settle. Is it capitalism, Whiteness, crime, stigma, racism, structure, culture, policing, or something else? The choice of what is relevant, including what needs to be described at the data level, seems to depend on the salience granted to different facts by different analysts. I don't see how to overcome this: perhaps social science is only possible if we have some common ground in the first place.

John Holmwood criticizes my view of Talcott Parsons, at least the few sentences that mention him in *Liberal Democracy 3.0* (2003), and defends him as having views similar to T. H. Marshall, and portrays him as a defender of democracy. I don't really disagree with his characterization of inclusion, but I think that in the American context it has a far less sunny significance, especially for his relation to democracy. My point in the passage cited is that Parsons' idea of professions did not include much about knowledge, but was more concerned with the interests they served in society.

I agree with Holmwood's claim that this was related to a social ideal, which Holmwood characterizes in terms of Marshall's "citizen complex." But I read the significance of this social ideal differently. In relation to both democracy and social theory, or social ideals, Parsons was taking a stance within American politics. What was it? That can best be seen in the efforts of his political mentor and fellow Heidelberg Ph.D. Carl Friedrich, who was the leader of the Harvard "defense of democracy" initiative, to which Parsons contributed. This was no incidental connection: Helen Parsons was an aide and assistant to Friedrich, and is thanked in his books of the period. Parsons' rise to power at Harvard was fueled by his role in training officers for occupation service, an initiative of Friedrich.

Friedrich was an authoritarian liberal. He was hostile to direct democracy and plebiscites, sought a revision of the US constitution to allow for its suspension, and valorized bureaucratic rule in the European manner (like Parsons and in contrast to Weber). Both Friedrich and Parsons were enthralled by the parallel to Weimar. The irony was that in Weimar, the opponents of the established order were enemies of the constitution. In the US, the people whom Parsons and Friedrichs wanted suppressed were defending the constitution. Friedrich wanted it made more authoritarian to "defend democracy." Before the war, he was obsessed with the aim of suppressing opposition to the war—the majority. He was concerned with the limitations of "coercive integration" and divided the public into cooperators and non-cooperators.

There is an especially revealing incident in Friedrichs' efforts to "defend democracy." A peace song by a group that included the young Pete Seeger was being distributed. Friedrich wanted it suppressed, both by legal and extra-legal means—to which he wanted to recruit voluntary organizations: "you never can handle situations of this kind democratically by mere suppression. Unless civic groups and individuals will make a determined effort to counteract such appeals by equally effective methods, democratic morale will decline."[1] This was a revealing inversion of Tocqueville: for him the vast range of voluntary organizations was a means of resisting central state power; for Friedrich they were means of suppression.

Parsons made several contributions to this program, including trying to identify potentially disloyal ethnic populations. But his most revealing contribution was in 1942, when Parsons advocated for a domestic propaganda agency modeled on psychoanalysis, which he said was "more than a mere analogy ([1942] 1954, 173). Parsons proposed a vast propaganda effort at a time when survey research by the government on morale was itself considered to be constitutionally questionable. His "principal thesis" was "that the structure of western society in its relations to the functions of social control provides an extraordinary opening for the deliberate propaganda of reinforcement as an agency of control" ([1942] 1954, 173). Dissent was to be understood as involving "deviant tendencies ... rooted in the conflicts, strains, and malfunctioning of the social system" ([1942] 1954, 176).

Susan Sontag, in her notorious 9/11 statement, said "Politics, the politics of a democracy—which entails disagreement, which promotes candor—has been replaced by psychotherapy" (2001). This was, in a nutshell, Parsons' program. This puts Parsons' concerns with integration in a different perspective. Rather than accept democratic contention, Parsons wanted to prevent it. We can call Parsons' social ideal of "integration" by its continental name: corporatism. This informed his view of the professions. When he wrote about law as a profession, there was nothing about its role in defending rights and the constitution, or

---

[1] Wikipedia Carl Joachim Friedrich, note 2. https://en.wikipedia.org/wiki/Carl_Joachim_Friedrich.

legal expertise as knowledge. Unlike a contemporary like Michael Polanyi, he did not treat it as a strongly traditional epistemic community which set its own goals and standards. For Parsons, the profession was there to serve an interest: it was "interstitial" and "along with that of other professional roles "collectivity-oriented" in contrast to business, which was self-interested ([1952]1954, 375).

Parsons dismissed the liberal democratic idea that "the public must be taken fully into government's confidence and treated as responsible adults" as a "compound of rationalistic and utopian bias" and compared it to the idea that "medical practice should be abolished since it is incompatible with the human dignity of a sick person to submit to being helped by someone more competent than himself" ([1942] 1954, 172n). Julien Benda, in 1947, ascribed the debacle of the twentieth century to those who "believed that there existed categories of men destined to command and that the good of the whole, bound up with the supremacy of these men, might very well necessitate their overriding the convenience of those whose function it is to obey" (1947, np). This was Parsons.

References

Banfield, Edward. 1958. *The Moral Basis of a Backward Society*. Glencoe, IL: the Free Press.

Barsalou, Lawrence W. 2013. "Mirroring as Pattern Completion Inferences within Situated Conceptualizations." *Cortex* 49: 2951–2953.

Bear, Adam, and Joshua Knobe. 2017. "Normality: Part Descriptive, Part Prescriptive." *Cognition* 167(October): 25–37.

Benda, M. Julien. 1947. "The Attack on Western Morality: Can European Ideals Survive?" *Commentary*, November. https://www.commentarymagazine.com/articles/julien-benda/the-attack-on-western-moralitycan-european-ideals-survive/.

Bezemek, Christoph. 2019. The 'Normative Force of the Factual': A Positivist's Panegyric. In *The Normative Force of the Factual: Legal Philosophy Between Is and Ought*. Nicoletta Bersier Ladavac, Christoph Bezemek, and Frederick Schauer, eds. New York: Springer, pp. 65–77.

Bicchieri, Cristina, and Peter McNally. 2018. "Shrieking sirens: Schemata, Scripts, and Social Norms. How Change Occurs." *Social Philosophy and Policy* 35 (1): 23–53. doi:10.1017/S0265052518000079.

Bicchieri, Cristina. 2017. *Norms in the Wild: How to Diagnose, Measure, and Change Social Norms*. Oxford: Oxford University Press.

Davidson, Donald. [1974] 2001. On the Very Idea of a Conceptual Scheme. *In Inquiries into Truth and Interpretation*. Oxford: Clarendon Press, pp. 183–199.

Dumitrescu, Irina. 2020. "How to Write well: Rules, Style and the 'Well-Made Sentence'." *Times Literary Supplement*, 6 March. https://www.the-tls.co.uk/articles/good-writing-irina-dumitrescu-book-review/.

Durkheim, Émile. [1895]1982.*The Rules of Sociological Method and Selected texts on Sociology and Its Method*, ed. Steven Lukes, trans. W. D. Halls. New York: The Free Press.

Fodor, Jerry A. 2008. *LOT 2: The Language of Thought Revisited*. Oxford: Oxford University Press.

Friday, Nancy. 1977. *My Mother, My Self: The Daughter's Search for Identity*. New York: Bantam.

Gatti, Roberto Cazzolla Gatti, Roger Koppl, Brian D. Fath, Stuart Kauffman, Wim Hordijk, and Robert E. Ulanowicz. 2020. "On the Emergence of Ecological and Economic Niches." *Journal of Bioeconomics* 22: 99–127. https://doi.org/10.1007/s10818-020-09295-4.

Glymour, Clark. 1983. "Social Science and Social Physics." *American Behavioral Scientist* 28(2): 126–134.

Jellinek, Georg. 1905. *Allgemeine Staatslehre (General Theory of the State)*. Berlin: O'Häring.

Johnson, Charles S. 1922. *The Negro in Chicago: A Study of Race Relations and a Race Riot*. Chicago: The University of Chicago Press.

Mercier, Hugo, and Dan Sperber. 2017. *The Enigma of Reason*. Cambridge, MA: Harvard University Press.

Parsons, Talcott. [1942] 1954. "Propaganda and Social Control." In *Essays in Sociological Theory*. New York: The Free Press, pp. 142–176.

Parsons, Talcott. [1952] 1954. "A Sociologist Looks at the Legal Profession." In *Essays in Sociological Theory*. New York: The Free Press, pp. 370–375.

Patterson, Orlando. 2001. "Taking Culture Seriously: A Framework and an Afro-American Illustration." In L. E. Harrison and S. P. Huntington (eds) *Culture Matters: How Values Shape Human Progress*. New York: Basic Books, pp. 202–218.

Patterson, Orlando, and Ethan Fosse. 2015. *The Cultural Matrix: Understanding Black Youth*. Cambridge, MA: Harvard University Press.

Phillips, J., and Joshua Knobe, 2018. "The Psychological Representation of Modality." *Mind & Language* 33(1): 65–94.

Schmidt, Marco F.H., Hannes Rakoczy, and Michael Tomasello. 2011. "Young Children Attribute Normativity to Novel Actions without Pedagogy or Normative Language." *Developmental Science* 14(3): 530–539. DOI: 10.1111/j.1467-7687.2010.01000.x.

Sontag, Susan. 2001. "Tuesday, and After: New Yorker writers respond to 9/11, Tuesday, and After: New Yorker writers respond to 9/11, September 17." *The New Yorker*, 24 September. https://www.newyorker.com/magazine/2001/09/24/tuesday-and-after-talk-of-the-town.

Strawson, P. F. 1962 [1993]. "Freedom and Resentment." In *Proceedings of the British Academy* 48: 1–25.

Streeter, Joseph. 2020. "Should We Worry about Belief?" *Anthropological Theory* 20(2): 133–156.

Taylor, Charles. [1985] 2012. "Interpretation and the Sciences of Man." In *Philosophy and the Human Sciences* vol. 2. Cambridge: Cambridge University Press, pp. 15–57.

Turner, Stephen and William C. Wilcox. 1974. Getting Clear about the "Sign Rule." *The Sociological Quarterly* 15: 571–88.

Turner, Stephen. 1980. *Sociological Explanation as Translation*. Rose Monograph Series of the American Sociological Association, New York, Cambridge: Cambridge University Press.

Turner, Stephen. 1994. *The Social Theory of Practices: Tradition, Tacit Knowledge, and Presuppositions*, Oxford: Polity Press; Chicago: University of Chicago Press. http://www.press.uchicago.edu/cgi-bin/hfs.cgi/00/12674.ctl.

Turner, Stephen. 2003. *Liberal Democracy 3.0: Civil Society in an Age of Experts*. London: Sage Publications.

Turner, Stephen. 2011. Universalism, Particularism, and Moral Change: Reflections on the Value-Normative Concepts of the Social Sciences, in *Global Trends and Regional Development*, edited by Nikolai Genov. London: Routledge, 251–267.

Turner, Stephen. 2014. Mundane Theorizing, *Bricolage* and *Bildung*. In *Theorizing in Social Science: The Context of Discovery*, edited by Richard Swedberg. Stanford: Stanford University Press, pp. 131–157.

Turner, Stephen. 2015. Functionalism, Field Theories, and Unintended Consequences. In: G. Manzo (ed.) *Paradoxes, Mechanisms, Consequences: Essays in honor of Mohamed Cherkaoui*. Oxford: Bardwell Press, 229–251.

Turner, Stephen. 2017a. Naturalizing the Tacit. In Jassen Andreev, Emil Lensky, and Paula Angelova (eds.) *Das Interpretative Universum: Dimitri Ginev zum 60. Geburtstag gewidmet*. Würzburg: Koenigshausen & Neumann, 355–376.

Turner, Stephen. 2017b. "The Belief-Desire Model of Action Explanation Reconsidered: Thoughts on Bittner." *Philosophy of the Social Sciences* 48(3): 290–308. https://doi.org/10.1177/0048393117750076.

Turner, Stephen. 2018. *Cognitive Science and the Social: A Primer*. New York: Routledge, chap. 8.

Turner, Stephen. 2019. "*Verstehen* Naturalized." *Philosophy of the Social Sciences* 49(4): 243–264. https://doi.org/10.1177/0048393119847102.

Turner, Stephen. 2020. "Habit Is Thus the Enormous Flywheel of Society": Pragmatism, Social Theory, and Cognitive Science. In Fausto Caruana and Italo Testa (eds.) *Habit: Pragmatist Approaches from Cognitive Science, Neuroscience, and Social Theory*. Cambridge: Cambridge University Press. Pp. 320–336.

Weber, Max. [1904] 2012."Objectivity" in Social Science and Social Policy. In: H. H. Bruun and S. Whimster, eds. *Max Weber: Collected Methodological Writings*, trans. Hans Henrik Bruun, pp. 100–138.London/New York: Routledge.

Winch, Peter. 1958. *The Idea of a Social Science and its Relation to Philosophy*. Routledge & Kegan Paul, London.

Winch, Peter ([1964] 1974) Understanding a Primitive Society. In Wilson, B. R. (ed.) *Rationality*. Blackwell, Oxford. pp. 78–111.

Yeh, Wenchi, and Lawrence W. Barsalou. 2006. "The Situated Nature of Concepts." The American Journal of Psychology 119(3): 349–384.

Zahle, Julie. 2017. "Ability Theories of Practice and Turner's Criticism of Bourdieu." *Journal for General Philosophy of Science*, 48(4): 553–567.

Index

4E approach to cognition   40–41, 182–183, 194–195

affordances
  See Turner
anthropology   30–31, 36–37, 38, 111–113, 134–135
argumentation   40–41, 42, 110, 257
Azande   32, 33, 45

Banfield, Edward   253, 260
Bicchieri, Cristina   119, 253–254,
  norms   159, 164–167, 165n4, 168, 169–170
Boudon, Raymond   110–111, 113–114, 116, 117
Bourdieu, Pierre   76–78, 80–81, 87, 110–112, 184, 252
Bouvier, Alban   6, 256–258
Brandom, Robert   18–19, 136–137n5, 138–139, 139n10
brute data
  See Taylor

causal explanation   57, 90–91, 92–96, 94–95nn2–3, 99, 134–135, 251–252
  See also Turner, Weber
Chicago   1–2, 261
Chicago school   186–187, 192, 195–196, 259
cognition   40–42, 54, 56, 177–178, 180–181, 247–248, 257–258,
  See also representation
cognitive science   4–5, 7, 21, 23–26, 151–152, 158–159, 169
  culture and   180–181, 186–187
Cognitive Science and the Social (css in Roth, C1)   4–7, 23–27, 28, 31, 74, 150–151, 152–153
Coleman, James   113–114, 116–117, 120, 120–121n16, 122
collective beliefs   111, 117, 120, 122, 254
collective mental elements   75–76, 77
culture   4–5, 25, 59–60, 61–62, 64–65, 76, 244–245, 260
  bounded   31–32, 33, 35, 37, 38, 42–43
  and economic behavior   177–178, 183, 183n2, 184, 185, 197

  and rationality   38, 42–43, 45
  See also rules

Davidson, Donald   32–33, 35–36, 35n1, 43, 93–95, 93–94n2, 150–152, 254–255,
  "The Very Idea of a Conceptual Scheme"   32–33, 37
democracy   7–8, 222–223, 231–232, 235, 236–237, 261–263,
  See also Liberal Democracy 3.0, Parsons
deVries, Willem   134, 141–143, 141–142n12, 145, 147–148
Dennett, Daniel   24, 181, 188, 191
Durkheim, Émile   56, 111–112, 122, 122–123n20, 123–124, 194–195, 256

Edinburgh School   32–33, 36
Elster, Jon   110–111, 113–114, 117, 256
empathy   21–22, 23–24, 92–93, 100
  See also Turner, Weber
The Enigma of Reason (Mercier and Sperber)   41–42
Evans-Pritchard, E.E.   45, 112–113
Evidenz,   6–7, 22, 155–156, 157
  See also Weber
expertise   62, 222, 223–224, 225–226, 229–230, 231, 232, 236–237,
  See also Parsons, Turner
explanation   6, 36, 56–57, 87, 94–95n3, 134, 134–135n3, 137n8, 138–139, 140–141, 143, 145–146, 254–255,
  sociological   1–2, 12, 13–16, 54–55, 58, 59–60, 106–107, 171–172n5, 177–178, 189–190n5
  See also Good-Bad theories, normativity, *Sociological Explanation as Translation*, Turner (folk psychology), Weber (causality)
Explaining the Normative (EN in Roth, C1)   4–5, 6, 18–22, 51, 135–136

Fodor, Jerry   98–99, 181, 245
folk psychology
  See Turner
Friedrich, Carl   261–262
Fuller, Steve   222, 235–236

INDEX

Giddens, Anthony   72, 76, 80–81, 87
Gilbert, Margaret   122, 123–124
Goldman, Alvin   113–114n6, 115, 115n8
Good-Bad theories (GBT)   20, 59, 64–65, 182n1
  and normativity   59, 60–61, 65–66, 138–139, 147, 147–148n15

Habermas, Jürgen   227–229, 227–228n2
habits   79, 80, 245, 247, 248–249
Hayek, Friedrich   122–123n19, 177–178, 187, 189–190, 191, 195–196, 197
Holmwood, John   7–8, 261

ideal-type   246, 259
internal state   134, 152–153, 154–155, 164–165, 166
  See also Turner
interpretation   30–31, 32, 35, 43–45, 61–62, 102–103, 105–106, 157–159, 188, 191, 202
  See also Davidson, irrationality, Lachmann, translation, understanding, *Verstehen* bubble
irrationality   30–31, 32, 42–44, 45

Jones, Todd   212–213, 213nn6-7, 218–219

knowledge   51–52, 55, 56, 60–62, 84–87, 95–96, 103, 185, 186–187,
  See also Good-Bad theories, Menger, Turner
Kuhn, Thomas   120, 192

Lachmann, Ludwig   177–178, 189, 192, 259
learning   79–80, 83, 84–86, 247–248, 252
  See also practices
Levi-Strauss, Claude   245
Liberal Democracy 3.0   5, 222–223, 232–233, 234, 261
Lukes, Steven   34–35, 43–45

Marshall, T.H.   228–229, 229n3, 230, 234, 261
Marx, Karl   111–112, 226, 227
Mauss, Marcel   59–60, 255–256
Menger, Carl   7, 183–184n3, 186–187, 189–190, 200
  and cognitive science   180, 187
  and culture   177–178, 197
Mercier, Hugo   40–42, 114–115

methodological individualism   113–114, 116, 120, 120–121n17
mirror neurons
  See Turner

naturalism   30, 45
  See also Turner
Neurath, Otto   187–188, 189–190, 189–190n5
normativity
  See Turner
norms   38–40, 45, 138, 141–142, 143–144, 144–145n13, 147–148n16, 150, 204–205,
  culturally specific   30–31, 32–33, 43–45
  See also Bicchieri, rationality, Turner

O'Shea, James   134, 138–139, 140–141, 143–145, 144–145n13, 147–148
Olen, Peter   6, 122–123n20, 136–137n7, 250, 258–259

Pareto, Vilfredo   56, 111–112, 112–113n2, 113–114, 113–114n6, 116, 117, 122–123n19
Parsons, Talcott   224–230, 229n3, 231–232, 233–234, 261–263
patterns of activity   1–2, 34, 36–37, 38–39, 42–43, 50–51, 73, 74, 139n10, 143–144, 253
  See also Bourdieu, practices, Turner
Pettit, Philip   163–164
Popper, Karl   112–113, 153, 187–188, 189
practices   51–52, 61–62, 65–66, 71, 134–135, 136–137, 138, 143–144, 146–147, 147–148n15, 147–148n16,
  action and   204–206, 207–209, 210
  See also norms, normativity, patterns of activity, Taylor, Turner
professional knowledge
  See Parsons, Turner

Quine, Willard Van Orman   11, 45, 172

rational choice theory   94–95n3, 115
rational expectations theory   192, 195
rationality   5, 30, 110–111, 139, 147–148n15, 181, 183, 187, 254–255,
  and collective beliefs   111–113, 120
  See also Turner
Reid, Thomas   115, 116
representation   40–42, 153–155, 157, 166

INDEX 269

Rescorla, Michael   193–195
rhetoric   111, 257
Risjord, Mark   37, 42–43, 202, 244–245
Roth, Paul   4–5, 31, 56n3, 244–245
rules   34–35, 37, 76, 81, 82, 83–84, 86–87, 162, 166

Schatzki, Theodor   5–6, 252–253
Sellars, Wilfrid   6, 122–123n20, 134, 134n2, 136–137n7, 140–142, 143–145
Sellarsian tradition   136–137n6, 146–148, 147–148n16, 258
Simon, Herbert   33–34, 38, 259
Singleton, Michael   63, 64–65
Smith, Adam   100, 181–182, 184–185, 196n8
social, the   76–77, 87, 96, 100, 106–107, Weber   102–103
  See also Turner (social, social theory)
social explanation   1–2, 59–60, 106–107, 244
Social Explanation as Translation (SET in Roth, C1)   4, 12–15, 19, 20–21, 27–28, 30, 53, 244
social practices   50–52
The Social Theory of Practices (STP in Roth, C.1)   15–18, 17n2, 21, 57, 73, 204, 216, 252
sociology   224–225, 232
  See also Parsons, Turner
Sperber, Dan   40–42, 110–111n1, 113n5, 114–116, 117n14
Stueber, Karsten   6, 254, 255, 258
Strauss, Leo   55–56, 60–61

Taylor, Charles   203–204, 206, 212, 214, 218, 219
  and brute data   210, 210n3, 219
  and interpretivism   204, 206, 207
  and underdetermination   212, 217
theory of mind   23–24, 25, 104, 177–178, 180, 186, 191, 195, 197, 248–249,
  see also Turner (folk psychology)
Tocqueville, Alexis de   6, 117, 120, 122, 256
transmission problem
  See Turner
Turing, Alan   178, 197
Turner, Jonathan   223–224, 225
Turner, Stephen   1, 3, 111–112n1, 117n12, 122–123n20, 197, 221
  affordances   91–92, 104, 185
  causal world   245, 246

causality   14, 16, 17, 18, 20, 21, 23–24, 25, 245–246,
  and normativity   136–137, 136–137n6
  and practices   72, 75–76, 78, 85–86
early work
  See The Younger
empathy   21–22, 23–24, 80, 92–93, 102
expertise   7–8, 222, 224, 232–233, 235
explanation   12–17, 20, 21, 23, 25–26, 36–37, 58, 254, 258
  social   59–60, 72, 73–74, 90–91
  See also Good-Bad theories, *Sociological Explanation as Translation*
folk psychology/sociology   6, 12–14, 15, 16–17, 17n2, 21, 24, 25–26, 28, 90–93, 104
and history   12, 236–237
and internal states   153, 159
and knowledge   222, 223, 224, 231
mirror neurons   22, 23–24, 80, 91–92, 100, 155–248
naturalism   15, 22–23, 31–32, 57, 58–59, 90–91
normativity   18–19, 21, 26, 49, 101–103, 133, 134, 249, 253–254, 258
  See also Brandom, *Explaining the Normative*, Sellars
The Older   19–21, 26, 27
norms   21, 76, 90–91, 92, 139–140, 150, 216, 218–219, 246
  social   136–137, 150
  Verstehen bubble   154, 157
  See also Bicchieri, *Evidenz*, Taylor
practices   5–6, 14, 15–18, 57–58, 71, 90–91, 136–137n5, 139, 143, 204, 216, 245–247, 252, 253
  See also Pierre Bourdieu, Anthony Giddens, normativity, patterns of activity, *The Social Theory of Practices*
and professional knowledge   222, 223, 227, 232–233
rationality   5, 31–32, 54, 56, 94–95n2, 94–95n3, 139, 147–148n15, 254
social, the   12, 13–14, 16–17, 18, 20–22, 23–25, 27–29, 53, 54, 57–58, 74, 90–91, 248, 252, 253
sociology   3, 12–15, 16, 25, 27–28, 91–92, 155, 222, 223–224,
  See also folk psychology/sociology
social theory   12, 28–29

Turner, Stephen (cont.)
  tacit beliefs/presuppositions 203–218
  theory of mind 181–183, 185, 188
  transmission problem 17, 19, 23, 24–25, 28, 84
  underdetermination 216, 217, 219
  understanding 25, 27–29, 54, 56, 57–58, 221, 245–246, 254
    pre-scientific 12–14, 15–16
    See also Verstehen bubble
  and Weber 25–26, 53–55, 56, 74, 91–92, 106–107, 154–155, 156
  The Younger 4–5, 13–14, 19–21, 22–24, 25–27, 57
  See also *Cognitive Science and the Social, Liberal Democracy 3.0,* Parsons, *Verstehen* bubble

understanding 43, 54, 55–56, 81, 83–258,
  See also normativity, Turner, *Verstehen* bubble
universities 223–224, 231, 235

Verstehen, 23–24, 25, 101–102, 101–102n8, 152–153, 155, 177–178, 245

Verstehen bubble 7, 24, 26–29, 86–87, 90–92, 93, 94–95n3, 156, 245–246, 251–252, 254–256

Wason, Peter 38, 40, 41
Weber, Max 92–93, 122–123n19, 154–155, 185, 188, 189–190n5, 255–256,
  agency 101
  causality 101–103
  collective beliefs 120
  empathy 103
  Evidenz, 101–103
  action 74, 189–190, 191, 196n8, 245–246, 251–252
  See also social, Turner (mirror neurons, Weber)
"Where Explanation Ends" 58
Wierzchosławski, Rafał Paweł 5, 244–245
Winch, Peter 32, 34–35, 36, 37–38, 43, 45, 244, 245
  and Davidson 37
Wittgenstein, Ludwig 15, 28, 34, 36, 245
Woodward, James 95–97

Zahle, Julie 7, 255–256, 259–260